MASTER
VISUALLY

by Daniel Drew Turner

Visual

Mac OS® X Tiger™

Master VISUALLY® Mac OS® X Tiger™

Published by
Wiley Publishing, Inc.
111 River Street
Hoboken, NJ 07030-5774

Published simultaneously in Canada

Library of Congress Control Number: 2005923189

ISBN-13: 978-0-7645-7330-9
ISBN-10: 0-7645-7330-6

Manufactured in the United States of America

10   9   8   7   6   5   4   3   2   1

1K/SS/QW/QV/IN

Trademark Acknowledgments

Contact Us

For general information on our other products and services please contact our Customer Care Department within the U.S. at 800-762-2974, outside the U.S. at 317-572-3993 or fax 317-572-4002.

For technical support please visit www.wiley.com/techsupport.

WILEY

Sales

Contact Wiley
at (800) 762-2974 or
fax (317) 572-4002.

Praise for Visual Books...

"If you have to see it to believe it, this is the book for you!"
—PC World

"A master tutorial/reference — from the leaders in visual learning!"
—Infoworld

"A publishing concept whose time has come!"
—The Globe and Mail

"Just wanted to say THANK YOU to your company for providing books which make learning fast, easy, and exciting! I learn visually so your books have helped me greatly — from Windows instruction to Web development. Best wishes for continued success."
—Angela J. Barker (Springfield, MO)

"I have over the last 10–15 years purchased thousands of dollars worth of computer books but find your books the most easily read, best set out, and most helpful and easily understood books on software and computers I have ever read. Please keep up the good work."
—John Gatt (Adamstown Heights, Australia)

"You're marvelous! I am greatly in your debt."
—Patrick Baird (Lacey, WA)

"I am an avid fan of your Visual books. If I need to learn anything, I just buy one of your books and learn the topic in no time. Wonders! I have even trained my friends to give me Visual books as gifts."
—Illona Bergstrom (Aventura, FL)

"I have quite a few of your Visual books and have been very pleased with all of them. I love the way the lessons are presented!"
—Mary Jane Newman (Yorba Linda, CA)

"Like a lot of other people, I understand things best when I see them visually. Your books really make learning easy and life more fun."
—John T. Frey (Cadillac, MI)

"Your Visual books have been a great help to me. I now have a number of your books and they are all great. My friends always ask to borrow my Visual books — trouble is, I always have to ask for them back!"
—John Robson
(Brampton, Ontario, Canada)

"I write to extend my thanks and appreciation for your books. They are clear, easy to follow, and straight to the point. Keep up the good work! I bought several of your books and they are just right! No regrets! I will always buy your books because they are the best."
—Seward Kollie (Dakar, Senegal)

"What fantastic teaching books you have produced! Congratulations to you and your staff."
—Bruno Tonon (Melbourne, Australia)

"Thank you for the wonderful books you produce. It wasn't until I was an adult that I discovered how I learn — visually. Although a few publishers claim to present the materially visually, nothing compares to Visual books. I love the simple layout. Everything is easy to follow. I can just grab a book and use it at my computer, lesson by lesson. And I understand the material! You really know the way I think and learn. Thanks so much!"
—Stacey Han (Avondale, AZ)

"The Greatest. This whole series is the best computer-learning tool of any kind I've ever seen."
—Joe Orr (Brooklyn, NY)

Credits

Project Editor
Jade L. Williams

Acquisitions Editor
Jody Lefevere

Product Development Manager
Lindsay Sandman

Copy Editor
Marylouise Wiack

Technical Editor
Maarten Reilingh

Permissions Editor
Laura Moss

Editorial Manager
Robyn Siesky

Manufacturing
Allan Conley
Linda Cook
Paul Gilchrist
Jennifer Guynn

Screen Artist
Jill A. Proll

Illustrator
Ronda David-Burroughs

Book Design
Kathie Rickard

Project Coordinator
Nancee Reeves

Layout
Sean Decker
Jennifer Heleine
Amanda Spagnuolo

Proofreader
Vicki Broyles

Quality Control
Amanda Briggs

Indexer
Johnna VanHoose

Special Help
Apple Computer, Inc.

**Vice President and Executive
Group Publisher**
Richard Swadley

Vice President and Publisher
Barry Pruett

Composition Director
Debbie Stailey

About the Author

Daniel Drew Turner thought Emacs was his only option for writing English papers in college. This is not because he was so technically proficient, but because he didn't know any better. Despite that shortcoming, he has covered technology, business, and social issues for almost a decade for publications as diverse as *The New York Times, eWEEK, Salon, Feed, Publish, Lingua Franca, MacAddict, I.D., Nerve, Shift,* and more. He turned in the above-mentioned papers at MIT and went on to get a Masters degree in fiction writing while teaching at the University of Colorado in Boulder. Since then, he has practiced creating word processing in the San Francisco Bay Area.

Author's Acknowledgments

It's a truism that there are certain things that you do not want to see made; sausage and laws are two examples. Putting a book together, especially one about a moveable target, is another. Thanks to the crack team of project development editor Jade L. Williams, acquisitions editor Jody Lefevere, the eagle-eyed technical editors Maarty and Nick, and the many art and production folks at Wiley, you can enjoy the chewy goodness of this book without worry.

In addition, a big thanks to those who Spork — they know who they are — for support during the many beta days of Tiger, as well as for their humor that helped put everything in a saner perspective. Odd that the result should be sanity, given their inherent insanity, but there you go. And thanks to Tom Ierna of Shockergroup for keeping the digital packet trains running on time. On a personal note, thanks to Taitt, Fausto, and Zola for they know what.

PART I

PART III

PART II

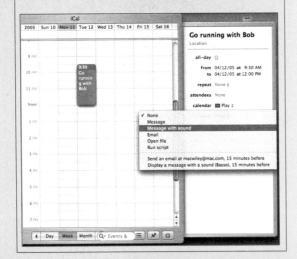

PART IV

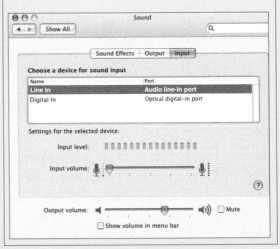

WHAT'S INSIDE

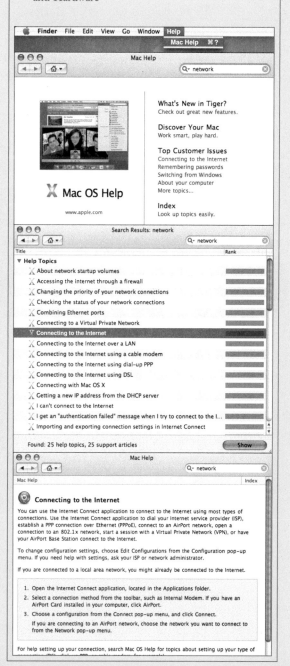

PART I — Getting Started

❶ Mastering Mac OS X Basics

❷ Finding and Viewing Files

TABLE OF CONTENTS

③ Working with Files

④ Maximizing Your Printing Capabilities

PART II — Mastering Mac OS X Utilities and Applications

TABLE OF CONTENTS

8 Managing Multiple Users

PART III — Making Mac OS X Your Own

9 Setting System Preferences

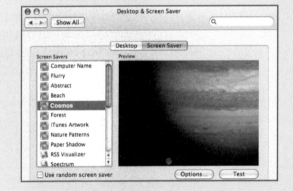

10 Using Fonts to Create Styled Text

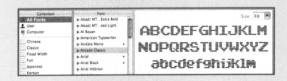

11 Applying Universal Access Features

PART IV   Working with Media on the Mac

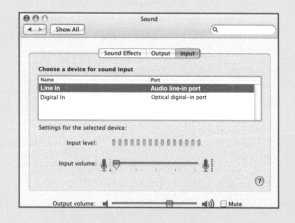

TABLE OF CONTENTS

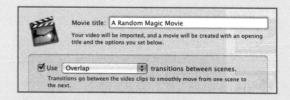

17 Using iDVD to Make a DVD

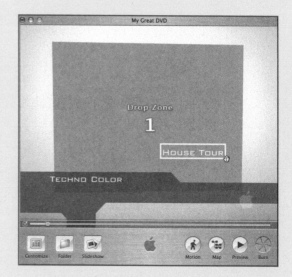

PART V   Managing Networking: Local and Remote

18 Setting Up and Working with a Local Network

TABLE OF CONTENTS

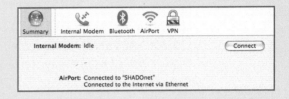

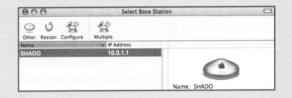

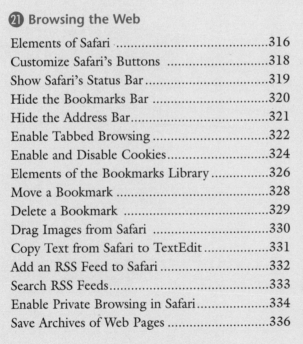

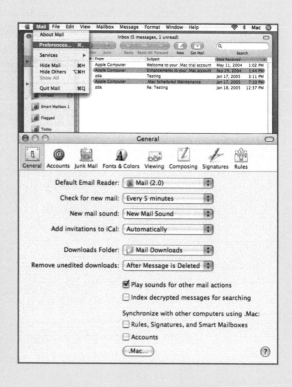

TABLE OF CONTENTS

PART VI   Troubleshooting Your Mac

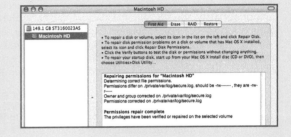

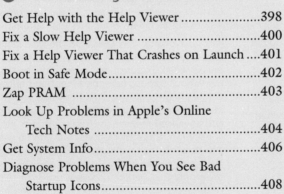

How to Use This Master VISUALLY Book

Do you look at the pictures in a book or newspaper before anything else on a page? Would you rather see an image than read how to do something? Search no further. This book is for you. Opening *Master VISUALLY Mac OS X Tiger* allows you to read less and learn more about the Mac OS X operating system.

This book is designed to help a reader receive quick access to any area of question. You can simply look up a subject within the Table of Contents or Index and go immediately to the task of concern. A *section* is a self-contained unit that walks you through a computer operation step-by-step. That is, with rare exception, all the information you need regarding an area of interest is contained within a section.

A chapter may also contain an illustrated group of pages that gives you background information that you need to understand the tasks in a chapter. Each task contains an introduction, a set of screen shots with steps, and, if the steps goes beyond one page, a set of tips. The introduction tells why you want to perform the steps, the advantages and disadvantages of performing the steps, a general explanation of any procedures, and references to other related tasks in the book. The screens show a series of steps that you must complete to perform a given task. The tip section gives you an opportunity to further understand the task at hand, to learn about other related tasks in other areas of the book, or to apply more complicated or alternative methods.

Who Needs This Book

This book is for a reader who has never used this particular technology or software application. It is also for more computer literate individuals who want to expand their knowledge of the different features that Mac OS X 10.4 has to offer.

Book Organization

Master VISUALLY Mac OS X Tiger has 26 chapters and is divided into six parts. Each part contains three or more chapters. Each chapter is divided into tasks.

Chapter Organization

This book consists of sections, all listed in the book's table of contents. A *section* is a set of steps that show you how to complete a specific computer task.

Each section, usually contained on two facing pages, has an introduction to the task at hand, a set of full-color screen shots and steps that walk you through the task, and a set of tips. This format allows you to quickly look at a topic of interest and learn it instantly.

Chapters group together three or more sections with a common theme. A chapter may also contain pages that give you the background information needed to understand the sections in a chapter.

Part I: Getting Started helps you get acquainted with the basic features of Mac OS X 10.4 Tiger. Chapter 1 shows you what to expect when you first boot up your Mac, how to work the Finder, how to move folders around, as well as how to use some of Tiger's new features, such as Spotlight. Chapter 2 illustrates how to find and view files, which are the basic unit of Mac OS X's Finder. Chapter 3 extends your competence in working with files, showing you how to change and share files. Chapter 4 helps you print out files, so you can make hard copies of the documents and images you create on screen.

Part II: Mastering Mac OS X Utilities and Applications turns the focus to the programs that help you be productive and creative in Mac OS X. In Chapter 5, the focus is on TextEdit, Mac OS X's bundled text editor, with which you can write and style text documents. Chapter 6 turns to Preview, which enables you to view and work with PDFs and most image types. Chapter 7 shows you how to use other Mac OS X utilities, such as the Address Book contact manager, the built-in calculator, the iCal calendaring application, and others. Chapter 8 enables you to set up and manage multiple users on your Mac.

Part III: Making Mac OS X Your Own turns to customizing settings as well as the look and feel of Mac OS X on your Mac. Chapter 9 talks about using the System Preferences to set your computer's clock, language, user interface appearance, and more. Chapter 10 helps you get the most out of Mac OS X's font capabilities. Chapter 11 helps you activate special settings to increase your computer's usability for those with seeing, hearing, or other disabilities. Chapter 12 demonstrates how to use Automator to create workflows that automate complex tasks.

Part IV: Working with Media on the Mac looks at the multimedia capabilities of Mac OS X and how you can use them to enjoy music, video, pictures, and more. Chapter 13 introduces you to the various options for sound input and output, as well as getting digital images out of a digital camera, as well as media options in Mac OS X's DVD Player. Chapter 14 goes over some of the basic and advanced features in iTunes, Mac OS X's music managing application. Chapter 15 goes over how to manage, as well as edit and present, digital images in iPhoto. In Chapter 16, you will learn how to use iMovie to create and share a movie from your own footage. Chapter 17 shows you how to take your movie and create a professional-looking presentation on an interactive DVD using iDVD.

Part V: Managing Networking: Local and Remote shows you the basics of working with local and remote networks. Chapter 18 helps you configure sharing files between computers on a local network. Chapter 19 takes on configuring the internal modem in your computer, if it shipped with one. Chapter 20 helps you make the step to a high-speed Internet connection and configure a wireless network with an AirPort Base Station. Chapter 21 focuses on making the most of surfing the Web, with tips on customizing Safari, Mac OS X's built-in Web browser. Chapter 22 enables you to access e-mail through Mail, the e-mail client included with Mac OS X. In Chapter 23, you will learn how to use Mac OS X's iChat instant messaging application to chat, audio chat, and video chat with friends around the world.

Part VI: Troubleshooting Your Mac helps you understand and fix potential problems that may crop up on your computer. Chapter 24 steps you through the features of Disk Utility, which can help you configure new hard disks and maintain the health of current ones. Chapter 25 shows you how to install and uninstall new software and hardware. Chapter 26 goes over more general troubleshooting techniques, including how to recognize hardware issues by the startup screens they present and how to use the Help Viewer to look up answers.

Using the Mouse

This book uses the following conventions to describe the actions you perform when using the mouse:

Click

Press your left mouse button once. You generally click your mouse on something to select something on the screen.

Double-click

Press your left mouse button twice. Double-clicking something on the computer screen generally opens whatever item you have double-clicked.

Right-click

Press your right mouse button. When you right-click anything on the computer screen, the program displays a shortcut menu containing commands specific to the selected item.

Drag and Release the Mouse

Move your mouse pointer and hover it over an item on the screen. Press and hold down the left mouse button. Now, move the mouse to where you want to place the item and then release the button. You use this method to move an item from one area of the computer screen to another.

The Conventions in This Book

A number of typographic and layout styles have been used throughout *Master VISUALLY Mac OS X Tiger* to distinguish different types of information.

Bold

Bold type represents the names of commands and options, which with you interact. Bold type also indicates text and numbers that you must type into a dialog box or window.

Italics

Italic words introduce a new term and are followed by a definition.

Numbered Steps

You must perform the instructions in numbered steps in order to successfully complete a section and achieve the final results.

Bulleted Steps

These steps point out various optional features. You do not have to perform these steps; they simply give additional information about a feature.

Indented Text

Indented text tells you what the program does in response to you following a numbered step. For example, if you click a certain menu command, a dialog box may appear, or a window may open. Indented text may also tell you what the final result is when you follow a set of numbered steps.

Notes

Notes give additional information. They may describe special conditions that may occur during an operation. They may warn you of a situation that you want to avoid, for example, the loss of data. A note may also cross reference a related area of the book. A cross reference may guide you to another chapter, or another section within the current chapter.

Icons and Buttons

Icons and buttons are graphical representations within the text. They show you exactly what you need to click to perform a step.

 You can easily identify the tips in any section by looking for the Master It icon. Master It offers additional information, including tips, hints, and tricks. You can use the Master It information to go beyond what you have learned in the steps.

Conventions That Are Assumed with This Book

This book assumes that you know how to navigate through the files in your computer and how to open, save, and close files. This book also assumes that you are familiar with Microsoft Excel but new to programming in Visual Basic for Applications.

Operating System Difference

This book is applicable to Mac OS X 10.4, also known as Tiger. It was written using an Apple Power Mac G5 on a Mac OS X 10.4 operating system.

System Requirements

You will need a Macintosh computer with a PowerPC G3, G4, or G5 processors, built-in FireWire, 256MB of RAM, and 3GB of free disk space.

2   Finding and Viewing Files

3 — Working with Files

4 — Maximizing Your Printing Capabilities

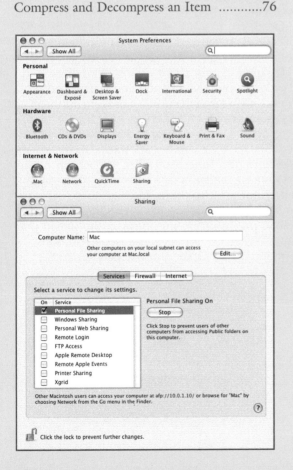

What Is New in Tiger

You can explore the many new features in Mac OS X 10.4 to help you work more productively, be more creative, and share your computer more efficiently with others. Mac OS X 10.4 includes over 200 new features and enhancements to the operating system and applications included with it.

Under the hood, Mac OS X 10.4 includes a new core that offers the power of the latest version of Unix and better multiprocessor support. To most users, this means better protection from system crashes, the ability to work with larger files, and, in computers with two processors, improved performance.

You can take immediate advantage of the new user interface features, new applications, and new versions of applications included in Mac OS X 10.4. You can use these to better work with files and folders, stay in touch with friends and family, synchronize your data across multiple computers, automate regular tasks, personalize news feeds, work with your computer if you have a disability, and more.

Spotlight

You can use Spotlight to find files, whether they are text documents, images, folders, applications, PDFs, e-mail contacts, or calendars. You can access Spotlight by clicking the Spotlight icon in the upper-right corner of the screen; this reveals the Spotlight search field. You can enter words that relate to the item you want to find — part of its name, when it was accessed or created, the kind of content, the author, or other criteria — and Spotlight shows you a list of possible matches organized by type. Spotlight indexes your hard drive and updates as changes are made to items to keep its information current. You can also access the Spotlight feature by using the Spotlight search field in the Toolbar of any Finder window. For more information, see "Use Spotlight to Find Files in the Finder."

Dashboard

You can use Dashboard, Mac OS X 10.4's new interface layer, to work with a special class of applications, called widgets, which can help you organize your work and your life. When you press one key, Dashboard zooms onto the screen, displaying the last widgets you have opened and Dashboard's Favorites Bar, from which you can launch other widgets and connect to Apple's Web site for more downloadable widgets. The widgets that come with Mac OS X 10.4 include a stock tracker, a dictionary, a world clock, an iTunes controller, stickies, an Address Book contact reader, a unit converter, a translator, a weather tracker, and more. Many of these can use your Internet connection to update their data invisibly. You can click anywhere on the screen that is not a widget to dismiss Dashboard. For more information, see "Open and Use Dashboard."

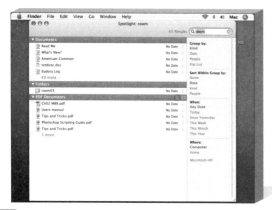

Safari

You can use Safari, the new version of Mac OS X's Web browser, to access Real Simple Syndication (RSS) feeds. These are article headlines and summaries provided by news organizations, personal Web sites, and blogs; Safari tracks these RSS feeds so you can see them together in a simple text format, free of ads. When you see a headline for an article you would like to read, you can click that headline and see the whole article. You can also select RSS feeds to bookmark. Once these are bookmarked, Safari automatically updates and notifies you whenever the feeds have new content.

Automator

You can use Automator, a new application included in Mac OS X 10.4, to automate nearly any task on your computer. You work with Automator by connecting together actions, which are small packages of instructions included in Automator. Actions tell the computer to do something, from creating a new folder to applying image-editing filters. You can drag and drop actions to create a string of them, which is called a workflow. Workflows can be as complex as retrieving a collection of images from a remote server, resizing and rotating them, organizing them by name or date, and placing them into a page layout application. Automator includes a library of actions that work with the applications on your computer as well as with the operating system.

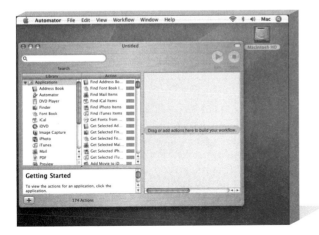

QuickTime 7

QuickTime 7 offers improvements to the video format, including support for the H.264 standard that allows QuickTime to play High Definition video (HDV). You can also use this new standard to capture and edit HD content. The new QuickTime also allows improved video conferencing capabilities in iChat AV, so that if you and a friend have FireWire-equipped Web cameras or digital camcorders, you can both enjoy smooth, full-color, two-way video and audio.

Mail

You can use new features in Mac OS X 10.4's Mail application to organize your e-mail correspondences more efficiently. Mail adds Smart Mailboxes, which automatically collect incoming messages according to criteria you set, so that work messages can go into one folder and family messages can go into another automatically. Mail also takes advantage of Spotlight, so that you can search all your e-mail messages more efficiently. For more information, see Chapter 22.

VoiceOver

If you or someone using your computer has a visual or learning disability, you can enable VoiceOver, Mac OS X 10.4's new spoken interface. VoiceOver, which is integrated into Mac OS X 10.4, reads the contents of the screen, including the interface as well as the contents of documents, Web pages, e-mail messages, and other files. This is useful if you have trouble reading the text of the interface on your computer screen. You can customize VoiceOver to work with any set of key combinations for navigation; these commands remain the same across all applications for ease of use. You can use VoiceOver in conjunction with other Universal Access options that allow you to navigate the screen, the Dock, the menu bar, window tools, and any other interface element with the keyboard. For more information, see Chapter 11.

Elements of the Finder Window

You can use the Finder as the master element of the interface between you and your Mac. Whatever system operation you want to perform — locate a file, folder, or application; organize files or folders; manage local and remote hard drives; move items such as folders, files, or applications; copy or delete items — you can do it all in the Finder.

The Finder is an application that is designed to run on your Mac and to provide you with certain functionalities. The Finder launches when you start up your Mac, and allows

you to manage all other applications and files through it. The Finder displays your desktop, as well as folders and their contents. For this reason, an open window that displays the contents of a hard drive or folder is called a Finder window.

Finder windows are different from application windows. The latter display the items, such as documents or images, which you are working on. The former display icons representing items on your computer's hard drive and, if you are connected to a network, a remote computer's hard drive.

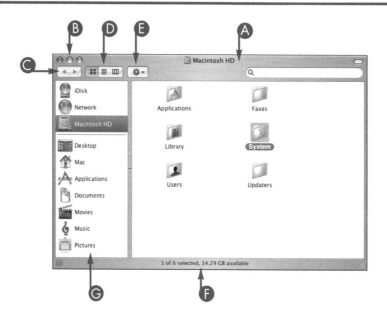

Ⓐ Title Bar
The Finder window's Title bar has window control buttons and an area that you can grab with the cursor to move the window around the screen. In addition, a Finder window's Title bar displays the current name of the hard drive or folder. The Title bar appears whether or not the Toolbar is visible. When the Toolbar is visible, the window has borders on the sides and bottom. You can grab to drag the window; when the Toolbar is not visible, you must use the Title bar.

Ⓑ Window Control Buttons
These three buttons enable you to close, minimize, and maximize the Finder window. The red button closes the window. The yellow button minimizes the window to the Dock. You can return a minimized window to its former state by clicking its icon in the Dock. The green button maximizes the window, allowing it to take up more screen space. When you move the cursor over the window control buttons, the X, minus, and plus symbols appear within

the buttons to remind you of their purpose. The Toolbar button, located in the upper-right corner of the Finder window, toggles the Toolbar off and on. The window control buttons appear whether or not the Toolbar is visible.

Ⓒ Back/Forward Buttons

If you have used a Finder window to view the contents of more than one folder, then you can click the Back button to return to the contents of the previously viewed folder. You can also click the Forward button to move through the content of viewed folders; this button is enabled only if you have already moved back. The Back and Forward buttons do not appear when the Toolbar is hidden.

Ⓓ View Buttons

In the currently open Finder window, you can use these buttons to display your folders in Icon, List, and Column view. The View buttons do not appear when the Toolbar is hidden. However, you can still change each Finder window's view type by clicking View in the Menu bar and selecting a view option.

Ⓔ Action Button

You can click the Action button to open a menu that allows you to perform various actions within the Finder, such as creating a new folder within the currently open folder in the Finder window or change the View options for the window. The options displayed in the Action button's menu change according to the context in which it is used. If you select a file or application within the Finder window, the Action button displays more options, such as opening the file or moving it to the Trash.

Ⓕ Status Bar

This area shows you how many files are displayed in the Finder window. When you change the contents of the Finder window, the count changes to reflect this. The second number displayed in the Status bar shows you how much space is available on your computer's hard drive.

Ⓖ Sidebar

The top section of the Sidebar displays the icons for your computer, your network if you are connected to one, your hard disk, any connected removable storage devices, and your iDisk if you have a .Mac account. The bottom section of the Sidebar displays icons for your home folder, the Desktop folder, the Applications folder, your Documents folder, your Movies folder, your Music folder, and your Pictures folder. You can click any folder icon in the Sidebar to display its contents in the Finder window.

You can drag and drop items such as documents, URLs, and folders to the Sidebar. When you drag and drop an item, you do not move the actual item; you move a pointer to the item. The exception is when you drag and drop an item into a folder in the Sidebar; in this case, the item will move from its original place into the folder. Note that the item does not now reside in the Sidebar, but in the folder in that folder's actual location.

You can remove an item from the Sidebar by dragging it out of the Finder window without deleting the original item. The icon of the item disappears in an animated puff of smoke. The original item remains in its actual location. If you remove a remote server's icon from the Sidebar, that server is unmounted and you are no longer connected to it.

Spotlight

Mac OS X version 10.4 uses a new built-in search engine called Spotlight, which can find items that meet a wide variety of criteria, anywhere on your computer. You can click the Spotlight button and enter text in the search field. Spotlight displays its results within the Finder window. You can sort the results by name, date modified, size, or kind, just as you would normally sort files in a Finder window. Spotlight indexes your computer's hard drive when you install Mac OS X 10.4 or first turn on a new computer equipped with Mac OS X 10.4. When you make changes to files, Spotlight updates its database to track the change.

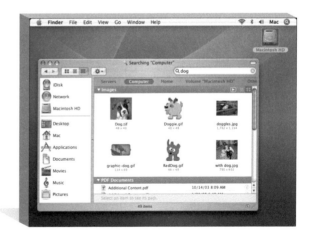

Create a New Folder on the Desktop and Within Another Folder

Y ou can create a new folder on the Desktop, or a subfolder within any other folder. This allows you to better organize your various files and applications. You can have as many levels of subfolders as you want.

Once you create a new folder, you can move files and other folders to the new folder. You can use folders to organize a project, such as a family photo collection.

You can do many things with folders that you can do with files. For example, you can move folders anywhere, except into areas that you do not have permission to access. You

can also rename folders as you would files. As with files, you cannot have two folders with the same name in the same directory. For more information about permissions, see Chapter 3.

You can give a folder almost any name that you want. However, certain characters and names are prohibited; if you try to create a folder with a forbidden name or using forbidden characters, then the Finder alerts you and asks you to choose another name.

Create a New Folder on the Desktop

1 In the Finder, click File.

2 Click New Folder.

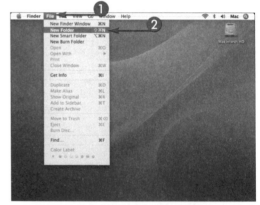

● A new folder with the name untitled folder appears on the Desktop.

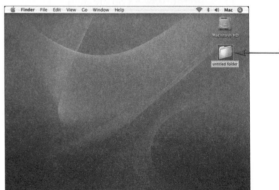

Create a New Folder Within Another Folder

1 Open an existing folder.

2 Click File.

3 Click New Folder.

● A new folder appears in the existing folder, with the name untitled folder.

Can I name a new folder?

▼ Yes. When you create a new folder, it appears with the name untitled folder. To change the name of the new folder, click the name. When it highlights, you can type a new name for the folder and then press the Return key to apply the name change.

What are the restrictions for naming a folder?

▼ You cannot use reserved names for folders because these names are used by the Finder. For example, you cannot call a folder System or Users, at the same level as these special folders. You also cannot use certain characters, such as a colon (:) or begin a folder name with a period (.).

Can I delete folders that I have created?

▼ Yes. Just as with a file, you can drag a folder to the Trash and empty the Trash to delete the folder. The contents of the folder are deleted at the same time.

Label Folders and Files

You can append labels to important folders and files in order to distinguish them visually. These labels appear as a colored bar around the item's name. This coloration appears whether you are viewing the item in List, Icon, or Column view. You can use labels to help organize folders and files. For example, business folders and files can have red color labels while letters to friends can have blue color labels.

When you have a folder or file selected, you may not be able to view the exact color of the label. To view the color of the label properly, click outside the icon of the folder or file.

The label remains constant if you change the folder or file. For example, you can change the name or move the folder or file, and the label remains the same color.

There is no preassigned meaning to a label color. For example, you can use red labels for personal or work items, for movies, for folders that are full, or for work that needs to be done. For more information about folder and file views, see Chapter 2.

Label a Folder

1 Click the icon of the folder that you want to label.

2 Click File.

3 Click the color that you want to use to label the folder.

● The filename displays with the color label that you selected.

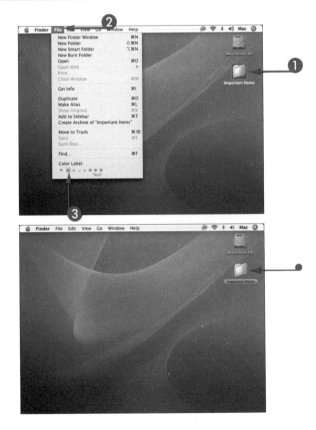

Label a File

① Click the icon of the file that you want to label.

② Click File.

③ Click the color that you want to use to label the file.

● The filename displays with the color label that you selected.

Can I change a label color to another color?

▼ Yes. You can repeat Steps **1** to **2** and then select a different color. The folder or file appears with the new label color that you selected.

Can I remove a color label from a file or folder?

▼ Yes. You can repeat Steps **1** to **3**, but instead select X (no color) in Step **3**. This removes any color from the title of the folder or file.

Will adding a label to an item affect the contents of the item?

▼ No. The label changes only the appearance of the folder or file in the Finder. The label remains the color you chose even if you share the item with another user; for example, a red-labeled file you e-mail to a friend will appear with a red label on your friend's computer.

Move and Copy Items in the Finder

Y ou can move items such as files, folders, and applications in the Finder. This allows you to organize items in the way that best meets your needs. You can also copy items as you move them. This is useful if you want to have multiple copies of an item. For example, if you have a birthday photo in your personal folder, you can move a copy of that birthday photo into another user's personal folder; you may also want to work on a letter while retaining a copy of the original in another folder.

When you move a folder, all items within it are moved along with the folder. Similarly, when you copy a folder to a new location, all items within it are copied to the folder's new location. Keep in mind that if you copy a folder that contains very large files, such as movies, this can take a good deal of time.

You can move or copy items anywhere on your computer's hard drive, such as to the Desktop, a folder, or another hard drive, as long as you have write permission for the target location. For more information about permissions, see Chapter 3.

Move an Item in the Finder

Note: *Before moving an item, ensure that you can clearly see the location where you want to move the item.*

① Click and hold the item that you want to move.

② Drag the item to a new location.

● The item moves to the new location.

● The item disappears from its original location.

Copy an Item in the Finder

Note: *Before copying an item, ensure that you can clearly see the location where you want to copy the item.*

1 Click and hold the item that you want to copy.

2 Press and hold the Option key as you drag the item to the new location.

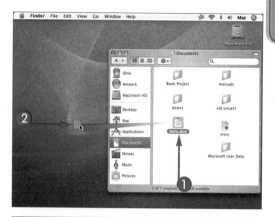

● A copy of the item appears in the new location.

Can I quickly move or copy a file to a commonly used folder?

▼ Yes. The Mac OS displays a list of commonly used disks and folders, such as Documents and Pictures, in the Sidebar of every open Finder window. You can use the methods described in this task to move or copy a file or folder to one of these locations. A blue highlight appears around the name of the target location.

When I drag an item to another hard drive, why does the Mac OS copy, rather than move, the item?

▼ This is a safety feature that ensures that you do not accidentally move an item to a disk for which you do not have read or copy access. When you drag a file, folder, or application to another disk, the Mac OS creates a copy of the item on that target disk. To move an item to another disk without copying it, press and hold ⌘ as you drag it.

Use Contextual Menus in the Finder and Windows

You can increase your productivity by using contextual menus to quickly access a variety of commands and actions. These commands and actions would normally require multiple clicks in the Menu bar.

You can display the contextual menus by holding down the Control key while clicking the Desktop or an item. The options that you see in the menu change, depending on the item that you select prior to Control-clicking. When you press the Control key, a small menu icon appears next to the cursor icon, to indicate that you can display the contextual menu.

These menus are called contextual menus because they change according to their context. For example, when you Control-click the Desktop, a contextual menu appears with general actions related to your computer and the Finder. When you Control-click a file or folder, a contextual menu appears with actions listing what you can do to that particular file or folder.

If you have a multiple-button mouse, the right mouse button calls up contextual menus by default. You can change this behavior in the Keyboard and Mouse Preferences. For more information, see Chapter 9.

Use Contextual Menus in the Finder

① Press and hold the Control key and click the Desktop.

● A contextual menu appears.

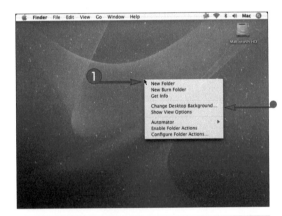

② Scroll to the action that you want to select.

The Finder applies the action that you select.

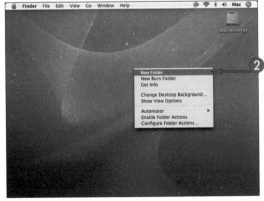

Use Contextual Menus in Windows

1 Press and hold the Control key and click in a window.

● A contextual menu appears.

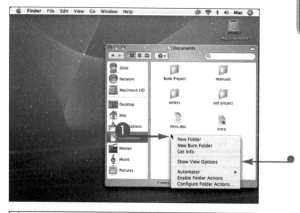

2 Scroll to the action that you want to select.

The Finder applies the action that you select.

Is there another way that I can display a contextual menu?

▼ Yes. If you have a mouse with multiple buttons, you can use the right mouse button to call up a contextual menu. This is a default option, so you do not have to make any configuration changes.

Is there any difference between an action in a contextual menu in a Finder window and one with the same name that appears when I click the Action button?

▼ No. Although the contextual menu in a Finder window displays some extra options, such as Help, the actions with the same name that appear when you click the Action button do the same thing. For example, when you click a file in a Finder window, you can access the Open With feature either by clicking the Action button or Control-clicking the item.

Move and Resize the Dock

You can move the Dock from its default position at the bottom of the screen, as well as change its size. This is useful if you want to expand windows and files all the way to the bottom of the screen, or if you simply prefer the Dock on the side of the screen. Changing the size of the Dock allows you to either create larger and easier-to-read items in the Dock or to shrink the Dock in order to reclaim screen space.

When you place the Dock along the left or right side of the screen, the Finder will always be the topmost icon, with the applications directly below it, and then minimized windows. The Trash icon will always remain at the bottom.

You can also use the Dock to hold minimized windows. When you click the yellow control button in a Finder window, the window shrinks to a place on the right side of the Dock. To expand the window to its original size and position, click the window's icon in the Dock.

Move the Dock

① Click the Apple menu (🍎).

② Click Dock.

③ Click an option in the submenu.

You can select Position on Left, Position on Bottom, or Position on Right.

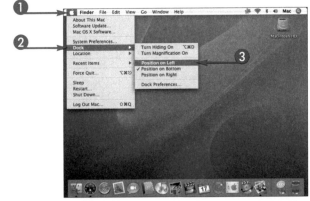

● The Dock moves to its new position.

To move the Dock back to the default position, repeat Steps **1** to **3**, and click Position on Bottom.

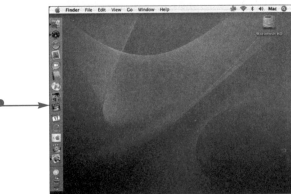

Resize the Dock

① Move the cursor over the dividing line in the Dock.

The cursor changes to an up/down arrow.

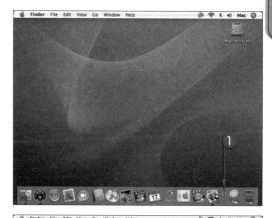

② Click and move the mouse up to enlarge the Dock, or move it down to shrink the Dock.

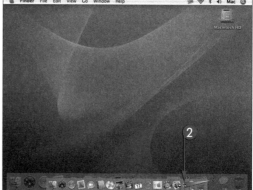

How can I identify the icons in the Dock?

▼ You can identify the icons in the Dock by name by moving the cursor over each item and holding it there. The item's name appears next to the item.

Can I identify which applications in the Dock are running?

▼ Yes. A triangle appears below the icon for each application that is currently open.

What is the purpose of the dividing line in the Dock?

▼ The vertical gap in the Dock divides the icons of applications from those of minimized windows and other items. For example, because it represents a folder, the Trash icon is always on the farthest right of the Dock.

Use Contextual Menus in the Dock

Y ou can use contextual menus in the Dock to hide or quit running applications, or reveal windows and documents related to running applications. You can display these menus by Control-clicking items in the Dock; the options that appear depend on the item that you have selected in the Dock.

If you have a multibutton mouse, you can also use the right mouse button for contextual menus. Instead of Control-clicking an item, you can right-click. You can

reassign this function to any mouse key in the Keyboard & Mouse preferences. For more information, see Chapter 9.

If you open files with a running application, you can bring these files to the front of the screen with the application's contextual menu. For example, you can Control-click your word processor's application icon and select an open text file, which then moves to the front. You can then repeat the process for another application, bringing it to the front.

Use Contextual Menus in the Dock

① Press and hold the Control key.

② Click a Dock application icon.

● A contextual menu appears.

Application icons appear on the left of the dividing line in the Dock, with running applications marked by a triangle.

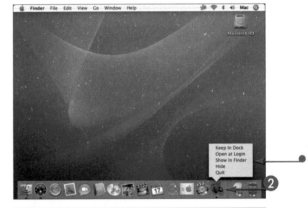

③ Scroll to and click the menu option you want.

That option is enacted.

Close Minimized Windows in the Dock

Y ou can use a contextual menu to close a window that you have minimized in the Dock. This is useful because it enables you to close a window without having to maximize it out of the Dock first.

This method does not work with windows associated with applications, such as a minimized Web browser window. You can identify minimized Finder windows because they include the Finder icon at the lower right of the minimized window icon.

Windows will always appear on the right side of the Dock, to the left of the Trash, if the Dock is at the bottom of the screen. If the Dock is along one side of the screen or the other, minimized windows appear along the lower part of the Dock, above the Trash.

The contents of the minimized windows reflect the contents of the window before it was minimized. That is, a Finder window will show its contents even in the Dock; a QuickTime window will show the movie currently showing.

Close Minimized Windows in the Dock

① Click a minimized window icon and hold down the mouse button.

You can also Control-click the icon.

● A contextual menu appears.

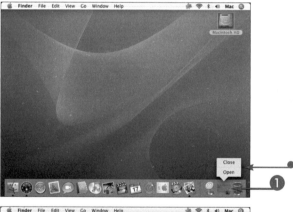

② Click Close.

③ Release the mouse button.

The window closes.

The closed window is not deleted.

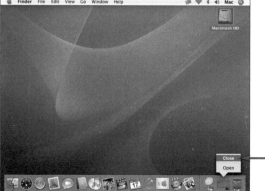

Switch Between Applications Using the Keyboard

You can quickly switch between running applications in Mac OS X using a keyboard combination. This is useful if you are working on more than one project, or want to copy and paste some text from a document into an e-mail, or to check your e-mail while browsing the Web.

Normally, you would use your mouse to click a running application's icon in the Dock to switch to that application. Running applications are indicated by a small triangle beneath their icon in the Dock.

However, it is often faster to switch using a keyboard combination, rather than taking one hand off the keyboard, locating the icon of the application that you want in the Dock, clicking it, and returning your hand to the keyboard.

In addition, the Finder remembers your most recently used applications. If you switch from one application to another, and then use the keyboard to switch applications, the Finder first allows you to return to the application you just used. If you have to move back and forth between two applications, this is the fastest way to do so.

① Press and hold ⌘-Tab key.

- A bar appears, displaying application icons and highlighting the most recently used application.

② Press and hold ⌘-Tab key again.

- The next application is highlighted.

③ Release the keys.

● The selected application is active.

● To skip to a specific application, you can click it with the cursor.

Why does an application end up at the right end of the bar?

▼ When you hide an application, either by selecting the Hide command from the File menu or by pressing ⌘-H, the Finder places it at the right end of the bar when you switch between applications. When you switch to that application, it is not hidden any more.

Can I reverse the direction of application switching?

▼ Yes. To cycle backward through running applications, press ⌘-Shift, and then, while holding these keys down, press the Tab key. Each press of the Tab key moves you one application backward.

Use Spotlight to Find Files in the Finder

You can use Spotlight, the system-wide search technology in Mac OS X, to look for any file, folder, image, e-mail message, calendar event, Address Book contact, or any item on your computer. In addition to helping you find a single item, Spotlight can help you find related items. For example, if you search for a friend's name, Spotlight shows you your friend's contact file, e-mail messages from that friend, documents with that friend's name in them, and more.

Spotlight indexes your entire hard drive when you first install Mac OS X 10.4, or when you first start up a new computer equipped with Mac OS X. Whenever you make a change to a file, Spotlight updates its information, so its results are current.

You can also search for items based on criteria that describe the item. For example, you can search for all images you have that are in landscape format by entering *landscape* and *image* into the Spotlight search box. Spotlight returns a list of images that match that description, along with other relevant items.

Use Spotlight to Find Files in the Finder

❶ Click in the search box.

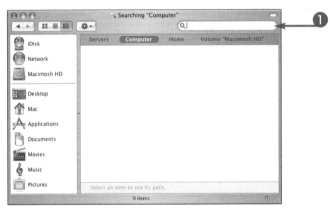

❷ Type a search term.

● Spotlight returns results of your search.

Show All Windows with Exposé

You can use Exposé, Mac OS X's window management technology, to reveal all open Finder and application windows at once. This is useful if you have open windows that may be hiding other windows that you want to use. Exposé can also help with other window management issues. For more information, see the sections "Show Application Windows with Exposé," "Reveal the Desktop with Exposé," and "Copy and Make an Alias of a File with Exposé."

The All Windows feature of Exposé shrinks and reorders all of the windows so that you can see them all at a glance.

If a window becomes too small to recognize, then you can move the cursor over that window; the Finder highlights the window and displays the name of the window.

Not all computers can support all the features of Exposé. Older computers with video cards that have less than 32MB of video RAM will not show a smooth scaling effect as Exposé moves windows on the screen. However, the features discussed in this book are available to all computers equipped with Mac OS X 10.4 or later.

Show All Windows with Exposé

1 Press the F9 key.

● All windows appear.

2 Move the mouse over the window that you want to bring to the front.

● The window's name appears.

3 Click the window.

You can quickly press the F9 key to keep the windows displayed; you can also hold the F9 key down to show the windows and let them return to their normal state when you release the F9 key.

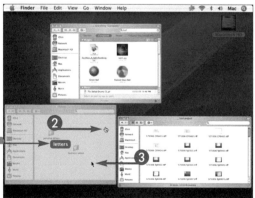

Show Application Windows with Exposé

You can use Exposé, Mac OS X's window management technology, to highlight only the windows associated with the currently running application. All other Finder and application windows appear dim and in the background. This is useful if you are working in an application with many open windows, such as a word processor with multiple text files, or an image editor with many images being worked on, and you need to see which files are open.

Exposé dims the background and other windows, while rearranging and highlighting the windows of the running application so that they are not blocking each other. You can click a window or press the Space bar to bring the selected window to the front. Exposé then returns your Desktop to its normal state.

You can change the keys used to activate Exposé features in the Exposé System Preferences. You can also set Exposé to activate when you move the cursor to a corner of the screen, or assign various Exposé functions to mouse buttons, if you have a mouse with multiple buttons.

Show Application Windows with Exposé

① Press the F10 key.

 ● The application windows highlight and rearrange themselves.

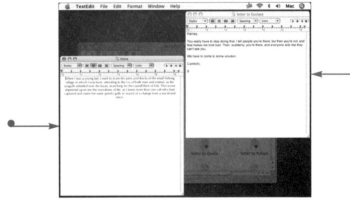

② Move the mouse over the window that you want to bring to the front.

 ● The window's name appears.

③ Click the window.

Note: *You can quickly press the F10 key to keep the windows displayed; you can also hold the F10 key down to show the windows and let them return to their normal state when you release the F10 key.*

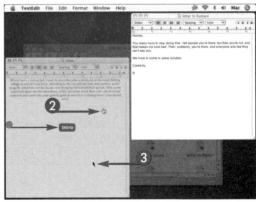

Reveal the Desktop with Exposé

Y ou can use Exposé, Mac OS X's window management technology, to move all existing Finder and application windows to the side of the screen to reveal the Desktop. This is useful if you need to access files or folders on your Desktop.

Exposé makes all existing windows appear to fly off the screen. If you tap the Exposé key, the windows remain at the sides of the screen. If you hold the key down, the windows remain out of the way until you release the key, at which point they return to where they were.

When you use this feature, all windows move to the side of the screen, including progress windows. This means that progress indicators, such as for file downloads, will not be visible.

You can change the keys used to activate Exposé features in the Exposé System Preferences. You can also set Exposé to activate when you move the cursor to a corner of the screen, or assign various Exposé functions to mouse buttons, if you have a mouse with multiple buttons.

Reveal the Desktop with Exposé

1 Press the F11 key.

● All windows move to the edge of the screen, revealing the Desktop.

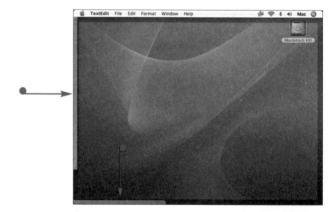

2 Press the F11 key again.

The windows return to their previous positions.

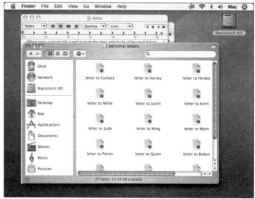

Copy and Make an Alias of a File with Exposé

Yου can use Exposé to easily copy files from one location to another, especially when other windows in the Finder hide your target location. You can use this feature to copy files, folders, and applications, either to the Desktop or to another folder.

You can also use this technique to select a file and attach it to an e-mail. If you have application icons on the Desktop, you can use this technique to select a file in a folder and drag it onto an application icon to open the file with the application. When you do this, you are not moving the file but placing a reference to the file. The original is not moved.

When you copy files from one location to another, the cursor changes to reflect the action you are taking. For example, a small plus sign in a green circle appears next to the cursor when you are copying a file. Similarly, if you are creating an alias to a file, a small arrow appears next to the cursor. For more information about aliases, see Chapter 3.

Copy and Make an Alias of a File with Exposé

Copy a file with Exposé

1 To copy a file to the Desktop, click and hold the file that you want to copy.

2 Press F11 to display the Desktop.

● Exposé moves all open windows to the edges of the screen.

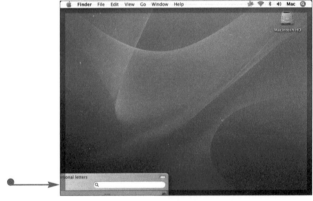

3 Press the Option key while releasing the file on the Desktop.

● A copy of the file appears on the Desktop.

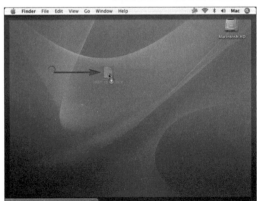

Make an alias of a file with Exposé

1 To make an alias of a file to the Desktop, click and hold the file.

2 Press F11 to display the Desktop.

● Exposé reveals the Desktop.

3 Press ⌘-Option and drag the file to the Desktop.

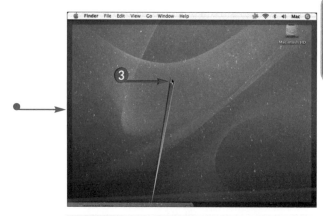

● An alias of the file appears on the Desktop.

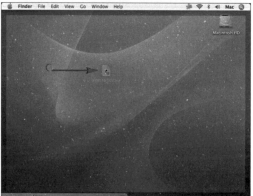

Can I move files with Exposé?

▼ Yes. To move rather than copy files, do not press the Option key in Step **3**. Keep in mind that if you are moving a file to a different hard drive, you must press the Option key to move the file, but not press the Option key to copy the file.

Can I cancel the procedure after I have started it?

▼ Yes. If you use Exposé to move the windows on your screen and decide to abort the procedure before you have released the mouse button, you can press the Exposé key again to return the windows to their previous locations and drag the file back to where it was originally.

Open and Use Dashboard

You can activate Dashboard, which overlays your screen with a collection of widgets. Widgets are a type of applications that can help you keep track of everyday tasks. These widgets are persistent, which means that they are always available without your having to launch them.

Dashboard is a Mac OS X technology that is similar to Exposé. When you click a button, a semi-transparent layer appears on your Desktop, displaying a variety of Widgets. Widgets are JavaScript- and HTML-based applications that can provide various functionalities, such as displaying livestock prices or the view from a favorite Web cam. They can access information over the Internet automatically.

Mac OS X comes with a variety of widgets installed. These include a calculator, calendar, address book, and others. Some, such as an iTunes controller or the address book widget, work with and share information with your existing applications. For example, the address book widget automatically includes contacts you have entered into the Address Book application.

You can enable and dismiss individual widgets when Dashboard is called up. You can also download and install new widgets from Apple's Web site.

Open and Use Dashboard

① Press the F12 key.

Note: On laptops, this is also the Eject key.

Dashboard appears.

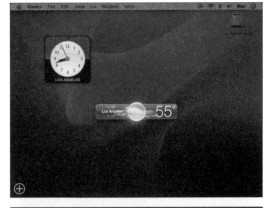

② Click a widget's name in the Favorites Bar to open it.

③ Move the mouse over a widget.

● A close control appears.

④ Click the close control.

The widget closes.

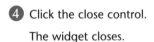

Can I dismiss the Dashboard overlay on my Desktop?

▼ Yes. As with Exposé functions, you can press the same key that calls up Dashboard to dismiss it. You can change the keyboard shortcut by opening the Exposé Preferences and using the Dashboard menu. You can also hold down the Shift, Control, ⌘, or Option key to assign Dashboard to a key combination, such as Control-D, for example.

Can I display more than one widget at once?

▼ Yes. You can open as many widgets as you like. You can also open multiple instances of many widgets. For example, you can open more than one World Clock widget, so that you can see the local time in many time zones, or you can open multiple Stickies so you can see more than one note to yourself at a time. If you cannot open multiple copies of a widget, the widget's name will be grayed out in the Favorites Bar when one copy of the widget is open.

Set Up Multiple Accounts

Y ou can set up your computer to host multiple accounts. This allows multiple users to share the same computer in separate workspaces with each user seeing its own files, preferences, and music, without affecting the workspaces of other users.

An account is a workspace dedicated to a particular user; the user logs in to the computer with its username and password, and is presented with its own Desktop. Each user can set individualized preferences, such as default icon size and desktop picture. Each user has a separate home folder and his or her own folders for Movies, Music, and Documents.

You can set an account login so that the user only has to click a picture, rather than a username, to log in. This is useful when configuring an account for children.

One user cannot access or change the personal files of other users. However, each user has a Public folder where one can place items for other users to access, and each user has a Drop Box in their Public folder, into which other users can place items.

① Click .

② Select System Preferences.

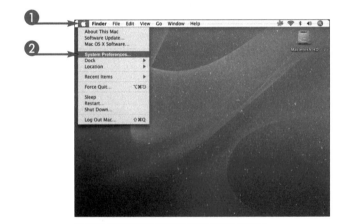

The System Preferences window appears.

③ Click Accounts.

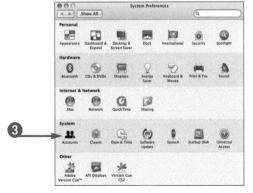

The Accounts window appears.

Note: *When you install Mac OS X on your computer, it automatically creates an Administrator account.*

④ Click Add (⊞).

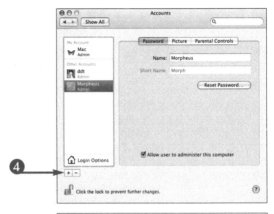

An account configuration pane appears.

⑤ Enter the full name and short name of the user of the new account.

Note: *Do not make the short name the same as the full name. A short name cannot contain spaces.*

⑥ Type a password for the user account.

⑦ Retype the password to confirm it.

⑧ Type a password hint.

A password hint is optional.

⑨ Click Create Account.

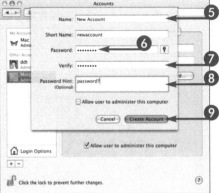

Are one user's personal files separate from those of other users?

▼ Yes. Mac OS X keeps your personal files separate from the personal files of other users. For example, your Photos folder contains only the images that you have created or downloaded from your digital camera. The exception is the Shared folder and its contents, which by default are accessible to other users on the same computer. You can also make other folders accessible to other users. For more information, see Chapter 3.

How can I personalize my user account?

▼ You can personalize the appearance of your user account by changing the Desktop picture, the default font size, the appearance of the Dock, screen resolution, and any other element that can be customized. This is useful if you have users with different abilities, such as vision-impaired users; you can configure one account with enhanced contrast or the Zoom feature on. For more information, see Chapter 11. Changes made to one account do not affect other user accounts.

continued

Set Up Multiple Accounts *(Continued)*

You can configure multiple accounts so that many people can share the same computer, though not at the same time, or set up multiple accounts for one user. The latter can be useful if you want to experiment with a variety of System settings, or try new kinds of software that can affect your computer on a system level. If these produce unwanted changes you cannot recover from, you can log back in to your other account.

You can delete user accounts, if you have an Administrator account. You may want to do this if a user will no longer be accessing the computer, or if you created a test account

that you no longer need. However, do not delete an account of an active user. Though you have an option to save the files of a deleted user account, restoring the account requires creation of a new user account and resetting of all user preferences, as well as manually moving over all the saved files.

You may also want to delete unused user accounts because each account fills a good deal of space on your computer's hard drive. Mac OS X uses free hard drive space to augment installed RAM, so the computer may slow down when free hard drive space is low.

Set Up Multiple Accounts *(continued)*

The Accounts window appears.

⑩ To select a picture for the account, click Picture.

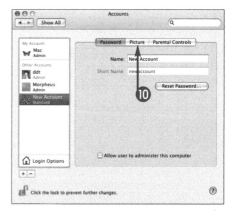

⑪ Click the picture that you want to use for the account.

⑫ To set this account as an Administrator account, click Password.

Note: *An Administrator can perform any task on the computer, such as installing new programs and adding user accounts.*

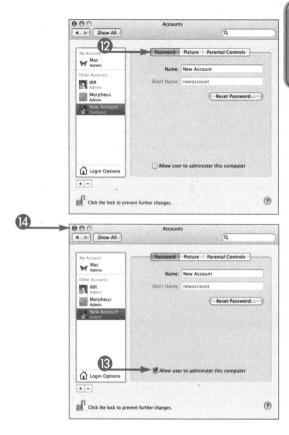

⑬ Click this option to allow the person to perform administrative tasks (☐ changes to ☑).

⑭ Click Close.

The new user can now log on to his or her account.

Can I edit the information for a user account?

▼ If you have an Administrator account, you can make changes to any user account on your computer. To make other changes, open the Accounts pane of the System Preferences and select the name of the user account you want to edit. You may be asked to enter your user password, or your user name and password. Then you can make changes to that user's account. If you do not have an Administrator account, you cannot make changes to other user accounts. Removing Administrator status is a good way to keep inexperienced or young users from affecting other accounts.

Can I delete a user account?

▼ Yes. If you have an Administrator account, you can delete a user account. To do this, open the Accounts Preferences, select the user account you want to delete, and click the Delete (-) button. You may be asked for your account name and password. You can choose to save the user's files or delete them immediately. If you save them, the files are stored as a disk image in the Deleted Users folder, which is inside the Users folder. You can double-click the disk image to see the files or delete the image.

Share Your Computer with Fast User Switching

You can move between user accounts quickly with Fast User Switching. When you enable Fast User Switching, a small Menu bar item appears in the upper right-hand corner of your computer screen that allows you to switch between user accounts quickly. This is useful if your computer is used by multiple people, each with a different user account, and more convenient than logging out and logging in as another user. It also enables one user to be on the computer without having to close another user account.

When Fast User Switching is on and you change users, the computer presents you with the login screen for that user.

You can enter the user's password to log in, if that user's account is password protected, or you can cancel. If you cancel, you are either returned to the previous user's account, if that does not require a password, or you see a general login screen, from which you can enter any user's name and password.

Switching between accounts does not affect either account. For example, one user can begin a file download, let another user log in to update his or her iPod, and then switch back. The original account is not affected.

Share Your Computer with Fast User Switching

① In the Accounts Preferences, click Login Options.

Note: *To open the Accounts Preferences, see "Set Up Multiple Accounts."*

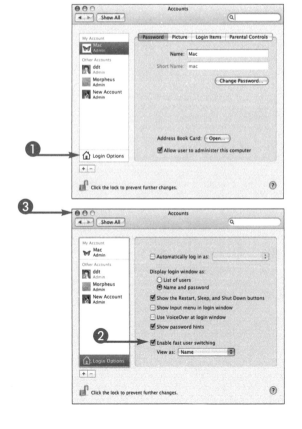

The Login Options pane appears.

② Click Enable fast user switching.

Note: *If an alert box appears, click OK.*

③ Close the Accounts Preferences.

④ In the Finder, click the name of the current computer user.

A list of user names appears.

⑤ Select a user account.

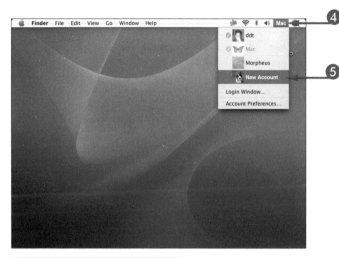

If you assigned a password to the user account, a login window appears, where you can enter a password.

⑥ Type the password.

⑦ Click Log In.

The computer switches to the selected user account.

Why does the login window shake when I try to log in?

▼ The login window shakes when you enter an incorrect password. If you enter the wrong password three times, you may see the password hint. You can then try to enter the password again. Check to make sure the Caps Lock key is not on, as this will affect the recognition of your password. If you have forgotten your password, you can click the Forgot Password button to get a hint or information on how to reset your password.

Does switching users log out a user?

▼ No. When you switch between user accounts, the user account switched from remains logged in. No applications quit and no files are closed. When you switch back, all files should be just as you left them. Background processes such as downloading files or image processing continue in a user account even when it is not the active account.

Solve a Problem with Help

Y ou can use Mac OS X's Help system to look for answers to many of your Mac-related questions. This is useful if you run across problems or want to use features that are new to you.

In Help, you can browse topics, explore new features, enter questions in plain language, and find troubleshooting tips. You can use the Back and Forward buttons in Help's toolbar to move between pages displayed in the Help window just as you would in a Web browser.

Each application on your computer has its own Help topics, most of which you can access through Mac OS X's

Help viewer. If you launch Help in the Finder, switch to another application such as Preview or Mail, and open that application's Help; then the Help page that you originally opened in the Finder will disappear. However, some third-party applications, such as Microsoft Office, have their own Help systems, which do not use the Help viewer.

If at any time you want to return to the main page of the Help viewer, you can click the Home button in the toolbar. You can use the Back button to return to the last page that you viewed.

Solve a Problem with Help

Note: *Be sure the Finder is the active application; Help opens a topic relevant to the currently active application.*

① Click Help.

② Click Mac Help.

Note: *The name of the Help command depends on the active application.*

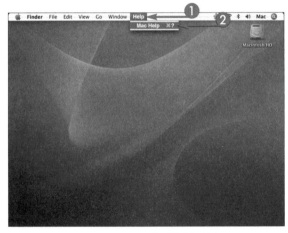

The Help window appears.

③ To search for specific help information, click here and type a word or phrase that is related to the topic and press Return.

Help topics that are related to your word or phrase appear in the Topic window.

④ Select a help topic.

⑤ Click Show.

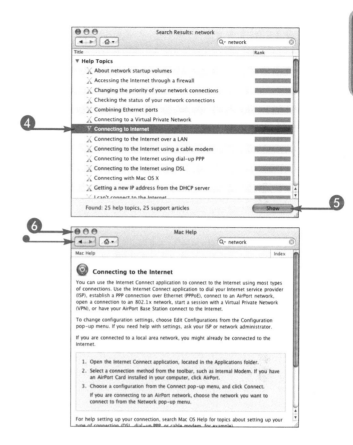

The help topic appears.

● You can click the Back and Forward buttons to move through the Help pages that you have viewed.

⑥ When you have finished reviewing help information, click Close.

Note: *You can click the Back button to return to the list of topics, or the Home button to return to the Help Viewer home page.*

The Help viewer closes.

What does the Tell me more link do?

▼ When you see the phrase Tell me more underlined, you can click the phrase to display a list of related help topics. You can then double-click the topics in the list for more specific information.

What happens if I let Help open an application or feature?

▼ Help can open an application or feature; it will then guide you on how to perform the task discussed in the help topic. You do not need to click the link that opens the application or feature.

Do I need to be connected to the Internet to use Help?

▼ No. Although the Help viewer uses an Internet connection to refresh its content to ensure that you have the most up-to-date information, you do not have to be connected to the Internet to use Help.

Look into the Applications Folder

The Applications folder is where you find all of the important programs, also known as applications, that you need to get your work done, play games, download images from a digital camera, and more. An icon and name represent each item in the Applications folder to help you locate and distinguish between the programs and folders.

The Applications folder is similar in content to the Program Files folder in Windows. However, unlike in Windows, you can easily launch applications and open files from the Applications folder.

Ⓐ Address Book
The Address Book application can help you to store and organize your contact information. For example, you can set up personal phone books and print mailing labels. You can also synchronize your Address Book information with a cell phone or personal digital assistant (PDA).

Ⓑ Automator
You can use this application to create workflows that automate common and repeated procedures. For more information, see Chapter 12.

Ⓒ Calculator
The Calculator application allows you to perform basic mathematical operations. You can customize the Calculator to show a record of your work, as though you had a paper tape record. If you want, you can also use it for trigonometric and logarithmic functions.

Ⓓ Chess
This is a 3D version of the classic game. You can play against the computer, another human, or watch the computer play itself. You can tell the computer to display hints while you play; you can even make moves using spoken commands.

Ⓔ DVD Player
This advanced DVD player can display subtitles in various languages, show multiple camera angles, and supports the Web features of many movie DVDs. It launches automatically when you insert a DVD into your DVD drive.

Ⓕ Font Book
This utility helps you organize and choose fonts for use in both your system and in your applications. For more information, see Chapter 10.

Ⓖ iCal
iCal is an application that you can use to manage your schedule. You can also share calendars over a network or over the Internet.

Ⓗ iChat
The iChat instant messaging application works with AOL Instant Messenger as well as with other iChat users. You can also have audio or video conversations with other iChat or AOL IM users.

Ⓘ iDVD
You can use iDVD to create and burn interactive DVDs from your own movies. For more information, see Chapter 17.

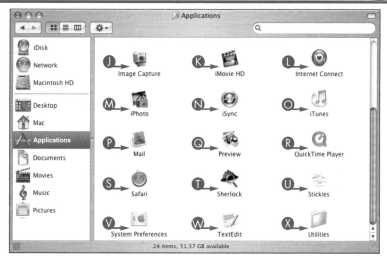

ⓙ Image Capture
The Image Capture application launches when you connect a USB- or FireWire-enabled camera or scanner to your Mac. This application helps you to import images to your computer.

Ⓚ iMovie HD
You can use iMovie HD to create your own movies from clips you recorded on and downloaded from a video camera. For more information, see Chapter 16.

Ⓛ Internet Connect
As its name states, you can use the Internet Connect application to connect to the Internet. You can do this either through your Mac's modem or a digital subscriber line (DSL).

Ⓜ iPhoto
You can use iPhoto with your digital camera to download, save, edit, and organize your digital photos. For more information, see Chapter 15.

Ⓝ iSync
The iSync application synchronizes contact and other data between your Address Book and cell phone or PDA. If you have a .Mac account, then iSync can also synchronize Calendar and Safari Web browser bookmarks between Macs on the same network.

Ⓞ iTunes
With iTunes, you can manage all your digital music files. You can also synchronize your iPod with your iTunes music, as well as purchase music through the iTunes Music Store.

Ⓟ Mail
Mail is the default e-mail client for Mac OS X. It is fully featured, so that you can use it to compose, read, forward, and manage all of your e-mail correspondence. It also has a powerful built-in junk mail filter.

Ⓠ Preview
Preview is the default viewer application for most image file types, including PDF. You can use Preview to rotate, crop, resize, and convert files.

Ⓡ QuickTime Player
You can use the QuickTime Player to watch movie files from your Mac or to view streamed media from the Web.

Ⓢ Safari
Safari is the default Web browser for Mac OS X. You can use this Web browser to view any Web page on the Internet and to store your own collection of bookmarks.

Ⓣ Sherlock
Sherlock is an advanced search application that can look for information on Web pages or your hard drive. For example, when you connect to the Internet, you can find movie schedules or stock prices.

Ⓤ Stickies
You can use Stickies in the same way that you use sticky note pads. You can write notes or reminders to yourself that stay on your Desktop until you close the application.

Ⓥ System Preferences
You can adjust almost anything about your Mac's operation from the System Preferences window.

Ⓦ TextEdit
TextEdit is a basic text editor. You can use it to write letters, notes, articles, and even to open Microsoft Word files.

Ⓧ Utilities
This folder contains various utilities that help you manage your computer and keep it in top shape. For more information, see "Explore the Utilities Folder."

Explore the
Utilities Folder

The Utilities folder resides within the Applications folder and contains many small but crucial programs that help you to maintain and troubleshoot your Mac. Your Mac automatically uses most of these programs, such as Keychain Access, when necessary. You can use other programs, such as Disk Utility, when something goes wrong with your system. For more information about troubleshooting, see Chapter 26.

Mac OS X also places assistants in the Utilities folder. Assistants are like wizards in Windows; these applications guide you through processes, such as setting up a wireless access point or a printer. You may also find folders that contain support files for installed extras. Although these files are located in the Utilities folder, you should never actually open or alter them.

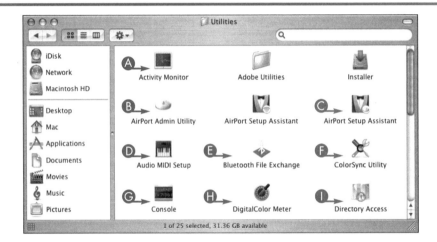

A Activity Monitor
The Activity Monitor utility displays information about your Mac's processor, disk, memory, and network activity. You can use it to check which applications are using more of your computer's resources.

B AirPort Admin Utility
If you have an AirPort wireless network connection and Base Station, then the AirPort Admin utility helps you to monitor and manage them.

C AirPort Setup Assistant
You can set up a new AirPort network or reset an existing one with this step-by-step assistant.

D Audio MIDI Setup
The Audio MIDI Setup helps you to connect audio and input devices that use the Musical Instrument Digital Interface (MIDI).

E Bluetooth File Exchange
The Bluetooth File Exchange utility allows you to select a file and send it to any Bluetooth-enabled device. You can choose to limit the file exchange to certain types of devices, such as computers, phones, or PDAs.

F ColorSync Utility
The ColorSync Utility uses your Mac's ColorSync color calibration technology to ensure accurate color representation. This utility allows you to fix damaged color profiles; set new ones; create color profiles for devices such as scanners, monitors, and printers; and adjust filters for individual documents.

G Console
You can view your Mac's log files with the Console utility. Log files help your computer to keep track of error messages and also help you to troubleshoot problems with your system.

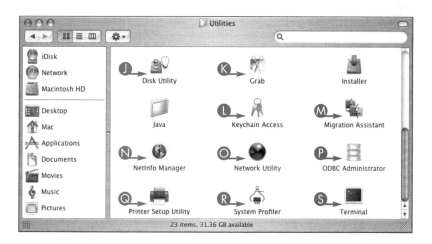

H DigitalColor Meter
The DigitalColor Meter utility opens a window that displays the color values of any point on which you place your cursor.

I Directory Access
The Directory Access utility is only for the advanced network user. This utility specifies how your Mac connects to certain network directory services. If you are using your Mac at home, then you do not need Directory Access unless you have a home network and server.

J Disk Utility
The Disk Utility is a basic management tool that you can use to configure and manage hard drives. For example, you can partition a disk or volume, erase a disk, restore it from a disk image, or verify and repair a damaged hard drive.

K Grab
You can capture screenshots with the Grab utility. Although Grab is an independent program, its interface does not appear in the screenshots that you capture.

L Keychain Access
The Keychain Access utility stores information about all of your Web site, application, and server passwords.

M Migration Assistant
The Migration Assistant helps you transfer your data, such as files, applications, passwords, and settings, from one Macintosh to another. It also transfers all users and their settings.

N NetInfo Manager
Primarily for network administrators, the NetInfo Manager utility handles and configures the central database of user accounts and configuration information.

O Network Utility
Also for network administrators, Network Utility collects network-troubleshooting tools. You should not need this utility if you are a home user.

P ODBC Administrator
The ODBC Administrator utility helps you to work with databases that use the Open Database Connectivity (ODBC) standard.

Q Printer Setup Utility
As the name suggests, the Printer Setup Utility allows you to set up and connect to printers.

R System Profiler
You can view detailed information about the hardware and software on your Mac with the System Profiler utility.

S Terminal
The Terminal utility allows you to enter and work with the Unix command line. You should only use the Terminal utility if you are familiar with Unix.

Tour the Home Folder

Your home folder, which is located in the Users folder, contains all of your personal settings and files. Each user has its own home folder, and you can switch between users in order to give each user a personalized and secure working environment.

Each home folder has the same name as its user's short name. For example, if a user's short name is Puppy, then the user's home folder is the folder named Puppy in the Users folder. You should not change the name of a home folder. For more information about setting up multiple accounts, see Chapter 8.

You can open your home folder in Finder by selecting Home from the Go menu. The active home folder appears as a house icon.

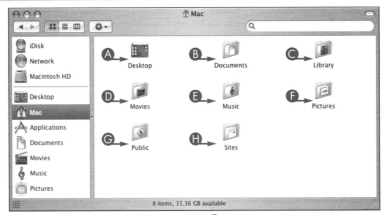

A Desktop
The Desktop contains all of the user's folders and files. These folders and files do not appear when another user logs on.

B Documents
The Documents folder is the default folder to which applications save text, data, spreadsheets, and other documents. As with other contents of your home folder, the Documents folder is not accessible by other users unless you allow them access.

C Library
Each user has a Library folder. The Library folder contains settings files that specify your preferences for your applications, as well as application support files, such as fonts. The operating system also has its own Library folder, which is at a higher level in the hard drive directory. You should not open or alter any of these files.

D Movies
Like the Documents folder, the Movies folder is the default folder to which applications save your videos and video project files.

E Music
This is the default folder to which applications save audio and music files. It is also where iTunes stores and organizes the MP3 and AAC files for its own music library.

F Pictures
Just as the Music folder stores iTunes files, the Pictures folder stores iPhoto files. You can save and organize photos and other images in the Pictures folder.

G Public
Unlike the other folders in your home directory, the Public folder is open to other users. These users can browse and copy files from this folder, as well as place files in the Drop Box within this folder. Your Public folder is useful for sharing information, projects, or files with other users on the same computer.

H Sites
The Sites folder is where you store the contents of your personal Web sites if you are hosting the sites from your Mac.

Customize Content Folders

Although you can use the default Mac OS X folder configuration to save all of your text files in the Documents folder and photos in the Pictures folder, you can also customize your folder structure for greater efficiency. This is helpful if you work with multiple projects or have hundreds or thousands of files.

Organize by Project
This is perhaps the most common method of creating and organizing files and folders. Instead of saving all of your text files into one Documents folder, you can create and name folders for each project. You can keep these folders within the Documents folder, on your Desktop, or in your Applications folder. This method allows you to keep relevant files together.

Organize by Topic
If you use the same research materials for various projects, or are saving text or movie files for later reference, then you can create folders for each topic. As a result, you can easily find information about specific topics. You can also group applications in subfolders in the Applications folder.

Organize Folders for Revision Control
You can create folders that help you keep track of which files are rough drafts, and which are in their final state. This method is helpful when you are organizing by project. As a result, you can quickly determine which items still need work.

Organize by Application
If you prefer to work in one application at a time, then you can create folders within the application folder for your work. For example, you may create illustrations in one application, and then quit that application to type a document in a word processing application. As a result, when you open the application's folder, all the files that you want to work with are organized in that folder. In addition, you can organize by project, so that each application's folder contains subfolders that you devote to each project.

Use Labels
You can use labels to color code folders and files so that you can find them quickly. You can also use labels to designate types of folders. For example, you can choose brighter colors to label folders that contain priority items, or darker colors for folders that contain less-important items. For more information on labeling folders and files, see Chapter 1.

Use Full Names
You can give folders descriptive names so that you can quickly determine folder content. You can also give related folders the same prefix, so that when you display them in List view, they are grouped together. For example, if you have three folders that contain photos of Andrew's first three birthdays, then you can name the folders Andrew Birthday 1, Andrew Birthday 2, and Andrew Birthday 3.

Use the Dock
You can place folders in the Dock by dragging the folders' icons to the Dock. You are not actually moving the folder, but you are placing a representation of the folder in the Dock. When you click the folder's icon in the Dock, the folder opens. You can also click and hold the folder's icon to reveal the folder contents.

Use Aliases
If you prefer to the store items on the Desktop for quick access rather than in the Dock, then you can create aliases to folders and place these aliases on the Desktop. When you no longer need to quickly open or move items to these folders, you can drag the alias to the Trash icon. Dragging the alias to the Trash does not affect the actual folder. This method works well with Exposé. For more information about using Exposé, see Chapter 9.

Control Access to Your Public Folder

You can specify the level of access that other users have to the Public folder in your home folder. By default, all other users can view the contents of your Public folder, as well as copy files from it. This is called Read only access.

You can eliminate this access to prohibit other users from even viewing the contents of your Public folder. You can also increase the access that other users have, to allow them to not only view and copy the files that you have in your Public folder, but also to place files in your Public folder.

The Public folder is useful when you want to share files with other users, especially if these files are too large to send through e-mail. For example, you can use the Public folder to facilitate collaboration on a project, or to share music or photos with other users.

Keep in mind that when you allow full access to your Public folder, other users on your Mac are able to delete your files, or to place files that you may not want in your Public folder. If you are concerned about this, then you can easily change the access permissions at any time.

Control Access to Your Public Folder

① In the Finder, click Go.

② Click Home.

Your home folder appears.

③ Click the Public folder.

④ Click File.

⑤ Click Get Info.

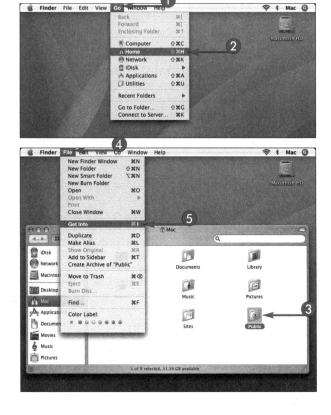

The Info window appears for the Public folder.

6 Click Ownership & Permissions (▶ changes to ▼).

7 Click Details (▶ changes to ▼).

8 Click Others 🔃 and select the access permissions you want from the pull-down menu.

You can choose to give other users Read & Write, Read only, Write only, or No Access permissions to your Public folder.

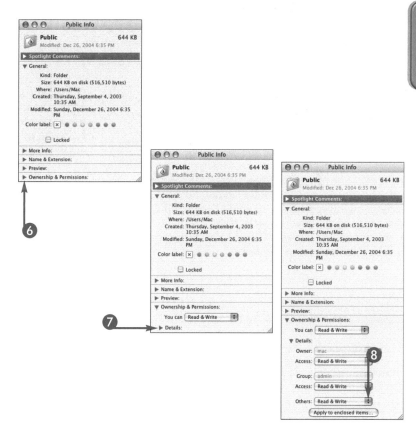

If I accidentally restrict my access to my own Public folder, can I correct this mistake?

▼ Yes. If you accidentally change the access permissions to No Access for the Owner rather than for Others, then you can change it back by following Steps **1** to **7**, and then selecting the Read & Write option from the Owner pull-down menu.

Can I change users' access to my other folders?

▼ Yes. You can select any folder and change its access permissions to allow other users to read the folder. By default all user folders other than the Public folder are inaccessible to other users. You should keep your own Library folder inaccessible, as this folder contains your user settings.

Can I change users' access to individual files?

▼ Yes. You can allow other users to read and write a file, which means that they are able to open and save the file. The default setting for your files is No Access, which means that other users can neither view nor alter your files.

Navigate Dialogs with Shortcuts

You can use keyboard shortcuts to navigate quickly through the dialogs that appear when you open and save a file, or save a file with a new name. Keyboard shortcuts are especially useful for users who are more comfortable using the keyboard than the mouse.

Many applications have their own keyboard shortcuts. These shortcuts appear next to the commands in the command menu, such as the standard Command-C shortcut for copying text. However, shortcuts may vary between applications, so you should familiarize yourself with each application that you use.

Certain keyboard shortcuts are standard across applications and in the Mac OS X Finder. If you familiarize yourself with these shortcuts, then you can increase your efficiency. For example, when you have to type something in a different field, instead of moving your hand to the mouse, using the mouse to click in the new field, and then returning your hands to the keyboard to begin typing, you can press the Tab key to move to the new field. In addition, because all applications use Open and Save dialogs, you can save time by using the keyboard shortcuts for these commands.

Select next area of the dialog

① Press the Tab key to cycle through selectable areas of the dialog.

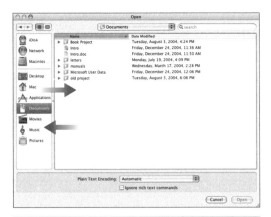

Select folders

① Press an Arrow key to select the item above the highlighted item.

● The Up arrow selects the item above, and the Down arrow selects the item below.

You can also press a letter key to move to a folder or file beginning with that letter.

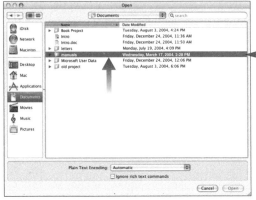

Scroll lists up or down

1 Press a Page key to move the list of folders or files up or down in the scroll window.

● The Page Up key scrolls the list one page up, and the Page Down key scrolls the list one page down.

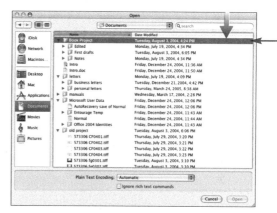

Navigate to a folder by name

1 Press ⌘-Shift-G.

The Go to the folder dialog appears.

2 Type the folder pathname.

3 Press Return or click Go.

The contents of the folder display in a Finder window.

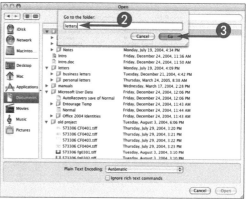

Can I select the Open or Save button in a dialog from the keyboard?

▼ Yes. Whenever a dialog has a default button, which appears blue and pulsing, you can press the Return or Enter key to select it. This is true for Open and Save dialogs, as well as any dialog with a default button.

Can I close the dialog from the keyboard?

▼ Yes. You can press Esc or the ⌘-. (period) combination. The result is the same as if you click the Cancel button in the dialog. This keyboard shortcut also works in most dialogs, such as the Shut Down dialog, to cancel an action.

When in the dialog, can I type the complete file or folder name to navigate to a specific file or folder?

▼ No. If you are trying to navigate to the folder named Foo and you type **F**, then the first folder that starts with *F* alphabetically is highlighted. As a result, if you have a folder named Fan, then that folder is highlighted. If you type **F** and then **O**, the dialog switches between the first folder starting with *F* and the first folder starting with *O*. Instead, you should type **F** and then use the Arrow keys.

Optimize the Sidebar

You can customize the Sidebar in any Finder or folder window to help you work more efficiently. For example, you can create links to the folders and applications that you use most frequently, increase or decrease the space that the Sidebar uses, unmount disks and hard drives, and store links to Web pages.

When you have customized the Sidebar, you can use one Finder window as your window onto the entire computer. When you click a location in the Sidebar, its contents appear in the right side of the window; you can click another item in the Sidebar to navigate directly to it.

All folders that appear in the Sidebar are drag-and-drop targets. As a result, you can drag files and other folders to the location icons in the Sidebar and drop the files to move them to a new location; you can also Option-drag the items to copy them. This method can save you a great deal of time that you would otherwise spend navigating layers of folders in order to move or copy a file.

Set Default Contents of the Sidebar

① Click Finder.

② Click Preferences.

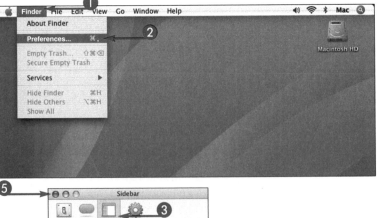

The General Preferences window appears.

③ Click the Sidebar icon.

④ Click the items that you want to appear in the Sidebar (☐ changes to ☑).

You can click selected items to deselect them (☑ changes to ☐).

⑤ Click ◉ to close the window.

Add and Remove Items in a Sidebar

Add an item to the Sidebar

1 To add an item, drag it to the lower part of the Sidebar.

● An alias of the item appears in the Sidebar.

The upper part of the Sidebar is reserved for hard drives, removable drives such as CD-ROMs, and network drives, including your iDisk.

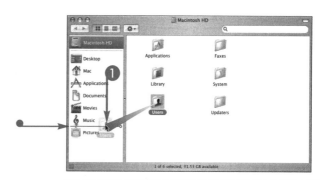

Remove an item from the Sidebar

1 To remove an item, drag it out of the Sidebar to the Desktop.

● The item disappears in an animated puff of smoke.

Although this action removes the alias of the item from the Sidebar, it does not delete the original file.

Can I change the size of my Sidebar?

▼ Yes, at least in terms of width. Place the cursor over the bar that divides the Sidebar pane from the main pane of the window. Click and drag the bar to the right or left to increase or decrease the Sidebar width.

Can I represent items in the Sidebar with only icons?

▼ Yes. When you decrease the Sidebar width, there is a point at which only icons appear for the items.

Can I open files that I place in the Sidebar?

▼ Yes. When you click a file that you have placed in the Sidebar, the Finder launches the application that is associated with that file and then opens the file. Unlike a file that is in a Finder window or on the Desktop, the file opens with a single click, rather than a double click.

Search in the Finder

Y ou can search for items, whether they are applications, folders, or specific kinds of files, within the Finder. This is useful not only because you can locate items, but searching allows you to see together items of a specific type, even if they are located in different folders or even drives.

The search feature in the Finder works with Mac OS X's Searchlight technology, which indexes your hard drive when you first install Mac OS X 10.4. Spotlight also automatically updates its index as you add, delete, or change files, so it is always up to date. The use of Spotlight

means that you can search for files based on a variety of criteria, such as keywords such as document or last week to find files by type or when they were last modified.

The search feature returns results displayed in categories such as folders, images, and so on. By default, the search results show only the top five results for each category but you can click a link to show all results in that category.

You can also add or delete search criteria in addition to name. This helps you narrow down search results, which is useful if you are searching for an item that has a commonly used name.

Search in the Finder

① Click File.

② Select Find.

The New Search window appears.

③ Type the name of the item.

④ Click ⊕ to add search criteria.

⑤ Select type of criterion from this pull-down menu.

Note: The menu to the right changes according to the criterion selected.

⑥ Click ⊖ to remove search criteria.

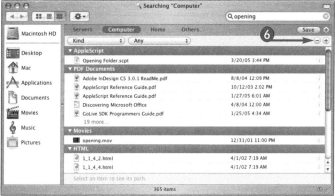

How can I open a file I have found by searching?

▼ You can double-click an item listed in the New Search window's results to open it. If you have not installed the application that created the file, Mac OS X prompts you to choose an application with which to open the file. You can also single-click an item to see where it is located. Its location is displayed at the bottom of the New Search window.

Can I move a file shown in the New Search window's results?

▼ Yes. You can click an item in the results to see where it is located; its location is displayed at the bottom of the New Search window. Drag the file to a folder or the Desktop to move it to that new place. The New Search window updates to reflect the change in the file's location.

Change Finder and Folder Views

Y ou can view Finder or folder windows in one of three ways: Icon view, List view, and Column view. The first two views are familiar to users of Mac OS 9 and earlier, while the last view is new to Mac OS X.

In Icon view, items appear as full-size icons, just as they would if they were on your Desktop. You can specify that the icons snap to a grid or that they appear randomly. This view is useful if you have a few items that you want to identify quickly. For more information, see the section "Change Your Desktop and Window Icon Sizes."

List view displays the contents of a window in a list that is organized alphabetically by name. List view can fit more items into a single window, and also displays other columns of information about each item.

Column view displays a visual representation of the folder hierarchy for the folder or file that you are viewing. This view is useful if you are working with multiple folders or need to move files to different folders.

These three views are available in all windows, whether or not the Sidebar is visible. For more information see the section "Optimize the Sidebar."

Change Finder and Folder Views

Change the view using the toolbar

① Click the Icon View button (▦).

The window changes to Icon view.

- The Snap to Grid icon appears if the Snap to grid option is selected in the window's View options.

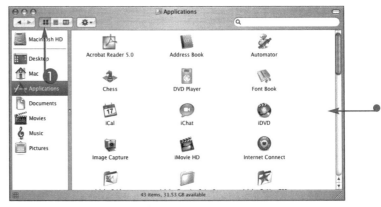

② Click the List View button (▤).

- The window changes to List view.

③ Click the Column View button (📖).

- The window changes to Column view.

To view the full folder hierarchy, you can scroll the window's content left and right.

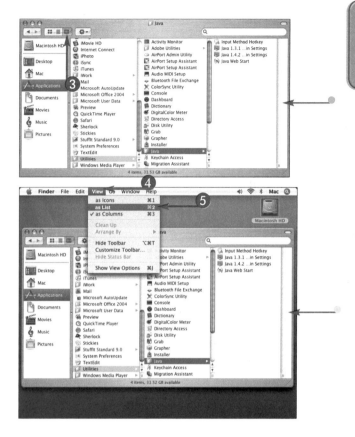

Change the view using the Finder menu

④ Click View.

⑤ Click a view option in the pull-down menu.

- The window changes to reflect your selection.

Can I use icon previews in a folder window?

▼ Yes. You can customize a window view so that it displays a preview of image files in the folder window. The preview becomes the file's icon. Click View➔Show View Options from the menu. In the View Options window, click Show icon previews (◯ changes to ◉). Close the View Options window. The Finder creates previews of the image files and uses the previews as the file icons. These previews only appear when a folder is in Icon view.

Can I change the width of the columns in Column view?

▼ Yes. Click and drag the bottom of a column divider to change the width of that column. To change the width of all columns at once, hold down the Option key while dragging the column divider.

Will the Finder remember my preferences for each window?

▼ If you have customized a window to display in Icon or List view, the window retains the same view settings the next time you open it.

Change Your Desktop and Window Icon Sizes

You can customize the file and folder icons that appear on your Desktop by changing their size. For example, you can specify sizes from 16 by 16 pixels to 128 by 128 pixels. The smaller icon size allows you to fit more icons onto your Desktop, although they are not as legible. In contrast, larger icons are easier to recognize, but require more space on your Desktop.

You can also set icon sizes for items in folder and Finder windows. In addition to specifying a default icon size for existing and new folders, you can also specify icon size

settings for individual windows. This is useful if you have certain folders that contain a small number of items that you want to make highly visible. In addition to changing icon sizes for a window in Icon view, you can also change the size of icons that appear in List view.

You can also customize the text size of icon labels. The type size can be from 10-point type to 16-point type, and you can specify whether these labels appear either below the icon or to the right of it.

Change Your Desktop Icon Size

① Click View.

② Click Show View Options.

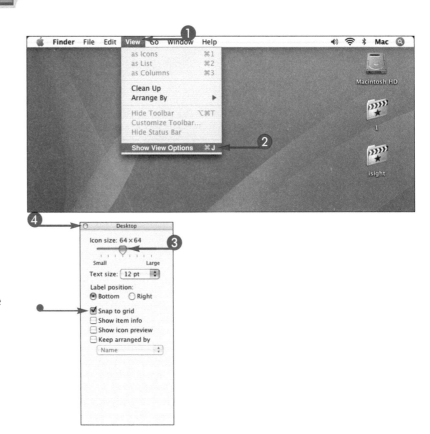

The Desktop View Options window appears.

③ Drag the slider to select a size for the icons on your Desktop.

You can select a label size in the Text size pull-down menu.

● You can arrange your Desktop icons neatly by selecting the Snap to grid option (☐ changes to ☑).

④ Click ◉ to close the window.

The Desktop icons reflect your changes.

Change Your Window Icon Size

1 Click a window.

2 Click View.

3 Click Show View Options.

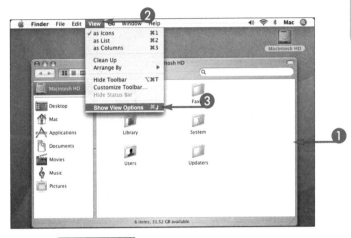

The View Options window appears for the window you selected.

4 Drag the slider to select an icon size setting.

● You can specify a label size in the Text size pull-down menu.

● You can apply your choices to all Finder windows by clicking All windows (○ changes to ⊙).

You can specify which columns appear in a window's List view by selecting them in the View Options window (○ changes to ⊙).

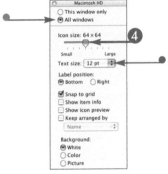

Can I specify the order in which items are arranged?

▼ Yes. Either on the Desktop or in a window in Icon view, you can use the Keep arranged by pull-down menu in the View Options window to arrange items by name, date modified, date created, size, kind, or label.

Can Desktop icons of images display thumbnails of the images?

▼ Yes. Click the Show icon preview option in the Desktop View Options window. When you save a file that has a preview, such as an image file, to the Desktop, the icon for the file appears as a preview of the image.

Can I set some Desktop or folder icons to one size and others to another size?

▼ No. Although you can specify that individual folders display their own icon sizes, whether in Icon or List view, you cannot display multiple icon sizes within a folder, Finder window, or on the Desktop. You also cannot specify icon sizes for individual folders if you have selected the All windows option in any folder's View Options window.

Change the Sorting Order
and Reorder Sorting Criteria

Y ou can sort items in any Finder window that is in List view. You can view the items in increasing or decreasing alphabetical order, by dates from newest to oldest or oldest to newest, or by kind. This feature is useful when you want to see which items have been accessed or modified recently, such as when a folder's contents have been changed. You can also see which files or folders use the most disk space, if you need to create space on your hard drive. Sorting by kind allows you to differentiate images from text files even if their names are similar.

In addition to changing the order in which each column is sorted, you can also change the order in which the columns appear from left to right. This feature is useful if you want to keep a window size small but also want to see a particular file attribute. For example, you may be more interested in viewing the kind of file rather than the date on which it was modified. The only column that you cannot move in the column order is the Name column, which always appears in the left-most column of the window.

Change the Sorting Order

① Open a folder or Finder window.

② Click the List View button (▤) to change the window to List view.

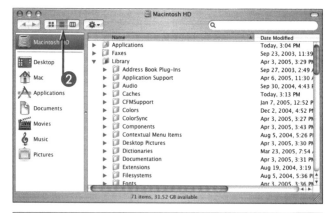

③ Click the Name heading to reverse the list sorting order (▼ changes to ▲).

The list switches between alphabetical and reverse alphabetical order.

You can click any number of times to toggle the order back and forth.

You can also click the Date Modified, Size, and Kind column headings to reverse their sorting order.

Reorder sorting criteria

① Click and hold the heading of a column that you want to move.

② Drag the cursor horizontally.

③ Release the cursor when the column is in the position you want.

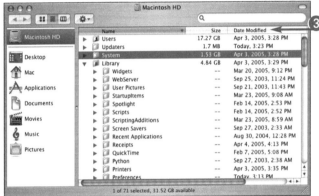

Why does a window have to be in List view when you change the column order?

▼ This is because you cannot sort the other two views, Icon and Column. For example, the Column view displays the contents of each folder by name in alphabetical order.

Can I arrange other folder views?

▼ Yes. In Icon view, you can click View, and then click Arrange in the Finder to reorder a selected folder's contents by name, date modified, date created, kind, size, or label.

Can I change the width of each column in List view?

▼ Yes. To change a column's width, position the mouse over the right edge of the column. The cursor arrow changes to a resize cursor. Click and then drag the column edge until the column is the width you want. Names that are longer than the column width are automatically truncated. The date information also automatically adjusts according to the width of the Date Modified column, and even changes to Today or Yesterday if the column is too narrow.

Add Parental Controls

Y ou can customize your Mac to limit the primary user interface for any of the computer's users. These parental controls offer less power and flexibility for users than the regular Finder, and prevent a user from changing important preferences and settings.

However, you can set controls to still allow users to access important applications, and you can also allow users to open and save documents, access the Internet, and share files with other users. This option does not preclude other users on the same computer from using the regular Finder and administering the computer.

These restrictions are useful for allowing inexperienced users to work on your computer safely. It presents fewer menu options and commands in the menu bar. It also adds three folders — My Applications, Documents, and Shared — to the Dock. Simple Finder users can neither add icons to the Dock, nor can they create new folders, although they can open folders that exist in the Documents and Shared folders. This allows for a less complex interface and simplifies troubleshooting if problems occur.

Add Parental Controls

Note: *The following changes must be made from an Administrator account.*

① Click the Apple menu ().

② Click System Preferences.

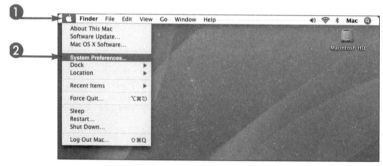

The System Preferences window appears.

③ Click the Accounts icon.

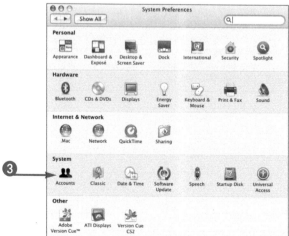

The Accounts window appears.

④ Click the name of the account that you want to simplify.

⑤ Click the Parental Controls tab.

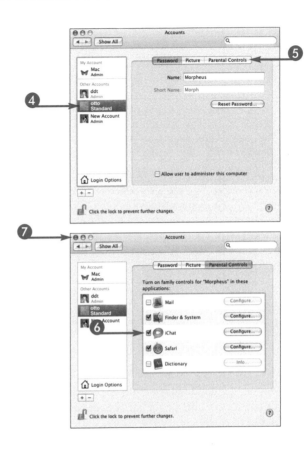

⑥ Click to check the applications and folders that you want the simplified user to be able to access.

⑦ Click 🔘 to close the window.

Note: *You should ensure that the Simple Finder tab is selected when you close the Accounts window. If it is not selected, then your changes may not occur.*

Can I switch back from the Simple Finder to the regular Finder?

▼ Yes. You can re-enable the regular Finder from an account that is using the Simple Finder without having to open the System Preferences. Click Finder, and then click Run Full Finder. You are prompted for your name and password. If you type the name and password of an Administrator, then Mac OS X returns you to the regular Finder. To enable the Simple Finder again, you can click Finder and then click Return to Simple Finder.

If a user has the Simple Finder, can I grant them access to any application, including utilities?

▼ Yes. In the Simple Finder tab, expand Utilities, Applications (Mac OS 9), or Others to display the applications and utilities that you can make available to the My Applications folder in the Simple Finder.

What if the Applications list does not display an application that I want to include?

▼ Click the Locate button at the bottom of the Limitations tab. A prompt appears, asking you to locate and choose the application. When you choose the application, it appears under the Others heading.

Select
Multiple Items

Y ou can select more than one item at a time. The items can be files, folders, or applications. This feature is useful when you want to open or delete multiple items, or move them to a new location.

You can select multiple items whether they are on the desktop or in folders. You can also select items in List, Icon, or Column view in a Finder window.

Once you select the items, you can do several things. For example, you can move the items by dragging them to a different location, or you can copy the items by holding

down the Option key and dragging them. You can also apply labels to the files, open the files by double-clicking them, and change permissions using the Get Info command. For more information see the section "Change Permissions with Get Info."

You can also select multiple items from different folders and even from different drives, including removable media. When selecting a large number of items, you can still deselect one item at a time. This allows you to select only the items you want to affect without having to start the selection process all over again.

Select Multiple Items

Select contiguous items

1. When in List or Column view, select an item by clicking it.

2. Hold the Shift key and click another item to select all items between and including the selected item and the one clicked.

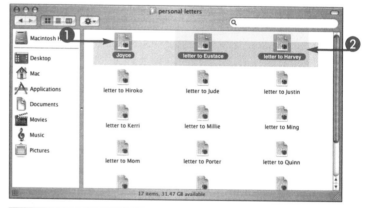

Select noncontiguous items

1. Click an item to select it.

2. Hold ⌘ and click another item.

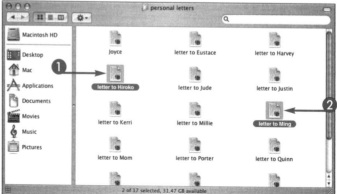

Delete Multiple Items

You can select multiple items, and then delete them all at once. This feature is useful when you need to delete a large number of files that you no longer need, such as earlier drafts of a project, or files that are cluttering up your work area. These files can be adjacent or nonadjacent items; they can even be in different folders. For more information, see the section "Select Multiple Items."

The items that you select can be files, folders, or applications. You can also select a hard drive or type of removable media, such as a DVD or CD-ROM. However, if you drag these items to the Trash along with items that you want to delete, the drives unmount and the DVDs or CD-ROMs eject.

You should be careful when disposing of long lists of items; you may accidentally include an application or file that you do not want to delete. You can open the Trash folder to check its contents before you empty it.

Delete Multiple Items

① Click an item to select it.

② Shift-click or ⌘-click other items to select them.

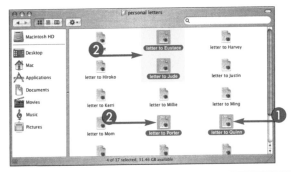

③ Drag the items to the Trash.

Note: The items are not deleted until you empty the Trash.

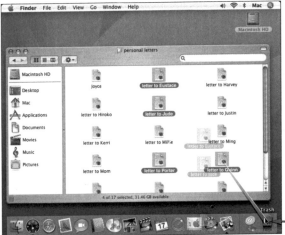

Share
Files

You can allow users to access and alter specific files if they are using the same computer as you or if their computer is on the network to which your computer is connected. This can be more convenient than e-mailing files back and forth, and saves you from having to manage multiple copies of revised files.

The downside of sharing a file is that other users may make changes that you do not want or may not even be aware of. Although certain applications, such as Microsoft Word,

offer features that allow you to keep track of changes, most do not. As a result, it is best to keep a copy of the file in your unshared user directory for safekeeping.

If you have a .Mac account, you can also share your iDisk Public folder so that anyone with an Internet connection can view the files that you place there. However, they can neither alter the files without downloading them, nor can they upload them to your iDisk folders.

Share Files on the Same Computer

① Double-click the hard drive icon on the Desktop.

The Finder window appears for your hard drive.

② Click your user icon in the Sidebar.

Your user directory appears in the right pane.

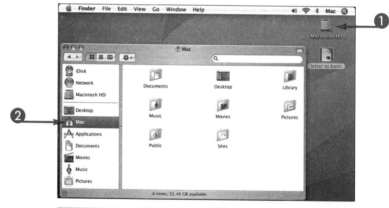

You may have to scroll up or down in the Finder window to locate your Public folder.

③ Drag the file that you want to share to your Public folder.

This file is now accessible to other users on your computer.

You can also Option-drag a file to place a copy in the Public folder, rather than the original.

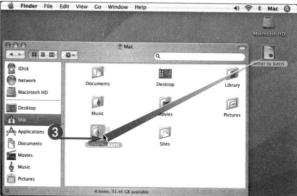

Share Files over a Network

① Click the Apple menu (🍎).

② Click System Preferences.

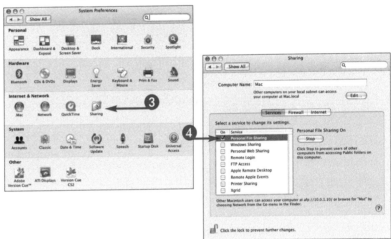

The System Preferences window appears.

③ Click the Sharing icon.

The Sharing window appears.

④ In the Services tab, click the Personal File Sharing checkbox (☐ changes to ☑).

The Start button changes to a Stop Button as File Sharing starts up.

⑤ Click ⬤ to close the Sharing window.

Any files in your Public folder are now accessible to users on the same network.

Can I transfer a file to other users on the same computer?

▼ Yes. You can transfer a copy of a file by dragging the file's icon to the Drop Box inside another user's Public folder. The user can now open, alter, and save that copy of your file.

Do I need to alter a file's permissions before I can share it?

▼ No. When you place a file in your Public folder, it is automatically accessible to other users on the same computer. The same is true for other users on the same network, provided that you have turned on Personal File Sharing. For more information on permissions, see the section "Change Permissions with Get Info."

Can I share files with Windows users?

▼ Yes. In the Sharing window, select Windows Sharing and then click Start. All Windows users on the same network can now access your Public folder.

Delete Files Securely

When you put files in the Trash, you can take an extra step to ensure that they are deleted securely. Although you delete files when you empty the Trash normally, specialized file recovery software can still recover at least portions of these files. If you regularly handle sensitive or personal information and are worried about other users gaining access to the data, you can use the Secure Empty Trash feature.

This feature overwrites all deleted files with random ones and zeros, to ensure that even dedicated recovery efforts

cannot reconstruct your data. However, the flip side to this is that any file that you may have accidentally deleted in a secure manner is beyond recovery.

Using the Secure Empty Trash feature can also take more time than the regular Empty Trash feature. This is due to the disk overwriting that is required for security. How long the secure deleting takes is based on the size of the file or files that you are overwriting.

Delete Files Securely

① Click the files that you want to delete securely.

② Drag these files to the Trash.

The Trash icon changes to show that it contains items.

③ Click Finder.

④ Click Secure Empty Trash.

The files that you selected are removed securely.

Delete Locked Files

You may sometimes have to deal with files that are locked. The creator or another user of a file can protect the file from being changed or deleted by locking it. Although all users with access to the locked files can open them, they cannot put them into the Trash.

If you have proper permission to alter the status of a locked file, then you can delete it by changing its status. If you do not have permissions to change the file's status,

then you cannot delete it. For more information see the section "Change Permissions with Get Info."

Many applications load locked files onto your computer. These files are often instructions, or support files, that are necessary for the application to run. You should not delete or change a locked file if you are unsure whether the file is necessary.

Delete Locked Files

1 Click a locked file.

2 Click File.

3 Click Get Info.

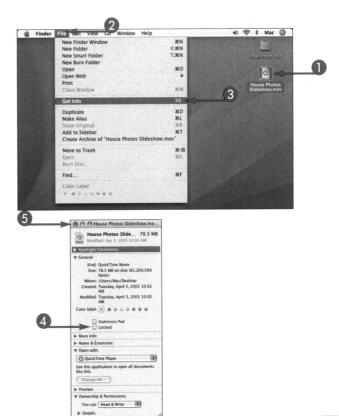

The Info window appears for the file you selected.

4 Click Locked (☑ changes to ☐).

5 Click ◉ to close the Info window.

The file is unlocked, and you can now drag it to the Trash to delete it.

Force Quit Recalcitrant Programs

You can force an application to quit when it is not responding to your input. A program can sometimes get caught in a loop, which is also called a hang, when it encounters bad data or a bug in the program. By forcing the application to quit, you can exit the program and relaunch it, so that you can continue to work.

When you force a program to quit, you lose all unsaved data, so you should save your data frequently. However, you do not cause any damage to the operating system when you force quit an application.

You may also choose to force quit applications that, for one reason or another, are using too much memory or processor time and you are not able to quit the application normally. If you notice that your computer is acting sluggish, and you have identified a specific application as the cause, then you can force quit and then relaunch the application. Keep in mind that in addition to losing all unsaved changes to your documents, you also lose any application settings that you have changed.

You can also force quit a Mac OS 9 application. However, this may also quit the entire Classic environment.

Force Quit Recalcitrant Programs

① Press ⌘-Option-Escape.

The Force Quit Applications window appears.

② Click the stalled program that you want to force quit.

③ Click Force Quit.

A dialog appears, asking you to confirm that you want to force the application to quit.

④ Click Force Quit.

The program is terminated.

Create an Alias

You can create an alias of a file, folder, or application. An alias is a pointer to the original file. Using aliases is often a way to collect pointers to various files and folders in one place. This can provide a more convenient way to access items that are sometimes buried in folders across your hard drive. For more information see the section "Create a Launcher with Aliases."

You can place an alias anywhere on your hard drive. An alias is visually distinguished from the original by a small arrow at the bottom left of the alias's icon and by the fact that the word *alias* may be appended to the alias's name.

When you double-click an alias, the action is the same as if you were double-clicking the original item. For example, when you double-click a folder's alias, the original folder opens on your Desktop. When you click an application's alias, the original program launches.

If you delete the original item, the alias no longer works. However, you can delete an alias without affecting the original item.

Create an Alias

① Click the item for which you want to make an alias.

② Click File.

③ Click Make Alias.

An alias of the original item appears next to the original item.

④ Drag the alias to a new location.

Create a Launcher with Aliases

You can use a menu that with one click launches often-used applications. This menu, called a launcher, groups aliases into a single, convenient location from which you can open your favorite applications. This saves you from having to first find them in your user, Applications, or Utilities folder.

Aliases are pointers to files, folders, or applications. Because they are not the original items, you can delete or move the aliases without affecting the originals. Aliases are useful because you can place them in multiple locations, as well as places you might not want the original. For example, you

may need to give users access to a certain application, but do not want to install the application in multiple user folders.

Although most of your applications are in your Applications folder, you may have organized your hard drive to place other often-used items, such as files or games, in their own folders. You may also want to use items from the Utilities folder regularly. By creating a launcher, you have quick access to all of these applications without having to move even one of them. Also, if you decide not to use the launcher, you can delete it entirely without affecting the original items.

Create a Launcher with Aliases

① Click an item that you want to place in the launcher.

② Press ⌘-L.

● An alias of the item appears.

You can distinguish aliases by the small arrow that appears by the file icon, and by the word *alias* appended to the filename.

③ Drag the alias to an empty folder.

Note: *To create a new folder, see Chapter 1.*

You can give the folder a name, such as Launcher or Favorites.

④ Repeat Steps **1** to **3** to add items to the launcher.

⑤ Drag the folder to the right side of the Dock.

● An alias of the folder appears in the Dock.

Note: *As with other items that you place in the Dock,*
the original folder is not actually affected.

⑥ Click and hold the folder.

A contextual menu of the folder's contents
appears.

⑦ Drag up to the name of the item that you
want to launch and release the mouse to
launch.

**Can I delete the original folder
and keep the one in the Dock?**

▼ No. The folder that appears in
the Dock is just an alias of the
actual folder. If you delete the
original folder, then the alias in
the Dock does not work. The
contents of the alias in the Dock
change to reflect changes you
make in the original folder.

**Can I create subfolders in the
launcher folder for better
organization?**

▼ Yes. You can create folders
within the original folder and
place aliases within any of these
subfolders. These subfolders
appear when you click and hold
the launcher folder in the Dock.
This is a good way to organize
applications, utilites, games, and
important files.

**Does it matter where the
original folder is located?**

▼ No. You can place the original
folder anywhere. However, you
should place it somewhere
accessible, so that you can easily
add or remove items to and
from it.

Change Permissions with Get Info

You can control access to your private information by imposing limitations on user permissions. Permissions are settings for files, folders, and even hard drives that tell your computer who can access the items on your hard drive and what they can do with them.

There are four permission settings: Read & Write, Read only, Write only, and No Access. Read & Write allows a user to open an item, view its contents, and make changes to it. Read only allows a user to open the item to view the contents, but not to alter or copy the contents. You can use

Write only with folders to allow other users to copy items to the folder, but not to view the folder contents or copy items from it. No Access prevents users from accessing the item at all — they cannot view the item, alter its content, or copy it.

Mac OS X automatically sets permissions for certain folders. For example, your user directory and folders are set to No Access for other users, aside from those with Administrator accounts. Each user also has a Public folder, which is set to Read only; inside each Public folder is a Drop Box, which is set to Write only.

Change Permissions with Get Info

① Click a file or folder to select it.

② Click File.

③ Click Get Info.

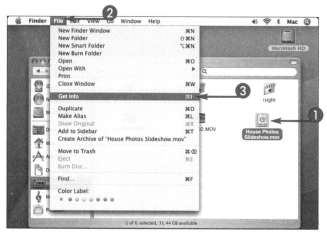

The Get Info window appears for the item you selected.

④ Click Ownership & Permission (▶ changes to ▼).

The permissions setting displays for this item.

5 Click Details (▶ changes to ▼).

6 Click Others ⬦ and select the permissions level for other users from the pull-down menu.

Folders offer the Write only (Drop Box) option, while files and applications do not.

7 Click ⬤ to close the Get Info window.

The permissions you selected are applied to the folder.

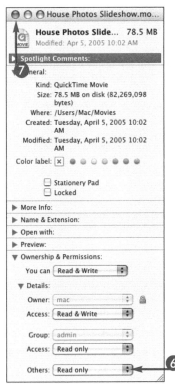

Can I apply a new permission to all items in a folder?

▼ Yes. To do this, click the Apply to enclosed items button. The same permissions that you specify for the folder automatically apply to all items in the folder.

Why are some menus in the Details or Ownership & Permissions sections dimmed?

▼ If any of the menus are dimmed, this means that you do not have ownership or sufficient permissions to change those settings.

What does it mean if I see a lock icon next to a pull-down menu?

▼ The lock icon signifies that only a user with an Administrator account can make a change to that setting. If you have an Administrator account, click the lock; you are prompted for your username and password. When you submit this information, it unlocks the menu and you can make changes.

Customize
Icons

You can apply customized images to folder, file, and hard drive icons using the Get Info window. This can give your desktop and folders a personalized look, as well as help you to visually distinguish items more easily.

The new icon can be any image file, whether a photo or vector illustration. It is scaled to the normal icon size that you have specified in the View options window. As a result, highly detailed images or photographs do not always make the best icons; they tend not to be recognizable at standard icon sizes. For more information about changing icon sizes in windows and in the Finder, see Chapter 2.

You can design your own icons in applications such as Adobe Photoshop or Illustrator. Some images in file formats that are native to certain applications may not transfer; you may need to experiment with your favorite graphics creation application.

There are sources online for icon collections, some of which are designed for Desktop usage, and others that are designed for maximum visibility when used as a smaller icon, as in a window's List view. To find these collections you can use your favorite search engine with terms such as "Mac OS X" and "icons."

Customize Icons

① Double-click the image that you want to use as an icon.

● The image opens in its default application.

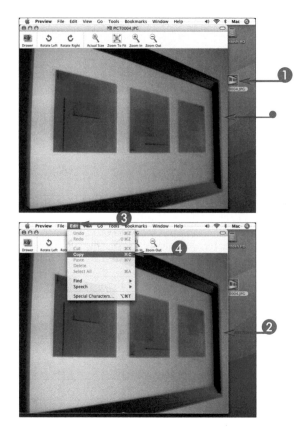

② Select the entire image.

③ Click Edit.

④ Click Copy.

If you only want to use a portion of the image, you can crop the image and save it before copying.

⑤ Click the item whose icon you want to change.

⑥ Click File.

⑦ Click Get Info.

The Get Info window appears for the item.

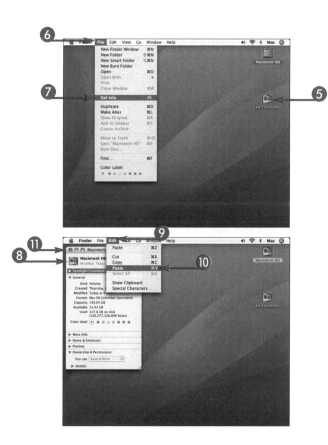

⑧ Click the icon.

⑨ Click Edit.

⑩ Click Paste.

⑪ Close the Get Info window.

The item's icon changes.

Can I restore an icon after I have changed it?

▼ You can undo the paste action (⌘-Z) as long as you have not closed the Get Info window. This gives you the chance to first see how the new icon looks. However, once you close the Get Info window, you cannot undo the change. You may want to keep a copy of the original icon in case you want to change back to it.

Why do some custom icons look blocky when I make them bigger?

▼ This situation occurs when you use a low-resolution pixellated image. An example of this type of image is a photo or a drawing that you create in a pixel-based editor such as Adobe Photoshop.

Will changing the icon change anything else about the item?

▼ No. Even though most icons help to identify what kind of file or folder, or which application, you are using, changing the icon does not change anything else about the item.

Use Undo in the Finder

You can undo various actions in the Finder, just as you can undo actions in most applications. For example, when doing things like altering filenames or removing files, you can change the file back to its original state before you made your change.

You can revoke actions such as the pasting of content from one place or file to another. You can also undo the action of moving a file, if you have placed it in the wrong folder, or have moved it to the Trash.

However, the scope of the Undo feature in the Finder is limited. For example, you cannot undo an action that has

since been superceded by another action. Also, if you paste text into a filename, then open and save the file, you cannot undo the original name change. In addition, you cannot undo the movement of a file to the Trash after you have emptied the Trash.

Whether or not an item is highlighted lets you know whether you can undo an action. For example, if a filename is still highlighted, you can undo changes that you have made to it. However, if you select another item, the filename is no longer highlighted, and you cannot undo the filename change.

Undo Copying a File

① Click a file to select it.

② Click File.

③ Click Duplicate.

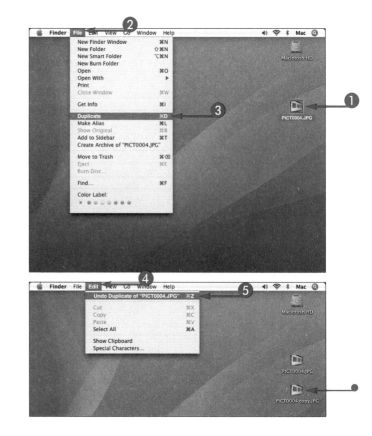

● A copy of the file appears next to the original.

④ Click Edit.

⑤ Click Undo.

The duplicate file disappears.

Undo a Move in the Finder

① Drag an item to another folder in the Finder.

It does not matter where you drag the item, as you will undo this action in the next step.

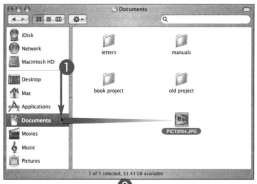

② Click Edit.

③ Click Undo.

● The item returns to its original location.

Can I undo multiple actions in the Finder?

▼ No. If you perform a series of actions, you cannot step back through the actions. This is because the Finder does not have an unlimited number of times that you can undo an action, as some applications do.

Can I redo the action if I have chosen to undo it?

▼ Yes. If you have undone an action, and want to redo it, then click Edit, and then click Redo. The menu command toggles between Undo and Redo.

Can I undo changes that I have made to the system, such as changing a System Preference?

▼ No. If you make changes to a System Preference, or enter new information into the Network Preference, you cannot use the Undo command to revert these changes. Similarly, you cannot use the Finder Undo feature to roll back a change that you have made to a document, or to an image file. However, most applications have their own Undo feature, which is usually found in the Edit menu.

Compress and Decompress an Item

You can create compacted forms of individual files and folders. These compressed versions are useful for e-mailing files, as a smaller version transfers more quickly — the recipient can simply decompress the file when it arrives. You can also use compressed files or folders to archive files and applications because compressed files not only take up less disk space, you can e-mail compressed files with less chance of file corruption.

There are a variety of compressed file formats. You can usually identify a compressed file by its file extension. These extensions include .zip, .sit, and .hqz. They can all be shared with Windows users.

No data are lost when you compress or expand a file. The compression process searches files for redundant items, such as words or bits of code, and creates shorter notes for each item that appears more than once. The compression utility also creates a dictionary that refers the shorter note to the original content. When there is a great deal of redundancy in a file, replacing multiple instances of an item with the shorter note can save a great deal of space. When the file is expanded, the utility refers to the dictionary and replaces each shorter note with the full item.

Compress and Decompress an Item

Compress an item

1. Select the item that you want to compress.

2. Click File.

3. Click Create Archive.

   The Finder compresses the item and creates a file with the filename and .zip file extension in the same location as the original.

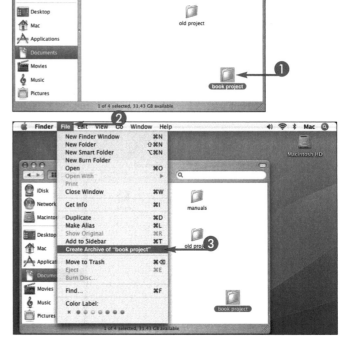

Decompress a file

④ Click the file that you want to decompress.

- Compressed files can have the extension .zip, .sit, or .hqz.

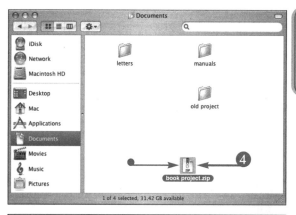

⑤ Double-click the compressed file.

- The Finder expands the file and places the decompressed item in the same location as the compressed file.

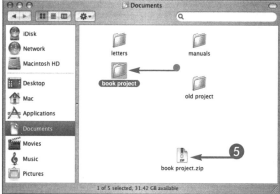

Do some files compress better than others?

▼ Yes. Text files usually compress very well, because most human languages use the same words many times. Programming languages also compress well, because they use a smaller vocabulary and so have higher content redundancies. Graphic images usually do not compress as well. However, if the image contains large areas of pixels that have the same color values, then the image compression will be better.

Can I compress music files such as MP3s?

▼ Yes. However, because audio files tend to have complex content and low redundancy, the compressed file may not be much smaller than the original.

Are all compression formats the same?

▼ No. Several different compression formats have originated from different computer platforms. Some formats and utilities have more efficient compression algorithms than others, and so these formats produce the smallest file sizes. However, regardless of the compression format that is used, as long as you have the proper decompression utility, you can expand a file that is sent in any format.

Elements of the Print Dialog

Mac OS X offers a standard Print interface that is available to all applications. You can use this dialog to choose which network printer you want to use, to select various printing presets, to choose which pages to print, to preview the resulting hard copy, to save your document as a PDF, or even to fax your document, if your computer is connected to a telephone line.

There are slight variations in the Print dialog, depending on the application from which you are printing. For example, some programs offer you a print preview within the Print dialog, while others do not. However, they all share the same basic features.

When a print dialog offers a preview option, this option takes advantage of Mac OS X's Preview application. This gives you access to a wide range of features, such as printing to PDF, zooming, and more.

Printer Menu

You can use this pull-down menu to select the printer to which you want to send your print job. If you connect to only one printer, such as in a home setup, that printer becomes the default printer. You may also see options in the pull-down menu for printers that were previously connected to your computer or network. For more information about adding a printer to your computer or network, see Chapter 25.

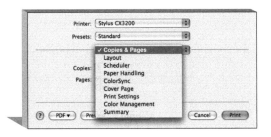

Printer Presets

This pull-down menu contains options for color and output presets. These settings contain color management information, such as color management, resolutions, layout, paper handling, ColorSync, number of copies and pages, and more. You can create and save presets in individual

applications, so that you can print black and white copies in your word processing application while printing full-color from iPhoto.

Print Options

This pull-down menu provides you with many options for your print job. The default option, Copies & Pages, allows you to choose how many copies and which pages of your document you want to print. The Layout option allows you to align multiple pages per sheet. The Output option allows you to save the file while printing in multiple formats. The Scheduler option can delay print jobs to any designated time, with any priority. The Paper Handling option tells the printer how to output the pages, such as in reverse or regular page order, as well as which pages to include.

The ColorSync option enables you to control color conversion. The Print Settings option accesses the printer's own print quality options, such as the type of paper you are using and the output quality settings. The Color Management option displays more detailed color controls, such as brightness and individual color levels. The Summary option displays an overview of your choices. Each application includes its own print-specific options in the Print Options menu.

Preview

When you click the Preview button in the Print dialog, you can view a high-quality image that is not a pixellated proxy, but a faithful, *what you see is what you get* version of your print output. Preview is useful as a proofing tool, so that you can catch any margin, layout, or other visual errors before you begin a print job. You can decide to print the document directly from the preview, or to cancel the print job, revise the document, and then print. Catching problems before you have printed the document can save you a great deal of time and effort, as well as paper.

Save As PDF

In past versions of the Mac OS, one needed specialized and sometimes expensive software to transform a document or image into a PDF. With Mac OS X, you can now use the Save As PDF button to create a PDF of any document or image directly from the Print dialog. You are then prompted to give a location to which you want to save the PDF version of the document. You can share PDFs with friends on any platform, and PDFs provide an accurate and dependable way to share documents that contain text and images. Recipients can use Mac OS X or the free Acrobat Reader application from Adobe Systems Inc. to view PDFs; users of the commercial Acrobat Professional application from Adobe can edit and add comments to PDFs.

Fax

You can use the Print dialog to fax files directly from your Mac to any other computer that is configured to receive faxes, or to any fax machine. If your Mac is connected via modem to a telephone line, then it is automatically configured to fax files. You can enter the fax number or choose a user from your Address Book. You can also include a cover page for your fax by clicking the Cover Page option and then typing a message in the Message field. You cannot fax through your modem if you are using the modem to connect to the Internet; however, the fax is sent as soon as you disconnect from the Internet. If you have a DSL line, you should contact your Internet Service Provider (ISP) for assistance in managing your phone line for faxing. If you use a cable modem, you may need to disconnet your computer from the Internet; again, contact your ISP for details.

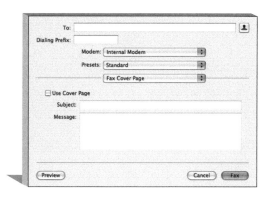

Create a Printer Pool to Output to Multiple Printers

Y ou can create a group of printers, called a printer pool, in Mac OS X. When you do this, your computer sends your print request to the first available printer. This is useful if you have multiple printers that are used by other people on your local network and you do not want to wait for another person who is using one particular printer. You can also use a printer pool to send your output to a specific printer based on the job. For example, if you have an inexpensive inkjet printer and a color laser copier, you can choose the former for text and drafts, while sending high-resolution art prints to the latter.

You can specify the order in which your computer chooses a printer from a group of available printers. This method allows your computer to search first for the nearest printer or your favorite printer; then, if that printer is in use, the computer moves down your list to the next preferred printer.

Because all printers do not offer the same quality of color reproduction or print resolution, you should create printer pools that contain printers that offer similar capabilities. As a result, you can ensure that a photo or résumé you send to a printer pool gets the quality printing that you want.

Create a Printer Pool to Output to Multiple Printers

① Click the Apple icon (🍎).

② Click System Preferences.

The System Preferences window appears.

③ Click the Print & Fax icon.

The Print & Fax window appears.

④ Click Printing.

⑤ Click Printer Setup.

The Printer Setup Utility window appears.

⑥ Select the printers that you want to pool in the Printer List.

You can select multiple printers by holding down the Shift key while clicking them, or multiple, noncontiguous printers by holding down the ⌘ key while clicking them.

⑦ Click Printers.

⑧ Click Pool Printers.

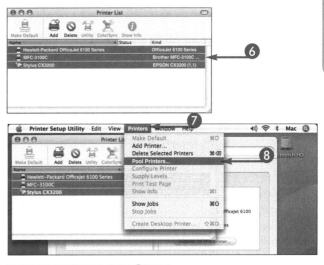

A Printer Pool sheet appears.

⑨ Type a name into the Printer Pool Name field.

Note: You can drag the printers into the order you want.

⑩ Click Create.

You can now select a printer pool when printing a document or photo.

How can I make sure my document will print as soon as possible if my primary printer is already in use?

▼ You do not have to choose manually which printer your document prints on, unless you want to make sure the document goes to a specific printer. If the default printer is in use, Mac OS X automatically sends your document to the first available printer in the pool.

How can I set printer options for the printers in the printer pool?

▼ You can set options for all the printers in the printer pool by selecting the first printer listed and setting options for it. All the other printers in the pool then take on the same option settings. You cannot set different settings for individual printers.

Enable Your Printer's Hidden Features

You can use the print utilities included in Mac OS X to enable extra features for your printer that may not be installed by default. For example, you can allow printing on both sides of a piece of paper or set a higher print resolution, depending on what extra features are available on your printer or printers.

Some printers may not have any extra features that you can install. This is because all of those printers' features are already enabled by default. Some manufacturers may make changes to their printers' firmware, which means that options may later become available.

If you cannot see your printer's name in the Printer Info window, then you should check the printer manufacturer's Web site for technical support. You may need to download the latest version of the printer drivers and install them. Before purchasing a printer, or a printer/copier/scanner combination device, check that the device has Mac OS X drivers available for it. This information is usually available on the product packaging or the manufacturer's Web site. If you are not sure, contact the manufacturer.

Enable Your Printer's Hidden Features

① Click .

② Click System Preferences.

The System Preferences window appears.

③ Click the Print & Fax icon.

The Print & Fax window appears.

④ Click Printer Setup.

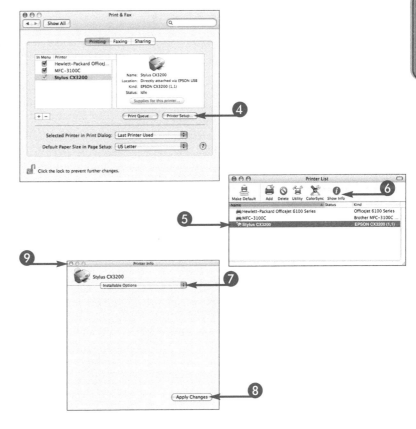

The Printer Setup Utility window appears.

⑤ Click a printer in the Printer List.

⑥ Click Show Info.

The Printer Info window appears.

⑦ Click ⊞ and select Installable Options from the pull-down menu.

You can click the options that you want to install.

⑧ Click Apply Changes.

⑨ Click ⊙ to close the Printer Info window.

Your printer now has access to the newly installed features.

Note: *Your printer may have no installable options available.*

What should I do if I do not see my printer's name after I choose Installable Options in the Printer Info window?

▼ If you do not see your printer's name after Step **7**, then choose Printer Model from the pull-down menu in the Printer Info window. Select your printer from the Model Name pull-down menu, and then select your printer from the Model Name list. Click the Apply Changes button and then choose Installable Options again. If your printer has any installable features, then the printer name should now appear. If your printer's name does not appear, then all of the available options for your printer are already installed.

What should I do if I cannot find the correct model of my printer listed in the Printer Info window?

▼ If you do not see the model name of your printer in the Printer List of the Printer Setup Utility window, or in the Printer Info window, then you may need to install, or reinstall, the software drivers for your printer. Check the manufacturer's Web site for the most recent version of the software drivers.

Share a Printer Wirelessly

Y ou can use an AirPort Extreme Base Station and a USB-based printer in connection so that all Macs on your local network can share the printer. As a result, all network users, whether they are connected physically or wirelessly, can use the printer.

The printer must be connected physically to the Base Station. You may have a limited choice of locations for the printer due to the Base Station's range, however. This, in turn, depends on whether the wireless signal has to travel through walls, doors, floors, or other media that can

interfere with AirPort reception. The better the signal strength, the fewer problems you will have with the wireless connection.

Earlier models of Base Stations do not work with USB printers. Check that your Base Station has a USB port; if not, it cannot connect to your USB-based printer.

All computers on this network must be running Mac OS X v10.2.3 or later. Not all printers are compatible with AirPort wireless networking. For more information, go to Apple's AirPort site at www.apple.com/airportextreme.

Share a Printer Wirelessly

① In an application, click File.

② Click Print.

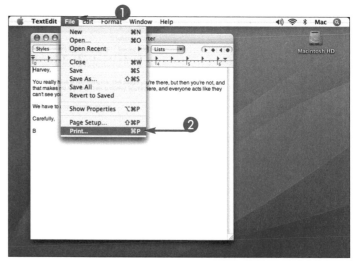

The Print dialog appears.

③ Click the Printer ⬧.

④ Scroll down to Shared Printers.

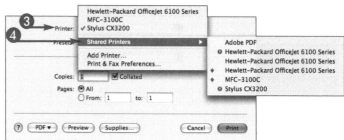

⑤ Click your printer in the sub-menu.

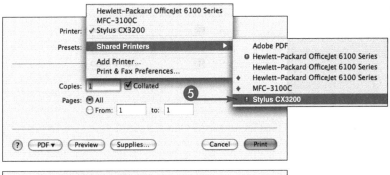

⑥ Click Print.

Your document goes to the printer you selected.

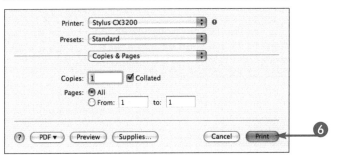

Do other computers on the network select the printer in the same way?

▼ Yes. All printers on the same AirPort wireless network use the same steps to select the printer that connects to the Base Station. However, the more computers connected to the same Base Station, the less bandwidth available for each computer.

Can I still see status or error messages from the printer?

▼ No. You may not be notified of errors or status changes, such as an "Out of Paper" notice, when the printer is connected to an AirPort network. Some printers have LCD or LED panels to show error messages; if you do not see your output, check these.

Can I use the Printer Utilities that came with the printer while it is connected wirelessly to my network?

▼ No. If you want to use the Printer Utilities to check the status of ink cartridges, to set the printer's resolution, or any of the utilities' other features, then you have to reconnect the printer directly to your computer.

Create a Desktop Printer

Y ou can create an icon on your Desktop that represents your printer, or any printer that is available on your local or remote network. This is a useful shortcut if you regularly print documents; instead of opening a document and then selecting the Print command, you can simply drag the file's icon to a Desktop printer.

This feature is also useful if you want to print out one or more documents on different printers. You can drag a file's icon to one or more Desktop printers to send your print job to multiple printers without having to open the file.

Otherwise, you must open the file, step through the Print dialogs to select a printer, and then start the Print command again to select a different printer.

When you have created a Desktop printer, you can easily monitor the individual printer's job queue. When you double-click the printer's icon, a window appears, displaying which documents are currently printing and are in the queue to print. You can also use this window to stop print jobs and to access any utilities that are available for your printer.

Create a Desktop Printer

① In the System Preferences window, click the Print & Fax icon.

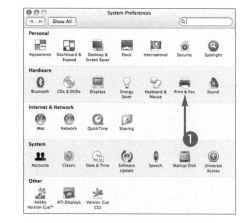

The Printing window appears.

② Click the Printer Setup button.

The Printer Setup Utility appears.

③ Click a printer from the Printer List.

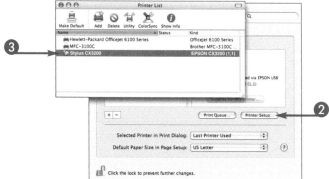

④ Click Printers.

⑤ Click Create Desktop Printer.

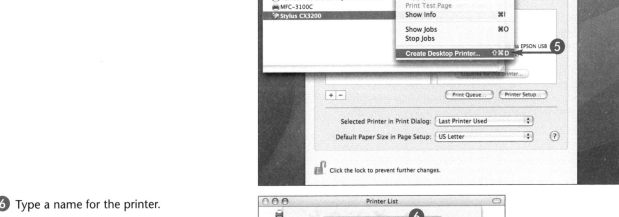

⑥ Type a name for the printer.

⑦ Click Save.

An icon for that printer appears on the Desktop.

Can I get rid of Desktop printers?

▼ Yes. You can get rid of Desktop printers by dragging their icons to the Trash. This neither affects your ability to print nor does it disconnect the printer. This is because Desktop printers are simply aliases that give you access to the print driver.

Can I place the Desktop printer somewhere other than the Desktop?

▼ Yes. When you are prompted for a name for the printer in Step **8**, you can choose to save it anywhere on your hard drive. If you have already created the Desktop printer, then you can still drag its icon to anywhere on your hard drive. If you have a lot of Desktop printers, then you can create a separate folder for them, in order to keep the Desktop tidier.

Can I drag multiple documents to a Desktop printer icon?

▼ Yes. Doing this saves you time if you want to print out multiple files; rather than opening each file and selecting the Print command, you can Shift-click the files to select them, and then drag them all to the Desktop printer icon.

Place Printers in the Finder Sidebar

Y ou can create an alias to your printer and place it in the Sidebar of a Finder window. This provides you with consistent access to your printer, whether or not any applications are open.

With a printer icon in the Sidebar, you can drag files and images to the printer icon for output. This is convenient when you have many files to print; instead of opening each file and selecting the Print command, you can simply drag

the files to the printer icon. This is the same as working with a Desktop printer. However, placing a printer in the Sidebar does not add clutter to the Desktop, nor is a Sidebar printer ever obscured by open Finder windows.

You can also place icons for different printers in the Sidebar if you regularly use multiple printers. You can then drag files to each printer, thus saving the time of specifying printer names in the Print dialog. Mac OS X groups printers together in the Sidebar, as it does hard drives.

Place Printers in the Finder Sidebar

① Click to select a Desktop printer icon.

Note: *To create a desktop printer icon, see the section "Create a Desktop Printer."*

② Drag the Desktop printer icon to the lower part of the Sidebar.

The printer icon appears in the Sidebar.

To remove the printer icon from the Sidebar, you can drag it out of the Sidebar. This does not delete your Desktop printer.

You can also monitor the printer by clicking the desktop printer's Sidebar icon.

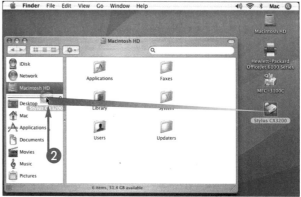

Print Sticky Notes

Y ou can print out Sticky Notes, or Stickies, which are digital versions of the paper sticky note pads. You can use Stickies to type notes to yourself or others. You can even paste text or graphics from other applications into Stickies or copy text or graphics from them. Printing Stickies is a useful way to get a hard copy of all of your notes or to print out selections from a long document.

Because Stickies store their data in Rich Text Format (RTF), you can print out formatted text that you have pasted from other applications and preserve the formatting. You can also stack multiple Stickies, to use as a to-do list. As you complete one task, you can delete the Sticky Note that reminds you of the task. This reveals the next Sticky Note, which reminds you of the next task.

Print Sticky Notes

① Click a note to select it.

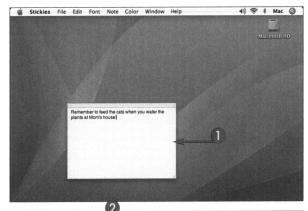

② Click File.

③ Click Print Active Note.

The Sticky Note prints.

Note: To print all open Sticky Notes, click File and then click Print All Notes.

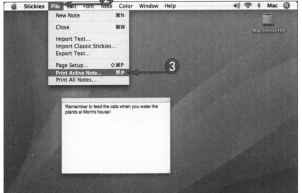

Add a Print Button to Safari's Bookmarks Bar

You can add a Print button to the Bookmarks Bar in the Safari Web browser. This useful shortcut makes it easy for you to quickly print out Web pages.

With the Print button in the Bookmarks Bar, you can click that button to call up the Print dialog for any page without having to select a menu item. The Safari Bookmarks Bar must be visible for you to use this feature. If it is not, you can click View in the Safari menu and then click Bookmarks Bar. You can remove the Print button by dragging it off the Bookmarks Bar.

This Print button is created through JavaScript, which is a scripting language usually used to build interactive features in Web pages. The task below does not require you to learn anything in particular about JavaScript or building Web pages, however.

Add a Print Button to Safari's Bookmarks Bar

① In any text editor, type
javascript:window.print().

② Select the text and drag it to Safari's Bookmarks Bar.

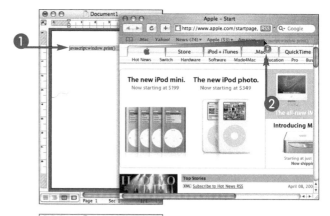

③ Type a name for the bookmark.

This example uses the name Print.

④ Click OK.

A Print bookmark appears in the Bookmarks Bar.

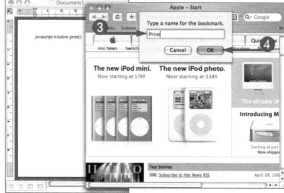

Share Printers with Other Users

You can allow other users on your local network to share any printer that is connected to your Mac. This is useful if your printer is the only printer on the network or if it has capabilities that the other network printers do not have. For example, your Mac may be connected to the only color printer on the network.

Some factors may affect the speed of the print process. This is because the print speed is dependent on network throughput, as well as the capacity of your computer. For example, documents that are waiting to be printed are stored on your hard disk, and so the process could be slowed or even cancelled if you do not have sufficient hard drive space available.

In addition, too many users printing large files can eat up the available bandwidth on your network. As with any other task that uses network resources, the more people and the more files going over the network, the slower the network will be.

Share Printers with Other Users

① Click .

② Click System Preferences.

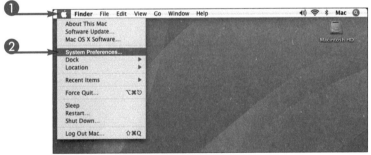

The System Preferences window appears.

③ Click the Sharing icon.

A new Sharing window appears.

④ Click Printer Sharing (changes to).

The printer sharing process begins automatically, and the Start button changes to a Stop button.

⑤ Click to close the System Preferences window.

Other users on your network can now use the printer connected to your Mac.

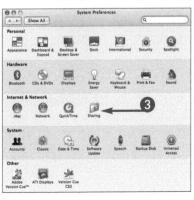

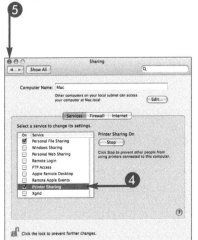

Purchase Printer Supplies Using the Print Dialog

Y ou can use any Print dialog to purchase ink online. This is useful because the Print dialog can provide information to Apple's online store about which ink you need and then send an order for the exact cartridge type and color you need.

Many printer utilities check ink status and alert you when the printer is about to run out of ink. When you go to print a file, Mac OS X automatically checks and confirms what brand and model of printer you have connected to your

computer, as well as any printers that you have access to over a network. You can purchase ink supplies for any of the available printers before you order; this option does not force you to buy ink for all available printers at once. This is useful if you are on a network that includes multiple printers, which use up ink at different rates.

When you decide to purchase ink through this feature, the Print dialog launches Safari and loads the proper Web page from the Apple Web site. You can then select from products that are available for your printer.

Purchase Printer Supplies Using the Print Dialog

① With a file open, click File.

② Click Print.

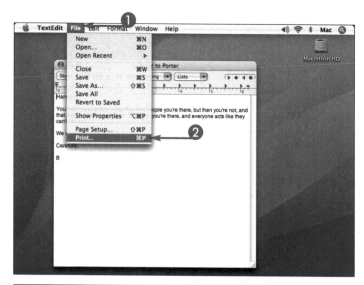

The Print Dialog appears.

③ Click Supplies.

Safari displays a Web page with products for your printer.

④ Select the product you want to purchase and click Add to Cart.

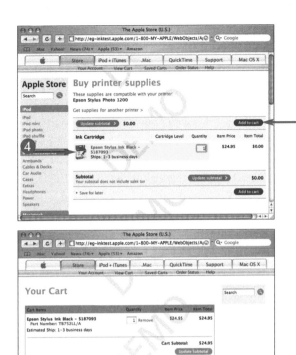

Safari opens a new Web page.

You can edit quantities, continue shopping, or check out.

Note: *If you have not purchased from the Apple Store before, you will need to enter your credit card info.*

The purchase is complete, and the product will be shipped to you.

Can I buy ink for my printer at other online stores?

▼ Yes. You can use the Printer Setup Utility for simple connection to the Apple Web site to purchase ink there, with the confidence that you are getting the correct type of cartridge and ink. However, this does not preclude you from shopping elsewhere. You will have to find and navigate to these other stores but you can use the information about printer model given to you by the Printer Setup Utility when you shop elsewhere.

Can I use the Printer Setup Utility to purchase ink if my printer is not connected to my computer?

▼ Yes. The Printer Setup Utility accesses the driver software to get the manufacturer and make of your printer. As long as you have installed the proper drivers for your printer, the Printer Setup Utility should direct you to the appropriate product. If you have already set up an account at the online Apple Store, you can purchase your ink with one click.

7 | Getting the Most Out of Mac OS X Utilities

8 | Managing Multiple Users

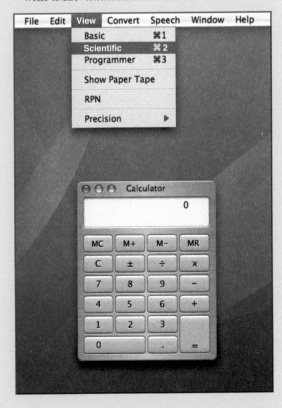

Elements of TextEdit

You can use TextEdit to create and edit text documents that contain advanced features such as styled text. TextEdit is the default word-processing application that ships with Mac OS X. Because TextEdit's native file format is Rich Text Format, it can handle Unicode editing, which also allows TextEdit to support languages such as Japanese and Greek.

TextEdit supports intelligent hyphenation, and includes a built-in spell check feature that can highlight questionable words as you type. You can also tell TextEdit to read any document aloud, using any of Mac OS X's built-in voices.

TextEdit can open files created in Microsoft Word, thus allowing you to share documents with users of the popular Office suite. TextEdit can also save its files in Word format so that Word users can open TextEdit files without losing formatting. However, TextEdit does not support all of Word's features, so document sharing may not be transparent.

Although it is not a full-featured HTML editor, you can use TextEdit to view HTML code. If you are familiar with HTML, then you can also use TextEdit to manually code Web pages.

Ⓐ Styles Menu

You can use this pull-down menu to format text. The Style menu for text allows you to select a font, color, size, and style, such as bold or italic. Paragraph styles also include paragraph and line spacing.

Ⓑ Alignment Buttons

You can use these buttons to change a paragraph's alignment to left, center, justified, and right. To change a paragraph's alignment, you can simply select a word or paragraph and then click any of the alignment buttons.

Ⓒ Spacing Menu

This pull-down menu allows you to specify the amount of space you want between lines of text. You can select the text and then choose Single, Double, or Other from the Spacing menu. If you choose Other, a dialog appears, giving you options for setting line height, inter-line spacing, and paragraph spacing.

Ruler

You can use the ruler to measure in inches where you want to place items such as tab stops, margins, and tables. No matter how you scale the TextEdit window, the ruler displays an accurate representation of the placement and size of the contents. You can show or hide the ruler from the Menu bar. To hide it, click Format, then click Text, then deselect Show Ruler. To make the ruler appear, if it is hidden, click Format, then click Text, and then select Show Ruler. You can set margins by dragging the left or right margin icon to where you want it. Similarly, you can drag the indentation icon to set where paragraphs indent. There are four types of tab stops and two types of margins. Triangular tab stops facing to the right are tab stops at which text is left-justified, and one facing to the left shows where text will be right-justified. Diamond-shaped tab stops show where text will be center-justified. A downward-facing triangle sets page margins, horizontal rectangles show the indentation of the first line of a paragraph, and circles are decimal tab stops, where numbers are justified around a decimal point.

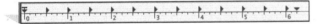

Tab Stop Palette

The tab stop buttons allow you to place any of the four types of tab stops into your document. The right-facing triangle is the left-alignment tab. The diamond tab stop is the center-alignment tab. The left-facing triangle is the right-alignment tab. The circle is a decimal tab stop; you can use this tab when you want columns of numbers to align on the decimal point. To place a tab stop into your document, click one of the tabs and drag it to where you want it on the TextEdit ruler. You can also click and drag existing tab stops to where you want them. To delete a tab stop, you can drag it off the ruler.

Font Menu

The Font menu, found under the Format menu, is where you can specify how your text appears. In addition to selecting fonts and styles, such as bold, italic, underline, and outline, you can access advanced features such as kerning and ligature if the font supports these features. You can also use the Font menu to copy and paste styles. When you want to see all fonts, TextEdit calls up a font palette, which is powered by Mac OS X's Font Book. This allows you to use all fonts available to you as a user on the computer; it also allows you to use all advanced font features, such as ligatures, available in Mac OS X.

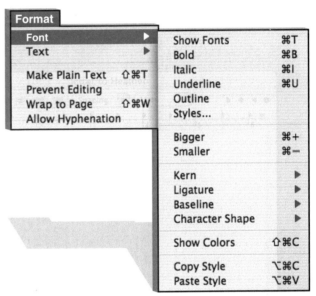

Save and Apply a Style

You can save customized text and paragraph styles in TextEdit so that you can then easily apply the saved style to any text or paragraph. This can save time when you are creating a long document that has areas that use and reuse certain styles. You can apply styles to text that include font, color, size, and style, such as italic or bold. You can also apply styles to paragraphs that include paragraph and line spacing. Once you have created a style, you can apply it to any section of text.

The Styles feature can make it easier for you to apply custom styles to your text. Rather than applying the

changes to each instance of text that you want to style, a process that requires making multiple selections from menus, you can simply select text or a paragraph and make one selection from the Styles pull-down menu.

Keep in mind that you cannot use styles in plain text documents; styles are only available for RTF and Word format files. For example, if you have created a file in either of those formats and save the file as a plain text document, then all of the styles are removed from the document.

Save a Style

① Click to highlight the formatted text to select it.

② Click Styles ▼.

③ Click Other.

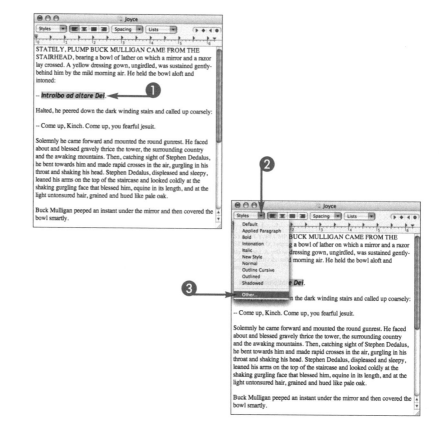

The Styles Favorites dialog appears.

④ Click Add To Favorites.

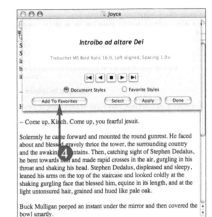

A dialog appears.

⑤ Type a name for the new style.

⑥ Click Add.

The new style now appears in the Styles menu.

Can I search a document for text in a certain style?

▼ Yes. You can use the Styles dialog to search for a select text that is in a certain style. To do so, select Other from the Styles ▼ pull-down menu; the Styles dialog appears. In the Styles dialog, click the forward or back buttons to move through the document. You can also choose to select one of your favorite styles and apply it to text in the open document.

Can I copy and paste styles?

▼ Yes. You can copy styled text and apply this style to other text you have selected. This changes the style of the selected text but not the text itself. To do this, select the text that has the style you want to copy. Then click Format, select Font, and then select Copy Style. Then select the text to which you want to apply and the style, then click Format, click Copy, and then click Paste Style.

continued

Save and Apply
a Style *(Continued)*

You have no limit on the styles that you can create. You can use any font that is available on your computer, and any combination of style elements offered by TextEdit. Some fonts even allow the use of ligatures and custom character shapes.

You may be limited in your choice of fonts for a style if that font is installed on the computer but your user account does not have permission to use the font. For more information on restricting font access for other users, see Chapter 8.

The Styles pull-down menu in TextEdit features some regularly used styles. These include bold, outline cursive, and others. When you create a new style and save it, the name of your saved style appears along with the others in the Style menu.

You can also use the Styles dialog to search your document for text that uses one of the styles shown in the menu. Once you have found the text, you can apply a new style or add the existing style to your favorites in the Styles menu.

Apply a Style *(continued)*

Apply a text style

1 Click to highlight the formatted text to select it.

2 Click Style 🔽.

3 Click a text style.

The text changes to the style you selected.

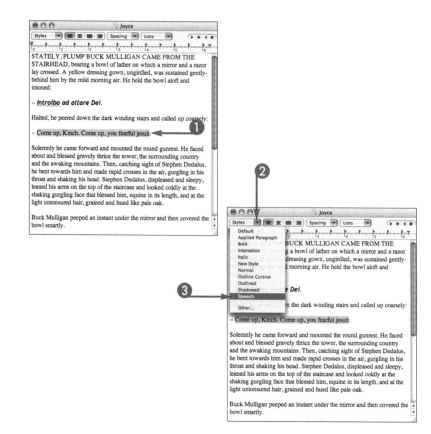

PART II

Apply a paragraph style

1 Select a paragraph.

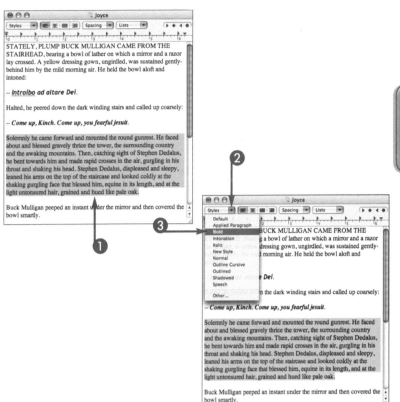

2 Click Style .

3 Click a paragraph style.

TextEdit applies the style to the paragraph.

When should I use the plain text file format for a text document?

▼ Plain text is the most universal file format across computer platforms, versions of operating systems, and word-processing applications. As a result, there is less risk of a recipient finding errors in your file. Plain text files are also usually more compact than RTF or Word files. If you send numerous documents where formatting is not critical, or you are sending files over a slow connection, then plain text files are the best choice. In addition, if you use TextEdit to code HTML files, you should save a file as plain text while still retaining a good RTF copy.

If a font has ligatures, how can I use them?

▼ You can use ligatures with selected text in your TextEdit document by clicking the Format menu, then clicking the Font submenu, then navigating to the Ligatures submenu, and then clicking Use All. You can turn off ligatures by clicking Use None. The Use Default option either displays or does not display ligatures, depending on whether they are available with the font. Ligatures do not appear in files saved as plain text.

Open and Save Word Files in TextEdit

You can use TextEdit to open documents that were created and saved in Microsoft Word. This feature allows you to read and share files with users of the Microsoft Office suite without having to purchase the software.

You can also save TextEdit files in Word format. This enables Word users who do not have TextEdit, such as Windows users, to be able to read documents that you have created in TextEdit without having to go through a conversion process.

Keep in mind that not all Word features are available in TextEdit. These features, such as tables, are not available to you when you open a Word file in TextEdit. However, text and paragraph styles, such as font choices and color, are preserved.

You can recognize Word format files by the .doc filename extension. In comparison, Rich Text Format (RTF) documents, such as native TextEdit files, use the .rtf filename extension. If you add graphics to an RTF document, the filename extension changes to .rtfd, which stands for Rich Text Format Directory.

Open a Word File in TextEdit

① Control-click a Word file.

● A pull-down menu appears.

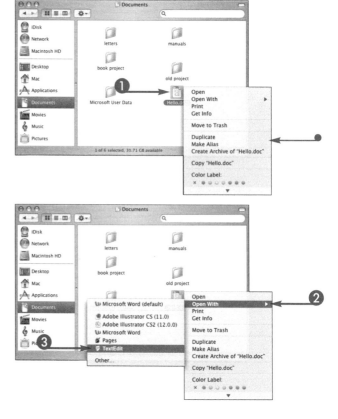

② Navigate to Open With.

③ Click TextEdit.

TextEdit opens the file.

Save a Word File in TextEdit

1 Click File.

2 Click Save As.

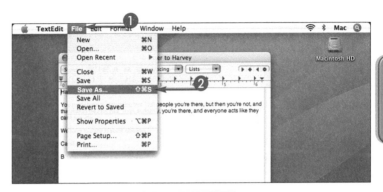

The Save As dialog appears.

3 Type a name for the document.

Note: You can select a different location in which to save the document.

4 Click File Format ⊞ and select Word Format from the pull-down menu.

5 Click Save.

TextEdit saves the document in Word format.

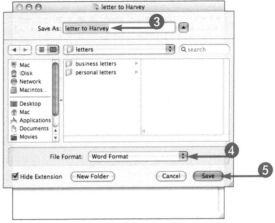

What should I do if Word users cannot open the files that I save in Word format?

▼ If Word users are having problems opening the files that you save in Word format, check to see that the saved files have the .doc filename extension visible. If it is not visible, ensure that the "Hide Extension" checkbox in the Save dialog is not selected.

Are there other ways to open Word files in TextEdit?

▼ Yes. You can drag the Word file onto the TextEdit icon in the Applications folder. If you have TextEdit in your Dock, you can also drag the Word file onto it. You can also click the File menu in TextEdit, then click Open, and then navigate to the Word file that you want to open.

If I open and save a Word file, and then send it back to the file's creator, will I have problems opening it in Word?

▼ There are some Word-only features that you will not be able to take advantage of in TextEdit, such as tracking changes. If you open a Word file that contains these features in TextEdit, save the file, and then send it back to be opened in Word, these features may no longer be available.

Set TextEdit as Your Default Text Editor

You can configure Mac OS X to open your text files and Microsoft Word documents automatically in TextEdit. This allows you to open all of these files by simply double-clicking them.

Once you have set TextEdit as your default text editor, all text files automatically open in TextEdit. When you open these text files in TextEdit, they list TextEdit as their creator application, regardless of the application in which they were originally created.

If you do not set TextEdit as your default application for Word files, and you do not have Word installed, then

an error message displays when you attempt to open a Word file.

You can change your default text application by following a few basic steps. You can apply these same steps to any other type of file in any other application.

When you open a Word file in TextEdit, you may see some garbled or nonsensical text. This happens when special features are used in Word that TextEdit does not support. You may have to delete some of this text; if you do so, and send the file back to a Word user, the user may notice some of their specially formatted text, or tables, may not have survived the round trip.

Set TextEdit as Your Default Text Editor

① Click a text file.

② Click File.

③ Click Get Info.

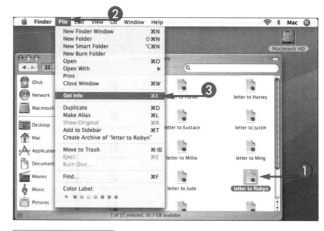

The Get Info window appears.

④ Click Open with (▶ changes to ▼).

PART II

⑤ Click ▣ and select TextEdit from the pull-down menu.

⑥ Click Change All.

*Note: By skipping Step **6**, you can specify that only this file, and not all files of this type, can now open in TextEdit.*

⑦ Click ◉ to close the Get Info window.

All text files now open in TextEdit.

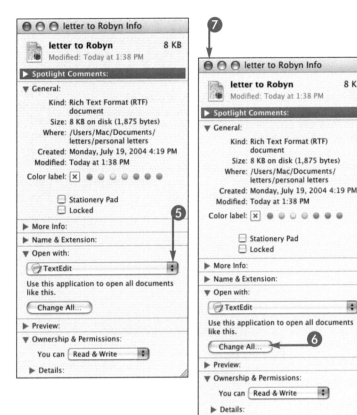

How does Mac OS X determine which files are the same type as the file I want to change using the Open With option?

▼ Mac OS X categorizes files by their filename extensions. It also keeps track of what application created each file. If you change the default application for one file and choose the Change All option in Step **6**, then Mac OS X opens all files with the same filename extension using the application you selected. However, not all files display their extension in the Finder, and as a result, some files will have a different default application. You can follow the steps in this task to change back to the default application.

If I create a file in TextEdit but save it as a Word file, does it open automatically in TextEdit, or in Word?

▼ If you save a TextEdit file as a Word file, it displays with a Word icon; double-clicking it opens the file in Word. If you open the file in TextEdit and save it as an RTF file, it opens by default in TextEdit. To change the default application to Word, you should follow the steps in this task, selecting Word in Step **5**.

Search for Words or Parts of Words

You can search for a word, or even a set of characters, in a TextEdit file. This allows you to find any or all occurrences of the text and then to edit them. TextEdit allows you to search and replace text, so that you can change a misspelled word outdated information such as a date. You can also search and replace all instances of a word, name, or date, and then change them to another word with one click.

When working with HTML or other code in TextEdit, you can use a simple click to search through a document to find each occurrence of a word or set of characters. This method allows you to step through a document from one instance to another of a set of characters, without having to start the search process from the beginning each time.

You can also search only within a selection of text. To do this, you simply select a paragraph or section of text that you want to search. When you apply the search feature, it only reviews the part of the file you selected.

Search for Words or Parts of Words

1 Click Edit.

2 Navigate to Find.

3 Click Find.

The Find window appears.

4 Click ⬍ and select Contains from the pull-down menu.

You can further limit your search by selecting Starts With or Full Word.

⑤ Type the characters you want to find.

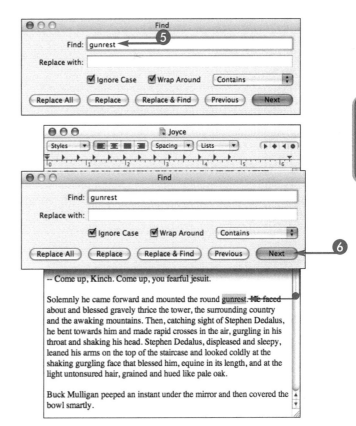

This example searches for the letters *gunrest*.

⑥ Click Next.

● TextEdit highlights the next instance of the text.

You can repeat Step **6** to see each occurrence of the set of characters.

Can you search backwards through a document?

▼ Yes. After you start to search your document for a word or part of a word, you can use the Previous button to search for the preceding instance of the text.

Can I use the Find feature to replace text only within a selection?

▼ Yes. If you want to replace all instances of a certain word within an area of selected text, hold down the Option key while the Find window is visible. The Replace All button changes to an In Selection button; click this button to search only in the selection.

Is there a keyboard shortcut for opening the Find window?

▼ Yes. ⌘-F is the keyboard shortcut. It is a standard shortcut for opening a Find feature in most applications as well as in the Finder.

Elements of Preview

You can use Preview, Mac OS X's built-in image viewer, to open and view image files. You can also use Preview to perform basic edits of images, as well as convert images from one graphics format to another. Though Preview is not a full-fledged image editing application, like Adobe Photoshop, it can provide basic services.

Preview can open many file types, including PDF, JPEG, GIF, TIFF, PSD, PICT, BMP, and PNG. JPEG, PNG, and GIF file formats are most commonly used for Web pages. TIFF and PICT files are often used in print publishing. PSD files are native to Adobe Photoshop. BMP is a standard file type often used in Windows. Adobe Systems created Portable Document Format (PDF) standard with the goal of faithfully reproducing and sharing text and graphics documents across various operating systems, including Windows and Mac OS X. PDF is the native file format that Preview uses. If you open PostScript and EPS files in Preview, then Preview first converts them to PDF files.

Mac OS X also uses Preview to enable you to view printed files. When you click the Preview button in a print dialog, the Preview application displays the image.

Ⓐ Drawer and Drawer Button

The Drawer button reveals and hides Preview's drawer. The drawer appears on the side of Preview's main window and shows thumbnails of the pages in a multipage document. If you open multiple image files in Preview at the same time, then the Drawer shows thumbnails of all of the images. You can move to each page or image by clicking its thumbnail. Preview will display in its main window one image at a time, or one page of a multipage document.

Ⓑ Rotate Left/Right Buttons

You can use these buttons to rotate the image one way or another. One click of the Rotate Right button turns the image 90 degrees in one direction and one click of the Rotate Left button turns the image 90 degrees in the other direction. This is useful if you have imported images from your digital camera that are oriented incorrectly, which often happens when you take a photo with the camera turned on its side.

Ⓒ Next/Previous Buttons

The Next and Previous buttons appear when you have opened a multiple-page document. The buttons move you sequentially through a multipage document. You can use this to scan pages of a multipage document or flip through a series of images. If you are looking for one image or page and cannot pick it out of the thumbnails shown in the Drawer, this

Ⓓ Actual Size Button

You can use the Actual Size button to view an image or text at its actual size. That is, you will view it at 100 percent zoom. Many high-resolution images actual size will be too large for your screen, however.

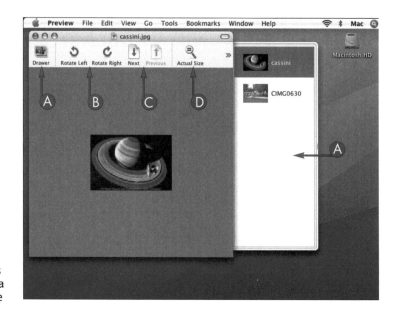

Zoom In/Zoom Out

You can use the Zoom In and Zoom Out buttons to increase or decrease the magnification of your document or image on-screen. This can help you to view small type or images, or get a whole view of an image that is larger than your screen. You may need to expand Preview's window to view all of a zoomed document or image; you can do this by clicking the bottom-right corner of the main Preview window and dragging it outwards. You can also use the scroll bars in the Preview's main window to navigate the image or document. If you zoom in very far on an image, you may start to see parts of the image look blocky. This means that you have zoomed in to the point where you are seeing the pixels that make up the image.

Tool Mode Buttons

You can access three tools through the Tool Mode buttons. You can use the Scroll tool when a document is too large to view in the main Preview window. This tool appears as a hand icon that you can select to click any point in the document, and then drag to move around the page. Note that this is different from scrolling, in that with the hand tool you drag the image itself, rather than a scroll button. The Text tool allows you to select text. This is useful if you want to copy text, though you cannot copy text in an image. The Select tool, which appears as a crosshair icon, allows you to select the contents of a document or an image area. You can use this tool by clicking and dragging over an area that you want to copy or paste. Keep in mind that you may not be able to copy from protected PDFs.

Custom Toolbar Options

You can customize Preview's toolbar to include a variety of buttons by clicking View and then selecting Customize Toolbar. Some toolbar items affect your image immediately, such as the Zoom, Actual Size, Zoom to Fit, Scale, and Rotate buttons. Other toolbar items affect the actual Preview application, such as the Drawer and Customize buttons. You can decide to place in or remove from the Back, Forward, Page Up, Page Down, and Page Number items; these help you to navigate multipage documents. You can use the Space and Flexible Space tools to alter text, and the Crop Image tool to crop an image. To add any tool to the toolbar, drag it from the Customize Toolbar sheet into the toolbar. You can also reorder tools by dragging them around the toolbar.

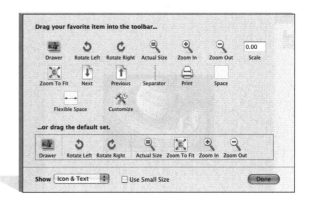

Copy Text from a Protected PDF

You can use Preview in conjunction with TextEdit to copy text from a protected PDF document. This allows you to extract and reuse text that may otherwise be unavailable to you.

Protected PDFs usually do not allow others to copy text directly from the document. The creator of a PDF document can protect the files in the same way that you can protect files and folders on your computer. The difference is that PDF creators can restrict whether other users can read, write, or print the document. For example,

you can password-protect the PDF document, thereby requiring a user to have a password to open the document.

Once you copy the text, it appears in a new TextEdit window. You can save the text as a new TextEdit document, or copy and paste the text from TextEdit into any other application, such as an e-mail client.

The new text appears in TextEdit as plain text, with all formatting and styles removed. However, if you add any styles or formatting to the text in the TextEdit file, you can retain this formatting by saving it as an RTF file.

Copy Text from a Protected PDF

1 Select the text that you want to copy.

2 Click Preview.

3 Navigate to Services.

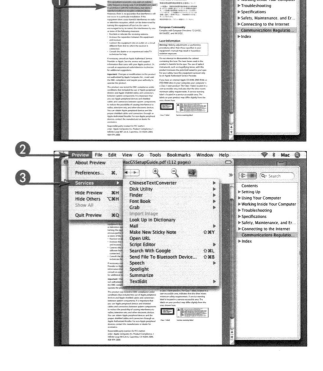

④ Navigate to TextEdit.

⑤ Click New Window Containing Selection.

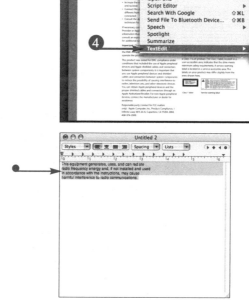

● The text appears in a new TextEdit window.

Note: *You may have to switch to TextEdit to bring this window to the front. See Chapter 1.*

Can I use this method to copy and paste images?

▼ No. You cannot copy and paste images in a protected PDF in this way. For more information on how to extract images from a nonprotected PDF, see the section "Copy Text with Formatting from a PDF."

Will the formatting of the original text be preserved when I copy and paste it?

▼ No. The text will appear in TextEdit as plain text, without any formatting. Line breaks may not be preserved in the process, also, resulting in lines running together. You can copy text with formatting from nonprotected PDF documents. See "Copy Text with Formatting from a PDF."

Can I perform this technique with a different word processor than TextEdit?

▼ No. Eventually, you can paste the text from TextEdit into any word processor or any other application that works with text. However, you cannot export the copied text immediately to another word processor from the Services menu. This action relies on underlying Mac OS X capabilites, and, as of this writing, most third-party applications do not take advantage of these capabilities.

Copy Text with Formatting from a PDF

Y ou can use Preview to copy text from a PDF document and preserve the line and paragraph breaks as well as any graphics in the document. This feature is useful when you have prepared a presentation or a letter as a PDF to print or e-mail to recipients, but you want to e-mail or edit portions of the text.

In order to copy text with formatting from a PDF, the file must not have been protected by its author from copying or writing. For more information about protecting PDFs, see the documentation accompanying your PDF creation software, such as Adobe Acrobat. First, you must be able

to view the PDF, so you cannot copy text from a PDF that is password protected for opening the file. For more information see the section "Copy Text from a Protected PDF."

If you are copying text that is in a font that you do not have on your system, then you may run into a few problems. For example, you may be able to copy the text, but Preview may substitute the unavailable font with one that approximates it, or use its default font. If you then export that text into a word-processing application and then save it as plain text, the line breaks may be preserved, but the graphical elements may not.

Copy Text with Formatting from a PDF

① Click Tools.

② Click Text Tool.

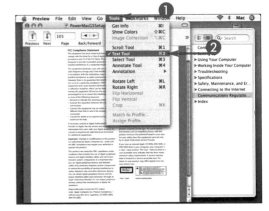

③ Press and hold the Option key.

● The cursor changes to a crosshair (+).

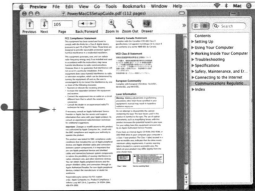

④ Drag the cursor to select the text that you want to copy.

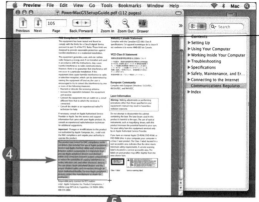

⑤ With the Option key still held down, click Edit.

Note: You can Copy text without holding the Option key; however, holding the Option key preserves formatting.

⑥ Click Copy.

You can now paste the text into another application.

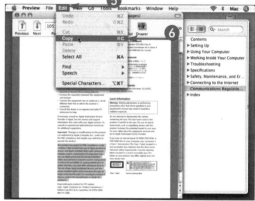

Why would I want to preserve line breaks?

▼ You may want to preserve line breaks so that text that has been prepared in paragraphs, such as in longer documents, is easier to read when you paste it into another document or into an e-mail. Without preserving line breaks, all of the text that you copy may appear as one long paragraph. Other applications that read PDF documents may not offer this feature.

Can I preserve all font, color, and other text formatting when I copy and paste text?

▼ No. Certain features of the copied text, such as its being all in capital letters, or its font size, may be preserved when you copy and paste it from a PDF document; however, because many PDF documents use fonts that you may not have on your computer, all of the font styles may not be preserved when you copy the text over.

Can I paste the text into any application?

▼ Yes. Unlike when you extract text from a protected PDF document, you can paste the text from an unprotected PDF document into any application that works with text. You can still paste the text into TextEdit, but you do not have to use TextEdit. For more information see the section "Copy Text from a Protected PDF."

Change the Background Color in Preview

You can change the background color of the main Preview window. When you use a background color of a higher contrast than the default background color, this can help you to read small text more easily, or to view details of a complex image. Conversely, when you use a background color of a lower contrast, this can help reduce eyestrain if you are working with many images.

When you change the background color of the main Preview window, it does not change any of the colors in the actual image or document. To change the background color of an image, you need to use an image-editing application such as Adobe Photoshop; to change the background color of a text document, you need to use a word-processing application.

However, if the image you are viewing in Preview has any transparent areas, you can see the background color of the Preview window through these transparent areas. For example, GIF or PNG images that are prepared for Web pages often have transparencies. These areas do not change to the Preview background color when you close the file.

Change the Background Color in Preview

① Click Preview.

② Click Preferences.

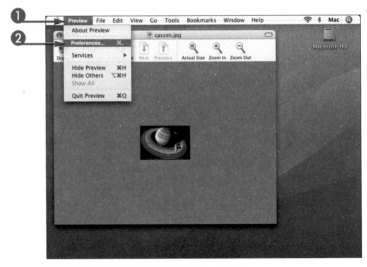

The Preview Preferences window appears.

③ Click the Window background color well.

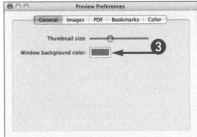

The Colors window appears.

④ Click a Color Space icon.

You can choose from Color Wheel, Color Sliders, Color Palettes, Image Palettes, or Crayons.

● The color space that you selected appears in the Colors window.

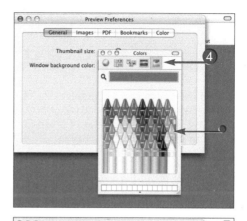

⑤ Click to select a color.

⑥ Click [icon] to close the Colors window.

● The main Preview window displays with the background color you selected.

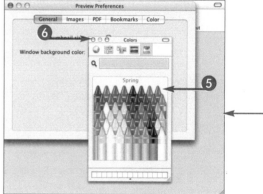

Can I use the Preview Color picker to change colors in an image?

▼ No. The Color picker only affects the Preview window, and not the image in the window. To change the background of the actual image, you can use a dedicated image-editing application such as Adobe Photoshop.

Can I revert back to the default color after I select a new background color?

▼ Yes. Although there is no shortcut method to do this, you can simply open the Color picker and select a white background from any of the color spaces.

Why would I prefer to use one color space in the Color picker over another?

▼ Different color spaces in the Color picker offer different tools and even different color ranges for selecting colors. For example, the Color Sliders color space allows you to choose individual elements of RGB, CMYK, or HSB color components. Others, such as the Color Palettes color space, allow you to choose individual colors from various sets, such as Web-safe.

Convert Graphic Files in Preview

You can use Preview to convert graphic files from one file format to another. This allows you to perform basic image edits instead of buying an expensive application such as Adobe Photoshop.

For example, you may want to share graphics files with users on other computer platforms, such as Windows users, who often find it easier to open BMP files than PICT files. In addition, because not all applications can open all types of files, you can use Preview to convert a file to a format that will work with your own applications.

You can also use Preview to reduce the size of a file by converting it to another file type. For example, you may want to convert a TIFF to a JPEG and then attach it to an e-mail or put it on a Web site.

Preview can convert PDFs to different file formats. You can also select images within a PDF and convert these images; you can then use these images in another application or put them on a Web site.

Convert Graphic Files in Preview

① Click File.

② Click Save As.

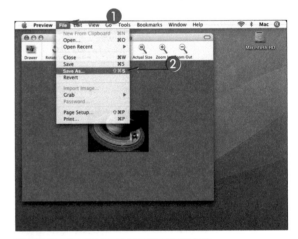

The Save dialog appears.

③ Click Format ⊡ and select the target file format from the pull-down menu.

If no options are offered, you can skip to Step **5**.

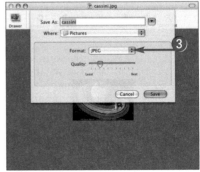

An Options dialog appears for the format you selected.

Different file formats offer different options.

④ Drag the slider to select the quality level you want.

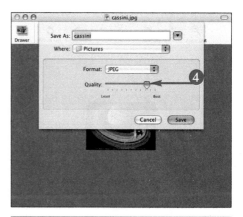

⑤ Type a new name for the file.

⑥ Click Save.

Preview saves the file in the format you want.

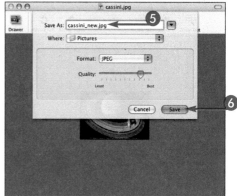

What file types can I convert an image to using Preview?

▼ Preview can convert image files to the BMP, JPEG-2000, JPEG, PDF, PSD, PICT, PNG, SGI, TIFF, and TGA file formats.

Which file formats should I convert an image to if I want to use that image on the Web?

▼ The most common file formats for images on Web pages are the GIF and JPEG formats. The PNG format is also used, although it is not as common.

How can I reduce the file size of an image after I convert it?

▼ You can save the image in a file format that uses compression. For example, a JPEG version of an image requires less disk space than a TIFF version. The size of the JPEG file depends on the quality setting you select. However, you do not want to compress a file too much, as more compression means more data loss. That is, if you make an image file size too small, the image quality will suffer noticeably.

Crop Images in Preview

You can use Preview to crop an image. When you crop an image, you are trimming away the parts of the picture that you do not want. For example, you can crop a picture of a crowd in order to focus on one person. The Crop tool is a useful tool if you want to improve the layout of an image. When you use the Crop tool in Preview, you simply choose the part of the picture that you want to keep; Preview deletes the rest of the picture.

You can also perform multiple crops on a single image, paring away the parts of the image that you do not want. However, keep in mind that Preview does not have an Undo feature, and so you cannot step backwards through the changes that you have made.

The Crop tool is a useful tool for basic photograph preparation. For more advanced features, from red-eye reduction to color correction, you need a dedicated image editor such as Adobe Photoshop. You can also perform edits to your photos using iPhoto. For more information about iPhoto, see Chapter 15.

Crop Images in Preview

① Open the file you want to crop.

② Drag the cursor over the part of the image that you want to keep.

● The nonselected area of the image appears darker.

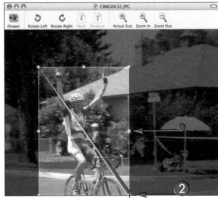

You can cancel the area selection by clicking Tools and then clicking Remove Crop.

3 Click Tools.

4 Click Crop.

● Preview crops the image.

5 Click File.

6 Click Save.

*Note: If you save the cropped image after Step **5**, or save it with the same name as the original image, the original image is overwritten.*

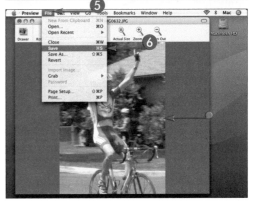

Can I adjust the crop selection?

▼ Yes. If you have selected an area for cropping but want to make an adjustment, move the cursor over one of the corners of the highlighted area. The cursor turns into a caret. You can now click and drag the corner of the highlighted area to adjust it.

Can I constrain adjustment of the crop selection to only one axis?

▼ No. Although in some image-editing applications, you can hold down a modifier key and drag a selection along only the X or Y axis, you cannot do this in Preview. To adjust only the height or only the width of a selected crop area, you must carefully adjust the corners of the selected area.

Can I move the selected crop area?

▼ Yes. When you move the cursor over an area that you have selected, the cursor changes to a hand icon. When you click the mouse, the hand icon changes to a closed hand icon. You can then hold down the mouse button and drag the selected area.

Search PDF Documents

You can use Preview to search a PDF single- or multipage document for a word or set of characters. This enables you to search a document for specific phrases or information, a feature that makes reviewing important documents much easier.

This feature is useful because most word-processing applications cannot open PDF documents, and many important documents are now released in PDF form. For example, judicial courts, federal governments, and businesses often use the PDF format when they release documents.

Preview's search feature uses a live search technique; the application starts to look for examples of your entry as soon as you begin typing. For example, if you are searching for the word automatic, Preview begins to return all instances of the letter "a" when you type the start of the word, then highlights instances of the letters "au," and so on. In most cases, you may not need to type the entire word that you are looking for before Preview displays all instances of its occurrence in the document.

If a search is taking too long, you can cancel it at any time by clicking the Stop button in the Search field. Keep in mind that Preview does not support Boolean terms or multiple searches.

Search PDF Documents

① If the drawer is not visible, click the Drawer button.

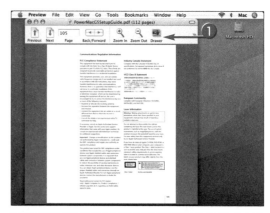

The drawer appears.

② Type the text that you are searching for in the Search field.

● The drawer displays all instances of the text.

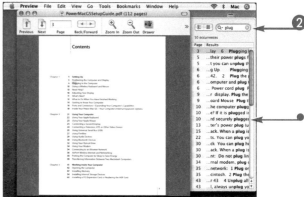

3 Click an instance of the text.

● The page that contains the text appears in the main Preview window with the text highlighted.

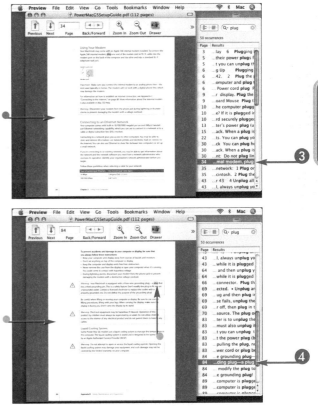

4 Click another instance of the text.

● The main Preview page displays and highlights that instance of the text.

Do I have to open the drawer in order to use the search feature?

▼ Yes. The Search field only appears in the drawer, and you cannot add the Search field to the toolbar in the main Preview window.

Can I also search for phrases in PDF documents?

▼ Yes. You can search for a phrase by typing it in the Search field, although you cannot use Boolean modifiers such as And or Or. You must use the exact phrase in the order that it appears in the PDF document. For example, if you are searching for the phrase "play the movie," you have to type that exact phrase; typing only the keywords "play movie" does not find the phrase.

How can I go back from seeing search results to seeing page thumbnails in the drawer?

▼ Once the search process is complete, you can click the Stop button in the Search field. The drawer hides the Search field and displays page thumbnails of the PDF document. To return to the search results, you have to retype the search criteria. Preview does not offer a shortcut that allows you to quickly switch back and forth between search results and page thumbnails.

Synchronize Address Book with Exchange

You can share e-mail addresses, phone numbers, and other contact information between Mac OS X's Address Book and Microsoft Exchange. Exchange is Microsoft's popular messaging and collaboration system, which allows you to keep all of your contact information in one place.

Organizations use Microsoft Exchange to keep all employees up-to-date on the scheduling of important events such as meetings and vacations. Exchange uses a centralized server that manages all contact and scheduling information from individual users, allowing them to share their schedules and contacts with other users. Users can also decide not to share certain information. Because of

open standards, Address Book can connect to the Exchange server and share similar information across a company network.

To connect Address Book and Exchange, you must know your Exchange username and password, as well as the Outlook Web Server address. If you have an Exchange account but do not know any of this information, you can contact your network administrator.

You can synchronize Address Book with Exchange Server 2000 or later. Earlier versions do not work with Address Book. Contact your network administrator for more information about which versions they have installed.

Synchronize Address Book with Exchange

① Click Address Book.

② Click Preferences.

The Preference window appears.

③ Click Synchronize with Exchange (☐ changes to ☑).

④ Click Configure.

A configuration window appears.

5 Type your username and password.

● You can select the Synchronize every hour option if you want the applications to update regularly (☐ changes to ☑).

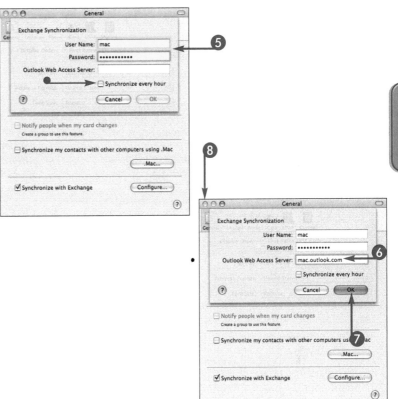

6 Type your Outlook Web Access Server information.

7 Click OK.

8 Click 🔘 to close the Preferences window.

Your Address Book contacts are now accessible in Exchange.

Can I synchronize Address Book with other applications?

▼ Yes. There are other applications for Linux and other operating systems that work with the Outlook Web Access (OWA) standard, a Web-based service that can manage a workgroup's list of e-mail and contacts. Microsoft Outlook is one of these.

Can Address Book synchronize across a network that uses the Windows Active Directory?

▼ Yes. Active Directory is a tool that allows many network resources to authenticate or provide reliable keys that allow users to access otherwise secure data. If you are working on a network that uses Active Directory and your network administrator has configured it to recognize Address Book, then you may not be asked to enter your username and password in Step **4**.

Attach an Address Book Contact to an E-Mail Message

You can attach a contact from your Address Book to an e-mail message in order to share that contact information with another Address Book user. This allows you to distribute contact information easily.

The recipient needs to have the Address Book application in order to read the contact information. Because Address Book is included in every installation of Mac OS X, you should be able to share contact information with all other Mac OS X users.

You can copy multiple Address Book contacts. This allows you to share some or all of your Address Book information with other users.

Attach an Address Book Contact to an E-Mail Message

① Select the contacts that you want to attach to an e-mail message.

You can select multiple contacts by Shift-clicking if they are contiguous, or by ⌘-clicking if they are not.

② Drag the contacts that you have selected to the body of an e-mail message.

Note: *For more information on using Mail, see Chapter 22.*

If you select multiple contacts, they are copied onto a single card. To copy them as separate cards, you can hold down the Option key as you drag them.

● The contacts attach to an e-mail message.

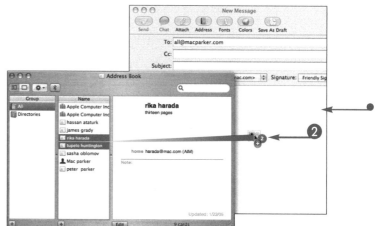

Use Searchlight to Search for Contact Info in the Address Book

You can search for any data stored in your Address Book using Spotlight, Mac OS X's advanced indexed search technology. This helps you to find contacts if you only remember certain bits of their contact info, such as a name, nickname, company name , AOL Instant Messenger handle, or even part of their names. You can even search for a person based on the notes you have attached to their contact information.

Spotlight begins searching as soon as you enter the first letter or number in the search field. As you enter more characters, the search results narrow down until you see the correct result.

Once you have located the correct contact information, you can double-click the result and see the entire contact information for that person, including notes. You can then work with that contact card to send an e-mail to that person, open iChat to contact that person, or share the contact information. To learn how to share a person's contact information, see the section "Attach an Address Book Contact to an E-Mail Message."

Use Searchlight to Search for Contact Info in the Address Book

① Click the search field in Address Book and type the name, address, or other information about the contact you want to find.

● Results appear in the Address Book.

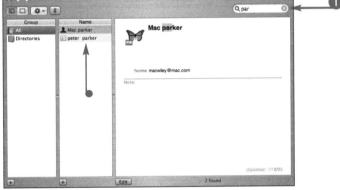

② Enter more characters to narrow the results.

③ Double-click the result you want to see the entire Address Book entry.

● The contact's information appears in a new window.

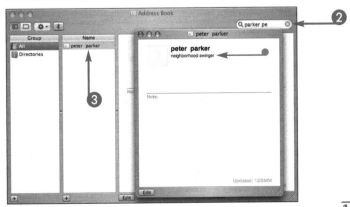

Turn on Scientific Features of the Calculator

Y ou can configure the Calculator in Mac OS X to add power features that expand the Calculator's power and usefulness beyond simple arithmetic functions. For example, in addition to trigonometric and logarithmic functions, you can also add the ability to work with exponentials and factorials, as well as switch between radians and degrees.

Another feature that you can add is a virtual paper tape that maintains an ongoing record of your calculations that you can save for future use. You can also use the Calculator to perform various conversions, including changing

Fahrenheit to Celsius and Imperial units to metric, and performing currency conversions. The Calculator can also update its currency conversion rates when your computer is connected to the Internet.

You can revert the Calculator to its basic configuration at any time, if you do not need the advanced features. This reduces the screen space that the Calculator requires. You can also hide the paper tape window at any time. However, if you do so, you cannot save or print the contents of the calculations that you have made up to that point.

Turn on Scientific Features of the Calculator

Add advanced functions

① Click View.

② Click Scientific or Programmer.

The Calculator displays extra function keys.

Add a virtual paper tape

1 Click View.

2 Click Show Paper Tape.

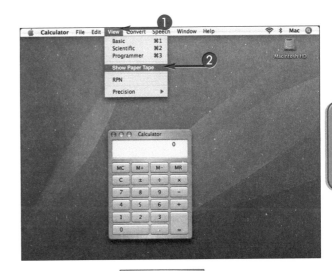

● The Paper Tape window appears.

Can I save the virtual paper tape of my calculations?

▼ Yes. After you have made a series of calculations, you can click File and then click Save Tape As. Calculator saves the record of your work as a text file that you can open and review.

Can I print out a paper tape of my calculations?

▼ Yes. After you make your calculations, click File and then click Print Tape. A standard print dialog appears, allowing you to select how you want to print the record of your calculations.

How can I perform unit conversions?

▼ You can use the Convert menu to translate between units of temperature, area, energy, length, speed, pressure, weight, power, volume, and currency. First type the number that you want to convert and then click Convert in the main menu. A menu appears above the main Calculator window, in which you can choose the conversion units. After you select the units, the result appears in the Calculator window.

Make a Desktop or Dock CPU Monitor

Y ou can create a small CPU monitor for either your Desktop or the Dock. This monitor displays a graphical representation of the demands on your system in real time. This feature is useful if you work with applications such as image or video editors, which often make great demands on your system.

When you work with graphics-intensive applications, your entire system can slow down due to each application's demanding CPU time. For example, windows may open more slowly and other processes such as searches may take longer than normal. This is not necessarily a sign anything is wrong with your computer.

A Desktop or Dock CPU monitor allows you to quickly determine whether the CPU is busy. If the monitor shows high CPU usage and you are not currently running powerhouse applications, then you can use the Activity Monitor to see if any processes are stuck in loops or otherwise using up more CPU resources than they should. If this is the case, then you can quit the process, which often returns your system to its prior performance level. For more information, see Chapter 3.

Make a Desktop CPU Monitor

① Launch the Activity Monitor application, which is located in the Utilities folder.

② Click and hold the Activity Monitor icon in the Dock.

A pull-down menu appears.

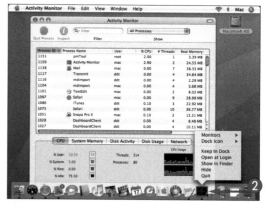

③ Select Monitors.

④ Select Floating CPU Window.

⑤ Click a display option.

You can choose either a Show Vertically or Show Horizontally option.

A Desktop CPU monitor appears.

Make a Dock CPU Monitor

1 Launch the Activity Monitor application.

2 Click and hold the Activity Monitor icon in the Dock.

A pull-down menu appears.

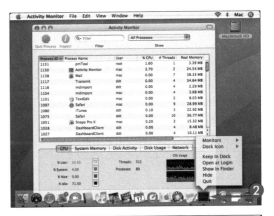

3 Select Dock Icon.

4 Click Show CPU Usage.

The Dock icon becomes a CPU monitor.

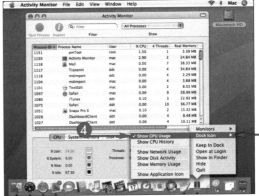

Can I move the Desktop CPU monitor?

▼ Yes. You can move the Desktop CPU monitor anywhere on the Desktop. To do so, click anywhere on the Desktop CPU monitor and drag it to where you want. Finder windows placed over the Desktop CPU monitor will cover it and hide it.

Why do some Desktop CPU monitors have one bar and others two bars?

▼ Each bar represents one processor. A single-processor Mac has a CPU monitor of one bar, while a dual-processor model has a CPU monitor of two bars. The same is true when the Dock icon shows CPU usage. In this example, made on a dual-processor Mac, there are two bars.

Can the monitors, either in the Desktop or the Dock, show anything other than CPU usage?

▼ No and yes, respectively. While the Desktop CPU monitor can only show CPU usage, the Dock icon can display CPU usage, CPU history, network usage, disk activity, or memory usage. In Step 3, when you select one of the other options, the Dock icon changes to represent that option.

Add a Calendar with iCal

You can create multiple calendars in iCal, Mac OS X's scheduling application. This is useful if you want to have one calendar for work, and another for personal or family events. You can also switch between calendars when you need to, or add events from one calendar to another.

If you have more than one person using the same account on your computer, then you can set up a calendar for each person. However, these calendars are not secure; anyone who logs on to an account can access all other iCal calendars on that account.

Users who have separate accounts can have their own calendars in iCal. Each user will not see iCal calendars created in other user accounts, unless the other user has chosen to share the calendars. Users can share events with other users, and even with people on other computers, by e-mailing event information.

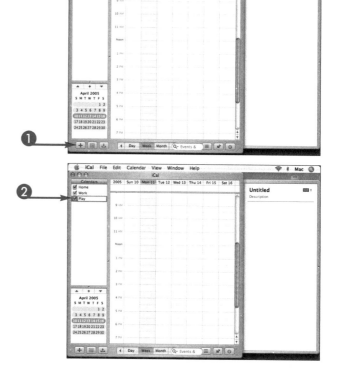

① Click Add ➕.

A new calendar appears in the Calendars list with the name Untitled highlighted.

② Type a name for the new calendar.

You can switch between calendars by clicking their names in the Calendars list.

Add an Alarm to an iCal Event

You can attach a variety of alarms to an event in iCal, to help remind you of the event. For example, this can be a useful way to remind you of upcoming obligations, such as a business meeting.

You can tell iCal to sound an alarm along with a message on your screen, to present the message silently, to send you an e-mail, or to open a file. The file can be a text document, a sound file, or even a movie. You can also tell

iCal to sound the alarm from minutes to days before or after you set a time.

If you choose to use an e-mail as an alarm for an iCal event, you should test how long it takes for an e-mail to reach you from the computer on which you are running iCal. In some cases, e-mails can take hours or even days; knowing how long the message takes to reach you can help you decide how long before the event to have iCal send the e-mail alarm.

Add an Alarm to an iCal Event

① Click an iCal Event.

② Click Info.

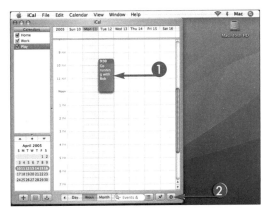

The Info drawer opens.

③ Click None, or the current alarm setting to open its pull-down menu.

④ Select the type of alarm that you want.

● iCal attaches the alarm to the event.

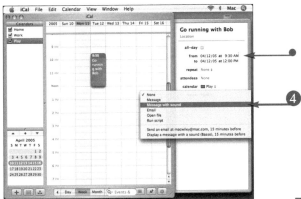

Synchronize Multiple Computers with .Mac

You can use a .Mac account to synchronize data across multiple computers. This is useful if you work on more than one computer in your office, or you want to take along important information while traveling.

You can transfer Address Book contacts, iCal schedules, and Safari bookmarks, so that you can have this information wherever you are. If one of the computers you are working with is not connected to the Internet, iSync records your information and updates all computers the next time they are online.

You must have an Internet connection and a .Mac account to be able to synchronize your data. If you do not have a .Mac account, then you can register for a free trial account; iSync prompts you to do this during the synchronization process. You also need to have entered your .Mac registration information in the .Mac section of your System Preferences.

Keep in mind that synchronizing data is not the same as using a remote Desktop solution. You cannot use a .Mac account to automatically transfer entire Desktops and other data, such as text documents.

Synchronize Multiple Computers with .Mac

① Click the Apple menu ().

② Select System Preferences.

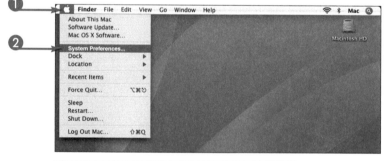

The System Preferences window appears.

③ Click .Mac.

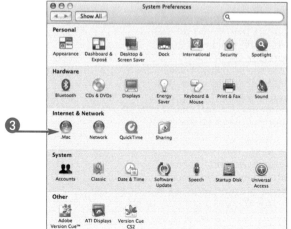

The .Mac pane appears.

④ Click the Sync tab.

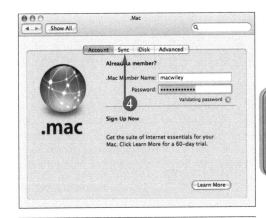

The Sync pane appears.

⑤ Click Synchronize with .Mac
(☐ changes to ☑).

Note: If you have not registered your .Mac account
on this computer, you will be prompted to
enter your account information.

The data that you selected is synchronized
through your .Mac account.

What if a window appears, prompting me to change my Data Alert Settings?

▼ If this prompt window appears before you set up automatic synchronization, then first click OK to close the window. Click Preferences and select the preferences you want. You can either deselect the Show Data Change Alert option or change the criteria of the alert. This note appears when iSync updates the data on each computer in excess of a certain amount.

Can I synchronize my information more frequently than every hour?

▼ Yes. After you click the .Mac button, you can click the Sync Now button. iSync updates all data immediately. However, only the computers that are currently connected to the Internet and that have access to your .Mac account are updated. If a computer is not connected, then it updates upon connecting.

How secure is this method of updating?

▼ If other users have access and you have registered these users with your .Mac login and password, they can see all of your information. If you cannot control access, you should delete the synchronized information and .Mac registration in the System Preferences once you are finished using the remote computer.

Set Up
Multiple Users

You can create multiple accounts in Mac OS X for multiple users. Individual users can log in to a personalized Mac OS X workspace, each with its own appearance, preferences, secure files, and applications. This allows you to share one computer among multiple users who may have different work or leisure requirements.

Each user has a home folder, which contains other folders for items that are required, such as applications, documents, movies, and music. By default, these folders cannot be accessed by other users, although a user can change this setting to give more access to others.

A home folder is not actually named *home;* instead, it displays a user's short name, which is assigned to the user in the Accounts preferences pane of the System Preferences window. Home folders reside in the Users folder, which is at the top level of the hard drive.

A user can protect access to his or her account by requiring a log on password. However, you can also specify that the account becomes accessible when a user clicks a picture or icon, for example, a child's account.

Each user can change the preferences for his or her account, such as altering screen resolution and the way that folders display, without affecting another user's account.

Set Up Multiple Users

① Click the Apple menu (⚫).

② Click System Preferences.

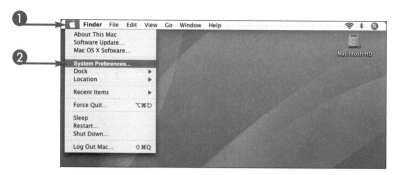

The System Preferences window appears.

③ Click Accounts.

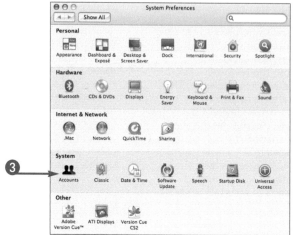

The Accounts pane appears.

If some options are dimmed, you can click the Lock icon and type an Administrator name and password to access them.

④ Click Add (+).

⑤ Type a new username.

You can also type a new short name in place of the one that is automatically assigned to the account.

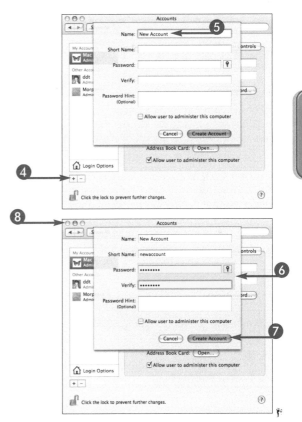

⑥ Type the new user's password in the Password and Verify fields.

You can also type a hint to remind the user of the password.

⑦ Click Create Account.

⑧ Click ⬤ to close the System Preferences window.

The new user can now log on to the computer.

Can I access my home folder from the Finder window?

▼ Yes. When you open a new Finder window that is displaying the Sidebar, your home folder appears in the Sidebar with a special icon. You can click that icon to open your home folder in the right pane of the Finder window. You can also navigate directly to your home folder by clicking Go in the Finder menu and selecting Home.

Can I change the short name after I have created the account?

▼ No. Once you have created the account, you can change the username, the user icon, the password, and other settings, but you cannot change the short name.

Can I set the computer to automatically log on users when the computer starts up?

▼ Yes. In the Accounts pane, click Login Options. You are presented with an option for the computer to log in automatically as any one of the available users. If that option is not checked, then the computer displays a login screen on startup; you must then type a username and password to start up the computer.

How can I determine whether I have an Administrator account?

▼ On the left side of the Accounts pane, there is a list of accounts on the computer. If your account has the word Admin under it, then you have an Administrator account.

Switch Users with Fast User Switching

I n Mac OS X, you can quickly switch between user accounts with Fast User Switching. This feature allows multiple accounts to be logged into simultaneously so that users do not need to log off one user, and then log on with another username and password to switch accounts.

With Fast User Switching, multiple users can remain logged on to the computer at the same time, while taking turns at using the computer. Switching between users does not affect open files, interrupt downloads, or change the workspace of the inactive users. In addition, switching back

to the original user leaves the processes of the other users active after they have begun. Because of this, you can switch back and forth between users an unlimited number of times without affecting the accounts of those users.

When you use Fast User Switching, the active username is visible in the upper-right corner of the menu bar, just to the left of the Spotlight icon no matter what application is currently in use. The other elements of the menu bar are not replaced, although they do move to the left. For more information on Spotlight, see Chapter 1.

Switch Users with Fast User Switching

① Click .

② Click System Preferences.

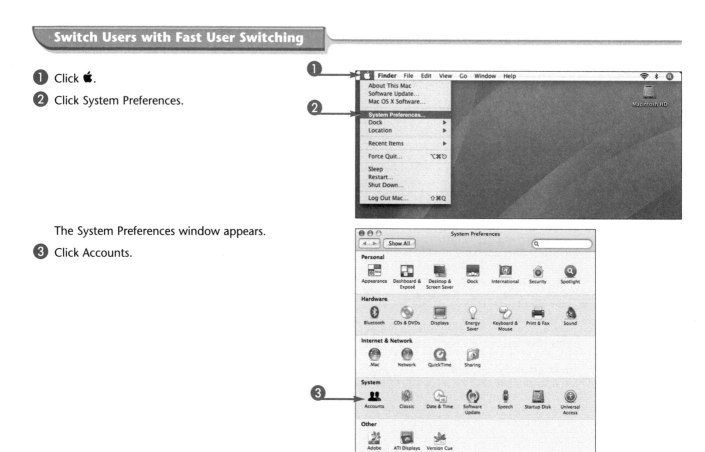

The System Preferences window appears.

③ Click Accounts.

The Accounts pane appears.

④ Click Login Options.

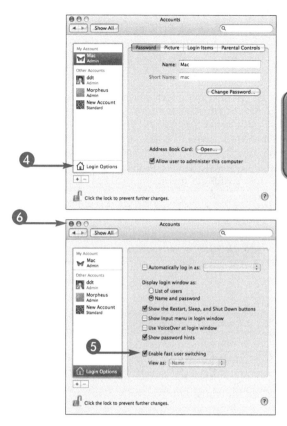

⑤ Click Enable fast user switching
(☐ changes to ☑).

⑥ Click ◉ to close.

What if I forget my password?

▼ If you forget the password to your user
account, you can ask a user of the
computer who has an Administrator
account to change your password for you.

Can another user see my password?

▼ No. Although other users can open the
Accounts pane in the System Preferences
window and are able to see your username
and your short name, they cannot see your
password. It is a good idea to write down
your username and password and keep it
in a secure place.

**What happens if I select Login Window
from the Fast User Switching menu?**

▼ If you select Login Window from the Fast
User Switching menu, the computer
switches to a new screen that allows you
to log in as any established user.
Depending on how you have configured
the Accounts preferences, you may be
asked to type in the username and
password of a user, or you may be asked
to click a user profile photo and enter a
password.

continued

Switch Users with Fast User Switching *(Continued)*

When you select another user's name to switch to that user's account, you may be prompted to enter a password. This is to protect unauthorized access to that user's account. If you have administrator access, you can set a user's account not to have a password. When you select this account name in the Fast User Switching menu, you will not be prompted for a password.

This can be useful when you share your computer with inexperienced users who may not be able to remember a password, or when you want to create an account for all users of your computer.

When you switch to another user account, Mac OS X displays that account's unique workspace. The user of the account may have set different screen resolutions, a different desktop, different placement of items on the Desktop, or any other different system settings. Each user can change his or her preferences without affecting those of other users.

On some Macintosh models, you will see the screen rotate when you switch user accounts. Older models that do not have video cards that support this feature will not rotate the screen.

Switch Users with Fast User Switching *(continued)*

The current user's name appears on the menu bar.

7 Click the name of the current user.

- A list of usernames appears.

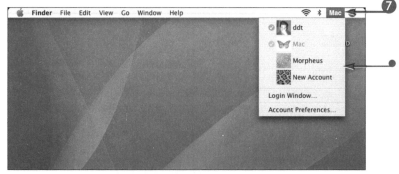

8 Click the username whose account you want to access.

If you assigned a password to the user account, then a login window appears.

If the user account does not require a password, skip Steps **9** and **10**.

9 Type the user's password.

10 Click Log In.

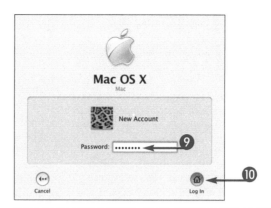

The computer switches to the account of the user that you selected.

Can I share files with users of other accounts on the same computer?

▼ Yes. You can drop files from your user space to another user's space by dragging a file to the user's Drop Box. However, depending on permissions and ownership of the file, you may or may not be able to access that file once you have done this. If you are uncertain, drop a copy of the file instead.

Can I share applications with users of other accounts on the same computer?

▼ Yes. All users of the same computer can access applications in the Applications folder of the computer. If an application is installed into one user directory, not all users on the computer may be able to access it. For more information on permissions, see Chapter 3.

Restrict File Access to Certain Users

You can restrict file access to ensure that your files are safe from use, alteration, or deletion by some users while also keeping the files available to other users on the same computer or on your network.

Mac OS X allows you to specify the level of access using different permission settings. You can use four settings: Read & Write, Read only, Write only, and No Access. By default, most of the folders in your home directory are secure from other users. This is because they are automatically assigned the No Access setting, so that other users cannot open these folders, let alone change their contents.

The exception is the Public folder. Items in the Public folder are visible to and can be copied by other users on the computer or the network. However, the Drop Box inside the Public folder is Write only; this means that other users can place files into this folder but cannot view or copy its contents. This applies to all users except for the account owner.

Restrict File Access to Certain Users

① Click a file or folder to select it.

② Click File.

③ Click Get Info.

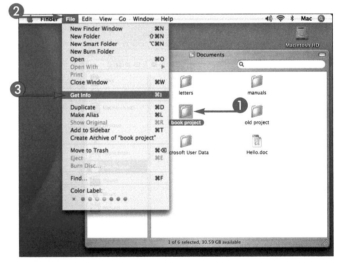

The Get Info window appears for the item you selected.

④ Click Ownership & Permission
(▶ changes to ▼).

The permissions setting displays for this item.

5 Click Details (▶ changes to ▼).

- You cannot make changes if the Locked option is selected. To deselect this option, click the check box (☑ changes to ☐). You may be prompted to provide an Administrator name and password.

6 Click Group ⬍ and select a user from the pull-down menu to whom you want to provide file access.

7 Click Access ⬍ and select the type of permission that you want to give the user from the pull-down menu.

- You can use the Others pull-down menu to specify the level of permissions that you want for all other users.

8 Click ⬤ to close the Get Info window.

The permissions that you selected are applied to the file or folder.

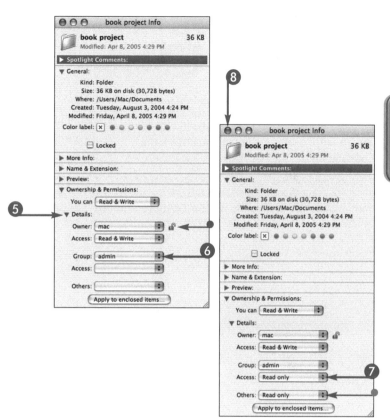

Can I make entire folders accessible, such as my Movies folder?	Can I change the access level of a file or folder back to its original state?	What if I am told that I do not have sufficient privileges to unlock the Get Info window?
▼ Yes. Follow all the steps, but in Step 1, select the folder that you want to be accessible rather than a file.	▼ Yes. You can follow the steps and change the access features back to their original state at any time. If you cannot remember the item's original state, then you can open the Get Info window of a similar item to help remind you of the original access state.	▼ Either you do not have ownership of the file, or the Administrator has not given your account the ability to change file access. Ask the person administering your computer whether you can make file access changes.

Restrict Font Access for Other Users

You can manage collections of fonts with Font Book to control whether users on the computer can or cannot have access to certain fonts. This is useful if you have a large number of fonts installed on the computer, and you want to avoid confusion for other users.

Some users may have unusual font requirements. For example, they may need a language font that does not use the Roman alphabet, such as Russian or Japanese. You can control font access to ensure that only the users who need these fonts have access to them.

Restricting font access can prevent other users from making changes to, or even deleting, a font. Whether accidentally or intentionally deleted, this can result in damage to an expensive font.

In addition, you can use this restriction to simplify the font menus for inexperienced users. These users might not understand the difference between slight variations of font families, and would appreciate a reduced set of font choices.

Restrict Font Access for Other Users

① Launch Font Book from the Applications folder.

The Font Book window appears.

② Click All Fonts.

3 Click Computer.

- The fonts that are available to all users on the computer appear in the Font column.

4 Click the font that you want to make available only to yourself.

5 Drag the font to the User icon in the Collection column.

- The font disappears from the Computer collection and appears in the User collection, at which point it is only available to you.

Can I restrict access to any font?

▼ Yes. However, there are certain fonts that are used by the operating system, such as Lucida Grande, and others that are used by Safari and other Web browsers. When you restrict access to these fonts, the substitute font can affect the appearance and spacing of text in the Finder and Web browsers.

Can I enable a font for all users?

▼ Yes. You can click and drag a font from the Font column to Computer in the Collection column. This removes the font from the User list and places it in the Computer list where it is available to all users on the computer.

Can I make a font available only to certain users on the computer?

▼ No. You can either make a font exclusive to a single user, or you can make it available to all users on the computer.

Can I share fonts between Mac OS X and Classic?

▼ Yes. If you install a font into the Fonts folder in the Mac OS 9 System folder, then it appears in the Mac OS X Font Book. However, you may need to quit and restart any running Mac OS 9 applications to use the font. Keep in mind that if you install a font into the Mac OS X Fonts folder, then it is not available to Classic applications.

Change User Limitations

You can change the limitations for other users on your computer if you have an Administrator account. This is useful when you want to manage users who may have various competencies with Mac OS X; you can give users no limitations, limit their access to applications and utilities, prevent them from accessing the System Preferences, or assign them to working in the Simple Finder.

The changes that you make come into effect when the user logs on to his or her account. For more information about changing between user accounts, see the section "Switch Users with Fast User Switching."

The changes can be subtle, such as restricting a user's access to applications. In this case, a user may notice no functional differences aside from not being able to work with a particular program. For more information, see the section "Restrict Applications Available to Other Users."

The change can also be more noticeable. For example, limiting a user to the Simple Finder restricts their workspace, providing a reduced set of commands in the Finder menu and locking the Dock so that it contains only a certain and unchangeable set of contents. This is useful when you provide an account to an inexperienced user.

Change User Limitations

① Click .

② Click System Preferences.

The System Preferences window appears.

③ Click Accounts.

The Accounts pane appears.

④ Click the account you want to change.

⑤ Click Parental Controls.

The Parental Controls pane appears.

6 Click Finder & System (☐ changes to ☑).

7 Click Configure.

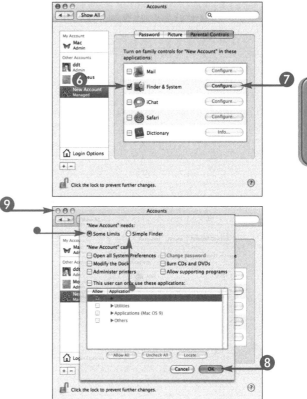

The Finder & System configuration sheet appears.

- Some Limits restricts applications and other access.

- Simple Finder restricts a user to the Simple Finder environment.

8 Click OK.

9 Click ◉ to close the System Preferences window.

The user account has the new limitations that you selected.

Can anyone change any other user's limitations?

▼ No. Only users with an Administrator account can change the limitations on other user accounts, as long as these other accounts are not also Administrator accounts. This is because Administrator accounts cannot be changed by other users.

Can I change my account back to its original state?

▼ Yes. You can simply follow the steps of this task and select different choices in the Limitations pane to return an account to its original state. By default, all accounts are created as standard accounts, which have no set limits, but are not administrator accounts.

Can I combine features, such as restricting application access to a user who is working in the Simple Finder?

▼ No. In the case of the Simple Finder, the user is already restricted in what he or she can access, so you cannot further prevent access to specific programs or files.

Restrict Applications Available to Other Users

I f you are the Administrator of a computer, then you can select and limit the applications available to other users on your computer. For example, if you share your computer with other users who have a range of experience, or with users who should be limited to working with a word-processing application and not playing games, then you can prohibit access to the System Preferences and password management.

However, you cannot restrict the applications of other users who have Administrator accounts. For this reason, you should only grant an Administrator account to users that you can trust with your computer and everything on it.

You can restrict user access for all applications and utilities. This includes all programs in the Applications and Utilities folders, as well as in the Applications (Mac OS 9) folder, which contains all applications that run in the Classic environment. In addition, you can select other programs that are elsewhere on your hard drive.

For more information on the contents of the Applications and Utilities folders, see Chapter 2. For information on restricting access to files, see the section "Restrict File Access to Certain Users."

Restrict Applications Available to Other Users

① Click .

② Click System Preferences.

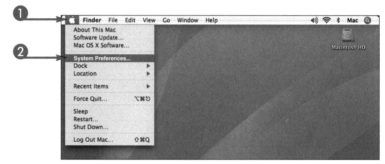

The System Preferences window appears.

③ Click Accounts.

The Accounts pane appears.

④ Click the account that you want to change.

⑤ Click Parental Controls.

The Parental Controls pane appears.

6 Click the application for which you want to set limits (☐ changes to ☑).

7 Click Configure.

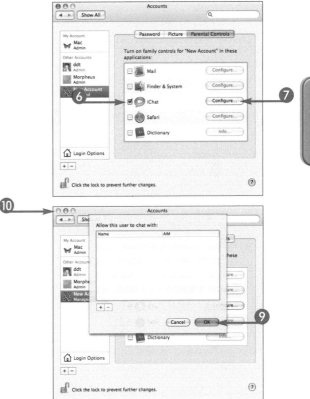

8 A sheet appears in which you can set limits for each application.

Note: *Sheets offer different options for different applications.*

9 Click OK.

10 Click ◉ to close the System Preferences window.

The user has limited access to the selected programs.

Can I select programs in other folders when I am assigning access?

▼ Yes. With the Some Limits pane open, click the Locate button. An Open dialog appears. You can navigate through your hard drive to find and select other programs that are not in the Applications, Utilities, or Applications (Mac OS 9) folders.

How is this different from the Simple Finder?

▼ Restricting a user's access to applications differs from assigning a user to the Simple Finder in that a user with restricted application access still has a full Finder and Dock. A user with the Simple Finder has a workspace with limited Dock and Menu options. For more information about the Simple Finder, see Chapter 2.

Can I assign other restrictions to users?

▼ Yes. You can choose to prevent a user from opening the System Preferences, changing passwords, altering the Dock, or burning CDs or DVDs. When you open the Some Limits pane, you can select or deselect these options without changing other restrictions. You must leave the Some Limits pane selected when you close the System Preferences window for the changes to take effect.

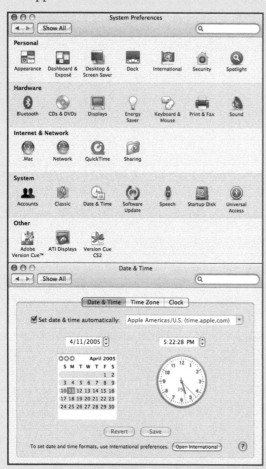

11   Applying Universal Access Features

12   Scripting Tasks with Automator

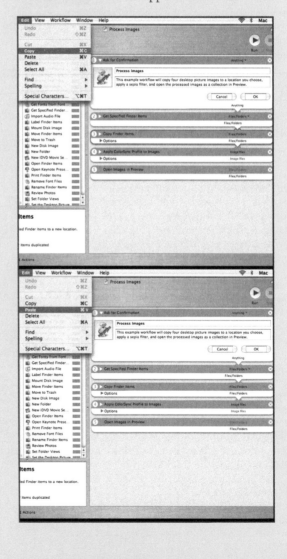

Elements of System Preferences

Just as each application has its own preferences, the operating system uses System Preferences. You can use the Mac OS X System Preferences to change and customize your computer. For example, you can use System Preferences to change the Desktop appearance, the Desktop layout, and to specify the users with whom you want to share your computer.

You can always access the System Preferences from the Apple menu in the upper-left corner of the menu bar. This easy access allows you to make changes to the system even while working in another application.

The System Preferences window is divided into sections that organize the various preferences by type. The Personal Preferences affect the appearance of your computer as well as how you interact with it. The Hardware Preferences can help you customize how you work with the peripherals

connected to your computer, even the ones connected wirelessly. The Internet & Network Preferences affect how your computer connects to other computers and to the Internet. The System Preferences affect the basic functions of your system, from who has an account to how you can access the system.

Some other applications and utilities may add their own preferences to the System Preferences. These preferences appear in another section, and generally control how third-party hardware and software interacts with your system, such as how your video card operates, or how utilities change your user interface.

When you select a preference icon in the System Preferences window, the options for that preference appear in the window's main pane. You can return to the full list of preferences by clicking the Show All button.

Appearance
You can change the general appearance of the user interface. For example, you can specify how buttons and highlighted items display, where scroll arrows appear in a window, and how windows minimize. These changes affect only the user currently logged in, if the computer is configured with multiple user accounts.

Desktop & Screen Saver
You can choose the background picture for your Desktop, either from an image that Apple supplies or from your own collection. You can also select one of the animated screen savers that are included in Mac OS X, or you can use one of your albums in iPhoto to create your own slideshow screen saver.

Dock
You can specify the placement of the Dock on-screen, change the size of Dock icons, choose to enable or disable magnification of Dock icons when the cursor hovers over them, alter the effect for minimizing windows, and decide whether to hide the Dock when it is not in use.

International
You can select the language that you want Mac OS X to use. You can also select the display formats for date, time, and numbers, as well as international keyboard layouts.

Dashboard & Exposé
Exposé enables you to specify hot corners. These are corners of the screen that can activate various Exposé functions. For example, you can set the preferences so that by moving the mouse to the lower right of the screen, you can activate Exposé's Show All Windows function. This preference can also set keys and mouse buttons as Exposé activators. Dashboard is another interface layer that appears when you press the F12 key by default; it presents a number of widgets, or mini-applications, that can translate text, control iTunes, and more.

Security
The Security preference enables you to access password protection for waking your computer when it is asleep, as well as giving you access to FileVault. FileVault is a security feature that works by encrypting the contents of your home folder. The process is a transparent one, encrypting and decrypting data as you use it, so you do not see a significant reduction in performance. However, it does use processor cycles, and so if you have a slower Mac, you should not enable FileVault unless you want to protect sensitive data in your home folder.

Bluetooth
You can set discovery and access criteria for communication between wireless Bluetooth devices and your computer. You

can also set how specific devices, such as Bluetooth-enabled personal digital assistants, handle the shared data. This preference pane will appear only on Macintoshes that have a built-in Bluetooth module.

CDs & DVDs
You can choose how your computer responds to blank DVDs and CDs, as well as to music and picture CDs and video DVDs. For example, you can specify whether a blank recordable CD launches iTunes or simply appears in the Finder, so that you can copy files and other items to the blank CD or DVD.

Displays
You can set the display resolution, number of colors, and refresh rate for your monitor. This preference also contains a color calibration utility and saves a list of established color profiles for your monitors.

Energy Saver
You can specify when your computer sleeps, as well as schedule automatic shutdown and startup times. You can also set your computer to restart automatically after an interruption in power, and choose how to manage processor performance in relation to power consumption, which is crucial for portable computers.

Keyboard & Mouse
You can customize the tracking and click speed of your mouse, as well as scroll wheel speed, if your mouse has a scroll wheel. You can also customize keyboard shortcuts and key repeat rate. You can also monitor signal strength from a Bluetooth-enabled wireless mouse and keyboard.

Print & Fax
You can choose printers on your network, monitor printing processes, and configure your computer to send faxes.

Sound
You can use this preference to adjust your computer's volume settings, choose sound effects for Mac OS X, and set up sound input and output options.

.Mac
This preference is the central point at which you can manage your access to the .Mac and iDisk services.

Network
The Network preference allows you to create and manage your network and Internet connectivity. You can enable multiple location settings for when you travel, configure AirPort and wired connections, and monitor the status of your current connections.

QuickTime
This preference allows you to select the settings for the kinds of files that QuickTime opens. You can also specify your Internet connection speed to optimize streaming media presentations.

Sharing
The Sharing preference is where you configure your computer for sharing files and services over a network. For example, you can arrange for personal Web sharing, printer sharing, and personal file sharing. You can also set up firewalls and shared wireless access.

Accounts
You can create and manage accounts for all users on the computer. You can also create and change passwords, as well as the level of access that each user has to the computer.

Classic
This preference helps you to maintain the Classic environment, in which Classic applications and utilities run. It appears whether Mac OS 9 is installed on your computer or not.

Date & Time
You can set the date and time that displays on the computer, as well as which time zone to use. You can also synchronize the computer's clock with a network timeserver. In addition, you can change time zones to check local time anywhere in the world.

Software Update
This preference allows you to obtain software updates over the Internet; it also keeps track of which updates you have recently installed.

Speech
In this preference, you can configure your computer both to recognize verbal commands and to read screen text aloud in a number of different voices.

Startup Disk
This preference allows you to choose the hard disk or partition from which the computer boots.

Universal Access
You can use the Universal Access preference to adjust the computer to make it easier for you to see or hear your Mac. For example, you can adjust screen contrast and zooming, and you can specify visual rather than audible alerts. You can also change keyboard access for easier use.

Use Spotlight with System Preferences

Y ou can use Spotlight, Mac OS X's built-in search technology, to help you locate which System Preference you need to use in order to change a specific feature of your computer. This is useful because the System Preferences contain many customization features, often in individual preference panes that you might not think are related.

In general, you can either browse for items or information, or search for them. Browsing the System Preferences would mean you would click an individual preference, see what it contains, then look in another for the feature you want to

find. Using the Spotlight feature, you can search, which narrows the field of relevant preferences.

Spotlight starts working as soon as you enter a character into the Search field in the System Preferences pane. The more complete you make the word in the Search field, the more accurate Spotlight's search results.

In addition, Spotlight works with many synonyms, so you can enter a word you think is related to what you are searching for, and Spotlight shows you potential matches. For example, you can enter "sleep" and Spotlight shows you the Energy Preferences.

Use Spotlight with System Preferences

① Click the Apple menu (🍎).

② Select System Preferences.

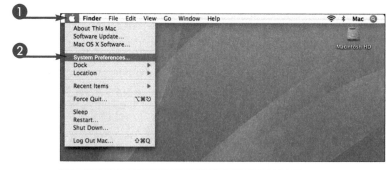

The System Preferences appear.

③ Enter your query text.

● Spotlight highlights relevant preferences and dims the others.

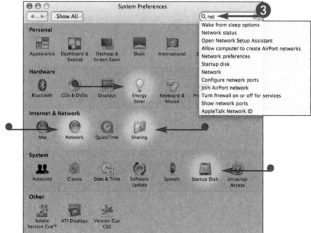

④ Click the closest answer in the pull-down menu.

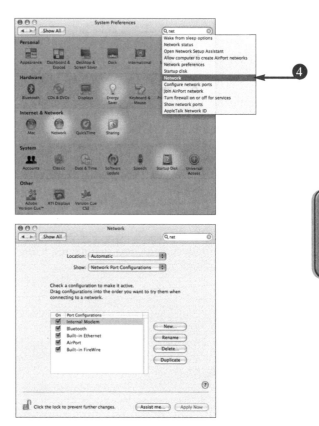

An individual preference pane appears.

Can Spotlight help me if I don't know the exact term?

▼ Yes. Spotlight can direct you to a particular preference even if you do not know the preference for which you are looking. For example, you know you want to work with a wireless network; enter "wireless" and Spotlight highlights the preferences that can help you configure your computer on a wireless network.

Can I cancel a Spotlight search of the System Preferences?

▼ Yes. If you have entered text in the Search field but want to try a different search, you can press the Delete key to erase letters and start typing again, or you can click the Show All button in the System Preferences window.

Does the search rank results?

▼ In a way. When you enter a search term, the most likely relevant System Preferences will be highlighted the brightest, while less relevant results will still be highlighted, but will appear more dim.

Change the
System Language

Although English is the default language for Mac OS X, you can change to another system language. When you change to a different language, the entire interface uses that language, from the menu bars to the button text. This is useful if you want to use your computer in a language with which you are more familiar.

Mac OS X supports languages that use the Roman alphabet and other languages such as Japanese, Korean, Chinese, Hebrew, and Arabic, as well as Slavic languages. Although your operating system can support many languages, some applications may not be able to. For example, you should check your word-processing application to see whether it supports Unicode — the standard for multilingual text — and right-to-left or vertical text. Some languages, such as Hindi, require that you install additional fonts; you can find these fonts on the Mac OS X Install Disc 2 CD-ROM.

You can view multilingual text documents without having to change the system's language settings. If an application supports Unicode, it should open documents that are created in any language. If your preferred word-processing application does not display the text correctly, then you can open the document in TextEdit.

Change the System Language

① Click .

② Click System Preferences.

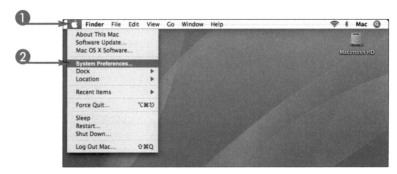

The System Preferences window appears.

③ Click International.

The International pane appears.

④ Click Language.

The Language pane appears.

⑤ Drag the language that you want to use to the top of the list.

Note: *You need to log out and log back in for changes to take effect in the Finder, or quit and relaunch applications for the changes to appear in their interfaces.*

The Finder and applications appear in the language that you selected.

Can I specify a second preferred language for applications that do not support my first language choice?

▼ Yes. For example, if you are comfortable working in Hebrew and French, and your critical application's menus and dialogs do not support Hebrew's right-to-left text, then you can tell the International preferences to present that application in a second language, such as French. If your first language in the list is presently Hebrew, then in the International Preferences pane, drag French directly below Hebrew. This tells the operating system to use French if Hebrew cannot be presented.

Can I use the International preferences to change how Safari displays Web sites?

▼ No. Changing the default system language changes Safari's menus and buttons, but does not translate the contents of Web pages. However, all modern Web browsers, including Safari, should properly display Web pages that are created with non-Roman characters, such as Japanese.

What if I do not see the language that I want to use?

▼ If you do not see the language that you want to use after Step 4, then click the Edit button. A list of languages appears; the languages that are presently visible in the Languages pane have selected check boxes next to them. Click the box next to the language that you want to appear in the Languages pane (☐ changes to ☑). Then click OK and proceed with Step 5.

Set Up a Screen Saver

When your computer is idle, you can enable screen savers in Mac OS X to have images or effects display on your monitor. This has the benefits of keeping casual onlookers from seeing what is on your screen and prevents the on-screen image from burning into the monitor.

You can choose any of the screen savers included in Mac OS X; these range from animated abstractions to a logo with the name of your computer. You can also choose a folder of your own photos or images that you can display on your screen in sequence, with transitional effects.

You can customize any of the screen savers. For example, you can choose how frequently images transition, how they zoom, or how the abstract screen savers behave.

In addition, you can specify hot corners for your screen saver. For example, you can tell Mac OS X to start showing the screen saver as soon as you move the cursor to selected corners of the screen, or set one or more corners to immediately disable the screen saver.

Set Up a Screen Saver

① Click ⌘.

② Click System Preferences.

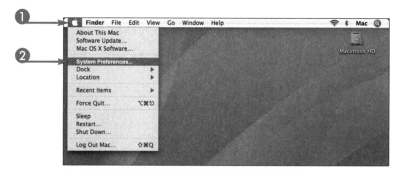

The System Preferences window appears.

③ Click Desktop & Screen Saver.

The Desktop & Screen Saver pane appears.

④ Click Screen Saver.

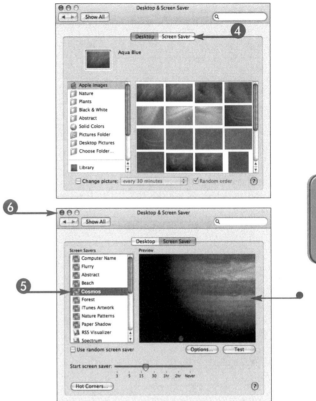

The Screen Saver pane appears.

⑤ Click a screen saver.

● A preview of the screen saver appears.

⑥ Click ◉ to close the System Preferences window.

The selected screen saver appears the next time your computer is idle.

Can I create a screen saver from a specific iPhoto Library or collection?

▼ Yes. At the bottom of the Screen Savers list in the Screen Saver pane are folders containing your iPhotos albums. Click one to select it.

Can I use other collections of images?

▼ Yes. Click Choose Folder in the Screen Savers list in the Screen Saver pane. An Open dialog appears. You can then choose another folder. Mac OS X displays all readable images from that folder in the screen saver.

Can I password protect my screen saver so that another user cannot wake my computer without a password?

▼ Yes. You can use your screen saver to lock your computer screen so that once it is running, a password is required to return to a useable screen. In the Security preferences, you can select the option to require a password to wake your computer from sleep or screen saver mode. Keep in mind that this method does not secure your entire computer. Other users can log in and access your account if they have an Administrator account.

Set Exposé Preferences

Mac OS X has a unique window management system, called Exposé. This system allows you to customize how you interact with your Mac to maximize your efficiency and enjoyment of working with multiple windows and files.

Exposé offers three new options to view the contents of your computer's Desktop and the windows that appear on it. You can choose the All windows option to scale down the windows and view them all simultaneously, thus enabling you to see all of the windows and their contents. When you choose the Applications window option, this feature dims all of the windows except for those associated with the currently selected application, so that you can see which items are opened in the currently running application. When you select the Desktop option, all open files appear at the edges of the Desktop, allowing you to see which items have been placed on the Desktop.

You can assign each of these Exposé features to any corner of the screen, so that they are activated when you move your mouse to these corners. You can also assign Exposé features to keys or mouse buttons. If you want, you can assign one feature to all corners, or separate features to different corners.

Set Exposé Preferences

1 Click .

2 Click System Preferences.

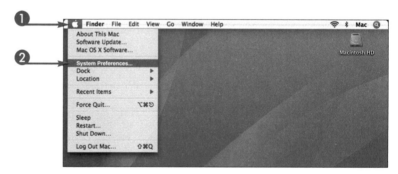

The System Preferences window appears.

3 Click Dashboard & Exposé.

The Dashboard & Exposé pane appears.

● To assign Exposé functions to screen corners, you can use these pull-down menus.

● To assign Exposé functions to keys, you can use these pull-down menus.

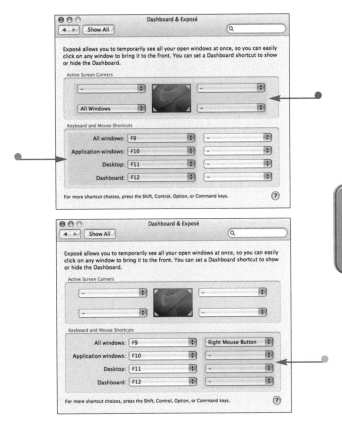

● To assign Exposé functions to mouse buttons, you can use these pull-down menus.

To create key-mouse button combinations for Exposé functions, hold down Shift-Control-Option, or ⌘ keys while using these pull-down menus.

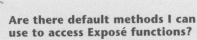

Are there default methods I can use to access Exposé functions?

▼ Yes. By default, the F9, F10, and F11 keys access All windows, Application windows, and Desktop functions, respectively. You do not need to make any changes to Exposé's preferences to use these features.

Can I set up Exposé to work in multiple ways, for example, with one function assigned to both a screen corner and a mouse click?

▼ Yes. You can use the Exposé preferences to access any Exposé function in a number of ways. For some users, setting a function to a screen corner works best when they are using their laptop without a mouse, but then they may prefer to use a mouse button when they connect a mouse to their laptop. Setting one method of using an Exposé function does not eliminate another method.

Can I set screen corners to both call up an Exposé function and to activate a screen saver?

▼ No. You can use a screen corner to either activate a screen saver or an Exposé function, but not both. However, you can set one corner to activate the screen saver, and the other corners to access Exposé functions, in the Exposé Preferences pane.

Set Your Computer to Sleep and Restart After a Power Failure

You can use the Energy Saver preferences to control when your computer goes to sleep, and to set it to restart after a power failure. This is an excellent feature if you regularly access your computer remotely. If a power outage occurs, your computer uses this feature to return to normal operation so that you can once again access it from a remote location.

You can also use the Energy Saver preferences to maximize battery life in a laptop. If you want to extend the time that you are away from a power supply, you can change the Energy Saver settings to put the computer or its display to

sleep if it is left idle for a specified time. Desktops with regular power supplies can generally be given a longer idle time before they sleep.

The option to change processor performance is also useful for laptops. You can use this option to tell Mac OS X to reduce the processor performance in order to trade off computing power for reduced energy consumption.

You can specify different idle times before the display and the computer sleep. This means that you can let the display, which often draws more power than the computer, go dark while the computer continues to process tasks.

Set Your Computer to Sleep

① In the System Preferences window, click Energy Saver.

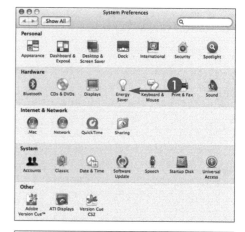

The Energy Saver pane appears.

② Click Sleep to open its pane.

③ Drag the slider to set the length of idle time after which the computer will go to sleep.

You can also specify the amount of idle time after which the display will go to sleep.

The computer and display will go to sleep after the idle time that you specified.

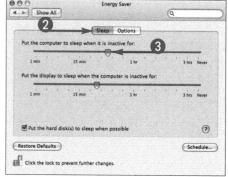

Set Your Computer to Restart After a Power Failure

① In the System Preferences window, click Energy Saver.

The Energy Saver pane appears.

② Click Options to open its pane.

③ Click Restart automatically after a power failure (☐ changes to ☑).

When power is restored, the computer restarts automatically.

Can I prevent my computer from ever going to sleep?

▼ Yes. You can set the sliders in the Sleep pane to Never, which means that your computer will never sleep. This is useful if you are running processor-intensive applications that would not run as efficiently when the computer is asleep.

Does setting the monitor to sleep affect the computer's performance?

▼ No. If you have an external monitor, then you can set the monitor to sleep or even turn it off, without affecting computer performance.

When should I choose to let the hard disk sleep?

▼ When you choose the option in the Sleep pane that tells the hard disk to sleep when possible, this affects how your computer performs disk-intensive tasks. The computer must wake up the hard disk when it needs to access data that is stored there, and this procedure of waking up and putting the hard disk back to sleep is time- and resource-intensive. However, allowing the disk to sleep when possible is still the most energy-efficient option that you can choose, next to allowing the display to sleep.

Change Keyboard & Mouse Preferences

Y ou can customize how your keyboard and mouse respond to your input by using the Keyboard & Mouse preferences. This helps you to set up both input devices so that they accommodate your personal style and increase your efficiency and comfort.

For the keyboard, you can change the speed at which the operating system displays key repeats, or how quickly it displays multiple characters on-screen while you hold down the character's key. You can also specify how long you need to keep pressing a key before the operating system

recognizes it as a key repeat. For example, if you are a rapid typist, then you may want a high key repeat rate and a low delay until repeat; however, if you are a slower typist, then you may want a longer delay until repeat.

For the mouse, you can set tracking, scrolling, and double-click speeds. Tracking determines how rapidly the cursor moves on-screen in response to mouse movements. Double-click speed determines how quickly you must click the mouse button twice for it to be recognized as a double-click.

Change Keyboard Preferences

① Click Keyboard & Mouse in the System Preferences window.

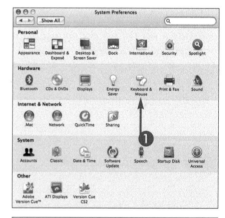

The Keyboard & Mouse pane appears.

② Click Keyboard to open its pane.

③ Drag the sliders to set the Key Repeat Rate and Delay Until Repeat settings.

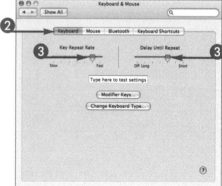

Change Mouse Preferences

① Click Keyboard & Mouse in the System Preferences window.

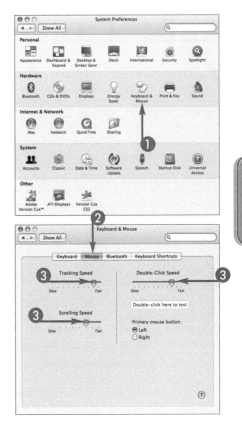

The Keyboard & Mouse pane appears.

② Click Mouse to open its pane.

③ Drag the sliders to set the Tracking, Scrolling, and Double-Click Speed Settings.

How can I test my changes?

▼ You can use the text boxes in both the Keyboard and Mouse panes to test how your changes affect how the mouse and keyboard respond to your input. For example, after you change the keyboard settings, click in the text box, and press and hold a key. Similarly, in the Mouse pane, you can use the text box to test how your changes affect double-click speed.

Can I change the trackpad preferences on my laptop?

▼ Yes. If you have a laptop and are not using a mouse, then you should see the Trackpad tab instead of the Mouse tab in the Keyboard & Mouse preferences. You can click the Trackpad tab to set tracking and double-click speed for the trackpad as well as the built-in trackpad button, exactly as you would adjust these settings for a mouse.

Can I reset my changes back to the default settings?

▼ No. There are no default settings for these preferences. However, you can adjust individual settings until you are comfortable with them.

Set the
Right Time

You can set the time manually or automatically in Mac OS X so that the system clock is always accurate. The system clock does more than just display the correct time in the menu bar clock; it also determines the creation and modification dates and time zones that appear on the files and folders in which you are working. You can also synchronize the computer's clock with a network time server. In addition, you can change time zones to check local time anywhere in the world.

You can set the time manually, or, if you have Internet access, you can use a network timeserver. This synchronizes your computer's clock with a precise time clock on a remote server.

Mac OS X synchronizes with the remote time servers automatically. You cannot force it to refresh the time.

The Mac OS X clock automatically resets according to Daylight Savings and Standard time. This means that you do not have to remember when the time change occurs.

Set the Right Time

① Click Date & Time in the System Preferences window.

The Date & Time pane appears.

② To set the clock manually, drag the clock's hands to the time you want.

● Alternatively, you can enter the correct time and date in the boxes above the clock and calendar.

③ To allow Mac OS X to set the time automatically, click the Set date & time automatically check box (□ changes to ☑).

The system clock displays the new time.

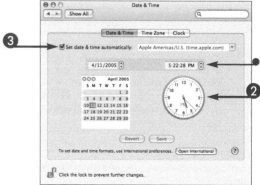

Set Appearance Preferences

Y ou can use Mac OS X's Appearance Preferences to change many features of how your computer's screen looks and how you work with it. You can change the overall look of buttons and highlight colors, where scroll arrows appear in windows, how scrolling works, as well as purely cosmetic changes such as font smoothing, which affects how text is rendered on your computer screen. In addition, you can change some elements of the Apple menu. These changes affect only the user currently logged in, if the computer is configured with multiple user accounts.

You can also change the color of buttons and menus, as well as of highlighted text. This can be useful for people with vision problems who find it hard to distinguish low-contrast colors.

In addition, you can customize the level of font smoothing. This is useful because different types of displays, such as CRTs or LCDs, display text better at different levels of smoothing.

Set Appearance Preferences

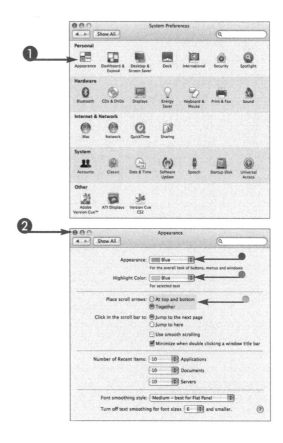

① Click Appearance in the System Preferences window.

The Appearance pane appears.

● To change the appearance of buttons, menus, and windows, select Blue or Graphite from the Appearance pull-down menu.

● To change the highlight color, select a color from the Highlight Color pull-down menu.

● To change the placement of scroll arrows, click an option to select either at the top and bottom or together (○ changes to ●).

② Click 🔴 to close the System Preferences window.

The appearance of the system reflects your new settings.

Elements of Font Book

You can use Font Book to view, organize, install, and manage fonts. A font is a complete set of type of a single size and style. For example, the text you are reading is set in one font, and the text of the chapter title is set in a different font.

You can also use Font Book to create, change, and manage collections of fonts. For example, you can create a font collection that contains all of the fonts that you plan to use on a project, all of the fonts that work well in Web pages, or all of the fonts of a particular language. This can help you to easily access sets of fonts that are important to one task without having to select them all individually.

Font Book validates all font files to check for corruption before it finishes installing the font. This protects you against damaged fonts, which can affect and even corrupt some of your documents.

Similar to Finder windows, Font Book features an Action button. You can click this button to add a font; disable, remove, or validate the currently selected font; preview a font; or show the font file.

The Font Book window also features a Search field. As with Finder windows, you can enter the name of a font you want to use and Font Book displays matching results. To launch Font Book, you can double-click its icon, which is located in the Applications folder.

Collection Column

You can browse through the Collection column to view a list of all of the font collections that are available to you. Although Mac OS X creates this default collection, you can create your own font collection for any project. This helps you stay organized, even when you have a large number of fonts installed on your computer. For more information, see the section "Create a New Font Collection."

Font Column

The Font column displays the available fonts in the selected collection. If that selected collection is All Fonts, Font Book shows all fonts installed on the computer. To view all of the styles included in a font, such as bold, italic, or condensed, you can click the arrow beside the font.

Preview Pane

The Preview pane displays a sample of every character in the font. The Preview shows you the font style that you have selected in the Font column. To see examples of all styles of a font, you can click each style listed in the Font column.

Install a Font

Y ou can purchase fonts on CD-ROM or download free fonts from the Internet. You can then install your new fonts in Mac OS X. Once you have installed them, they are available to all of your applications.

When you install a font, Font Book performs an automatic check of the font, called validation. If the font appears corrupted, incomplete, or otherwise damaged, Font Book asks you if you want to abort or continue installation. If you abort, you can try to acquire the font again and install that version.

You can also make the new fonts available to either all users on the computer, or to a single user. This can protect a valuable font from a novice user accidentally deleting it. It also can simplify the Font menu for similarly inexperienced users.

Fonts that you install into the Mac OS X Font Book are not available to Classic applications. However, the fonts in the Fonts folder in your Mac OS 9 System Folder are available to Mac OS X applications and appear in Mac OS X's Font Book.

Install a Font

① Double-click the font you want to install.

The font file can be one that you have downloaded or copied to your hard drive from a CD-ROM or another computer.

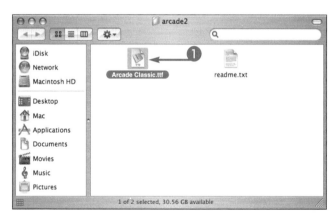

● Font Book opens and displays a preview of the font.

② Click Install Font.

The font is automatically added to the Library folder in your home folder.

To make this font available to all users on the computer, drag the font name from the Font List to the Computer folder in the Collection List.

Turn a Font Off and On

Y ou can turn an individual font or an entire font family off and on in Font Book. This is a useful way to keep your font menus short and manageable in your applications and in the Font Book.

Turning a font off means that the font does not display in the Font menus for any application. For example, if you have hundreds of fonts turned on, the Font menu in your word-processing application may take a few minutes to scroll through. As a result, simply opening the font menu can slow down your entire system performance. In addition, many fonts have similar names, which can confuse inexperienced users.

If you have turned off, or disabled, a font in a font collection, that font is not available, even if you or any user has access to that collection. To use that font, you must turn it on, or enable it, again.

Once you have learned how to turn fonts off and on, you can manage large font collections to streamline your work.

Turn a Font Off

1 In the Font column, click the font you want to turn off.

2 Click the Enable button to disable the font (☑ changes to ▣).

● The font is disabled.

Turn a Font On

1 Click a disabled font in the Font column.

A disabled font appears grayed out.

2 Click the Disabled button to enable the font
(☐ changes to ☑).

● The font is now enabled and appears in
application font menus.

Can I turn font collections on and off?

▼ Yes. You can turn entire collections of
fonts off and on, disabling either the
default sets of fonts or font collections
that you have created. Select an active
collection in the Collection column and
click the Disable button to disable it, or
click a disabled collection, and click the
Enable button to access the disabled
collection. When a collection is disabled,
it is not available to any application.

**When I turn a font off for one user, is
it turned off for all users?**

▼ If the font is available to all users on the
computer, then disabling it makes it
unavailable to all users. You can check to
see whether a font is available to all
users by clicking the arrow next to All
Fonts in the Font column and selecting
Computer; if the font is listed there, then
it is available to all users on the
computer. If it is only listed when User is
selected in the Collection column, that
font is available only to the current user
of the computer.

Create a New Font Collection

Y ou can create a new font collection in Font Book. This allows you to manage your fonts more efficiently, organizing different sets of fonts for use on different projects or for different languages.

Creating font collections also makes it easier for you to locate individual fonts. Before collections, you had to scroll through the entire list of fonts in Font Book's Font column. Using collections, you are now able to locate fonts by convenient groups, or collections. For example, you can store the fonts you want to use on a Web project in a Web font collection.

Once you create a new font collection, it appears in the Collection column in the Font Book window. You can click the collection's name in the Collection column to display the individual fonts from that collection in the Fonts column.

You can also add or remove fonts from collections. Fonts in the collections that you create are available to all users on the computer. The only exception is the User collection, which is the group of fonts available only to the current user of the computer.

Create a New Font Collection

① **Click Add (⊞).**

- A new collection appears with the name highlighted.

② **Type a name for the new collection.**

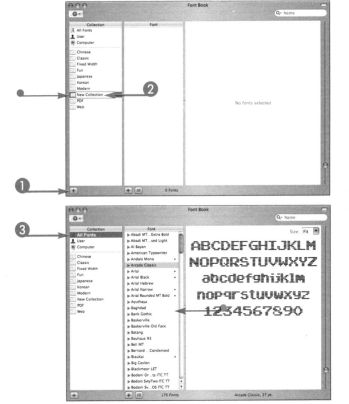

③ **Click All Fonts.**

- All installed fonts appear.

④ Select the fonts that you want for the new collection.

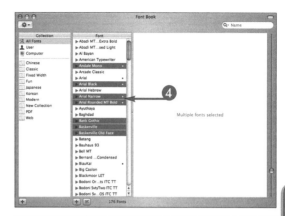

⑤ Drag the fonts to the new collection.

The fonts are now included in the new collection.

Can I create a collection that is available to all users on the computer?

▼ Yes. If you want the new collection's fonts to be available to all users on the computer, click Computer in Step **4**. Then select and drag fonts from the list that appears in the Font column; these are fonts that are available to all users on the computer.

Can I have one font in more than one collection?

▼ Yes. You can include any font in any number of font collections. This is often necessary, as many projects may need the same font or font family.

Can I create a font collection that is only available to me?

▼ Yes. You can click User in Step **4** and select the fonts that you want from the Fonts column. These fonts are only available to the current user, and so the collection created from these fonts is only available to the current user.

Understanding Access Options

You can use Mac OS X's Universal Access options to accommodate a range of visual or hearing disabilities, from color-blindness to hearing impairment. You can also set the computer to accept unique keystroke combinations for users who have difficulty using the keyboard, or to set keystroke replacements for mouse commands.

The goal of Universal Access is to allow users of all physical abilities to be able to use the computer. You can set different Universal Access options for each user account. Changing the options for one account does not affect other accounts. For more information about creating and managing user accounts, see Chapter 8.

The Universal Access preferences allow you to enable access for devices such as alternative pointers, and to turn text-to-speech capabilities on or off. The text-to-speech feature enables the operating system to read the options of the Universal Access Preferences aloud when the mouse moves over the option's text.

In addition, Mac OS X features VoiceOver, which is an alternative spoken interface. This is useful for people who have visual disabilities and need to hear what is displayed on the screen. VoiceOver speaks aloud the items that show up on the computer screen. For instance, when you click the System Preferences window, VoiceOver tells you what the window is, what application it belongs to, and how many items are in it. VoiceOver also says aloud the text in windows and in documents.

You can customize your computer for any language, but VoiceOver presents information only in English. You can visit Apple's Accessibility Web site at www.apple.com/accessibility for more information.

You can set up combinations of Universal Access options within a single account. You can also set up accounts that take advantage of a single Universal Access feature; for example, you can set up one account with Zoom on and another with keyboard options. Universal Access features that are turned on in one account do not appear in another account on the same computer.

Seeing

The Seeing pane contains all of the access options that pertain to how the user interface appears. It allows you to modify the interface in order that it is more visible to those users with difficulties seeing the screen in the default state. You can turn the Zoom feature on and off, as well as personalize its options, change to a white-on-black interface, and change the screen's contrast levels.

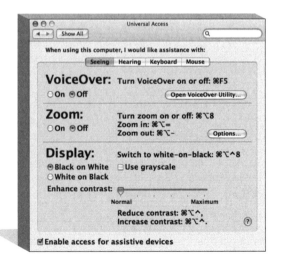

Hearing

The Hearing pane allows you to adjust the system volume, so that hearing-impaired users can hear alerts and other system sounds. For those with significant hearing loss, this pane has an option for the system to flash the screen to signify a system alert instead of making a sound. This option is also available for hearing users; a flashing screen alert is useful if you regularly work with the system sound muted but still want to be aware of system alerts.

Keyboard

The Keyboard pane has a number of options that help you work in various ways with the keyboard. For example, you can turn on and off or modify the Sticky Keys option, which helps users who have difficulties hitting more than one key at a time by "holding" one key press for you a number of seconds even if you are not physically holding the key down, allowing you to press another key as if the two were in combination. Being able to simultaneously press multiple keys is important when using key combinations, such as ⌘-O to open a file. You can also turn on and off a feature that makes the computer beep when a modifier key, such as Command or Option, is pressed. This helps you remember when you have used Sticky Keys to create a key combination. The Keyboard Preference pane also allows you to set up and customize Slow Keys, which allows a slight delay between when you press a key and when the operating system recognizes the key press. This can be useful for people who have dexterity issues. This feature makes Mac OS X more tolerant of less-than-precise typing.

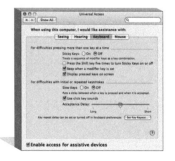

Mouse

The options in the Mouse pane are for users who have trouble operating a standard mouse. These options include fine-tuning the initial delay between when the user moves the mouse and when the cursor moves on-screen, limiting the maximum speed of the cursor and Mouse Keys. The Mouse Keys feature allows you to use your keyboard's numeric keypad instead of the mouse to control on-screen cursor movement. You can also change the size of the cursor, from normal to large; this is helpful for sight-impaired people who may have trouble locating the cursor on the computer screen.

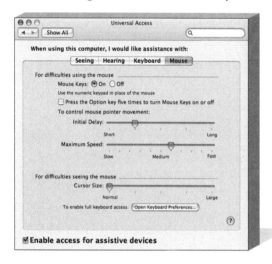

Turn On Zoom

You can use the Zoom feature in the Universal Access preferences to enlarge the image on your computer screen for easier viewing. Once the image is zoomed in, you can use the mouse to navigate around the screen. This is useful for people who would otherwise have difficulty reading text and other elements of the user interface at its normal size, even at lower screen resolutions.

Once you have turned on the Zoom feature, you can specify various options for how the Zoom feature works.

These options include limiting the maximum and minimum ranges for zooming, the ability to show a preview rectangle of the selected area while the screen is zoomed out, and how moving the mouse affects what part of the screen you see while zoomed in.

Once this feature is activated, you can zoom in and out using a key combination; you can use the Keyboard Shortcuts pane of the Keyboard & Mouse preferences to customize this key combination. This feature is most useful for users with difficulty pressing multiple key combinations.

Turn On Zoom

① Click the Apple menu (🍎).

② Click System Preferences.

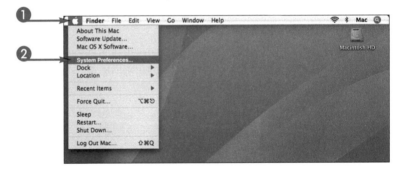

The System Preferences window appears.

③ Click Universal Access.

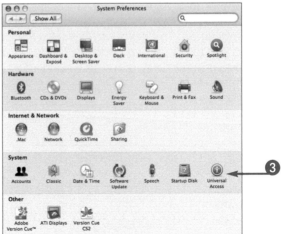

The Universal Access pane appears.

④ Click Turn On Zoom.

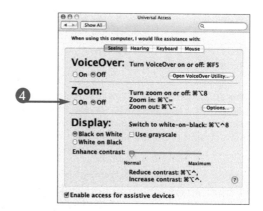

⑤ Press ⌘-Option-[equal sign key].

The screen zooms in.

⑥ Move the mouse to reposition the section of the screen that is showing.

You can press ⌘-Option-[minus key] to zoom out.

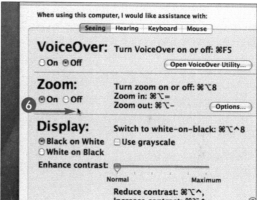

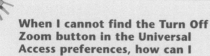

When I cannot find the Turn Off Zoom button in the Universal Access preferences, how can I turn off the Zoom feature?

▼ If you have zoomed in and want to turn off the Zoom feature, you can press ⌘-Option-8. The screen zooms out to its normal state.

If I find it difficult to use the zoom key combinations, can I change them to something easier?

▼ Yes. In the System Preferences, click Keyboard & Mouse, and then click the Keyboard Shortcuts tab to open the Keyboard Shortcuts pane. You can then scroll through the list of pre-assigned keyboard shortcuts to find one for Zoom In and Zoom Out. To change the key combination, double-click the one that you want to change and then hold down the new keys that you want to assign to that keyboard shortcut.

Can I change how the screen moves around when I am zoomed in?

▼ Yes. With the Zoom feature turned on, click the Zoom Options button in the Seeing pane of the Universal Access Preference window. An options pane appears; you can change the way the screen moves when zoomed in, from following the cursor, to only when the cursor reaches the edge of the screen, to keeping the cursor in the center of the zoomed screen.

Change Screen Colors and Contrast

You can choose to reverse the screen colors in Mac OS X, changing the standard black-on-white of windows and text documents to white-on-black. This can be useful if you find the usual set of screen colors difficult to read.

For some people, using a white-on-black color set is easier to read and less of an eyestrain than the standard black-on-white. This is due to the increased contrast that the white-on-black option provides.

If the reversed display in color does not provide a more readable interface, then you can also set the display to

grayscale, which removes all color from the user interface. You can also reverse the grayscale display, for a white-on-black environment without color.

In addition, you can simply adjust the contrast of the screen, independent of any hardware-based monitor settings. This allows you to fine-tune the display, so that you can further customize the contrast of the screen to provide the easiest-to-read monitor setting. Each user can have its own set of display color options without affecting other users.

Change Screen Colors and Contrast

① Click .

② Click System Preferences.

The System Preferences window appears.

③ Click Universal Access.

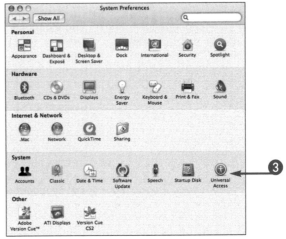

The Universal Access pane appears.

④ To reverse colors, click White on Black.

The screen colors reverse.

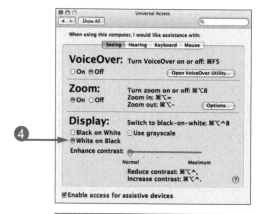

⑤ To enable a grayscale display, click Use grayscale (☐ changes to ☑).

The screen changes to grayscale mode.

⑥ To increase or decrease contrast, drag this slider.

The screen contrast changes.

Can I revert to the default display settings?

▼ Yes. You can undo any and all setting changes for the screen at any time. However, there is no shortcut for this; you need to set the screen to black on white, then color, and then move the Enhance Contrast slider to the Normal position.

Can I set the contrast to lower than Normal?

▼ You cannot reduce contrast below Normal through the Universal Access preferences. However, you can do this through the contrast controls on your monitor.

Can I combine grayscale and white-on-black settings?

▼ Yes. Doing so gives you a white-on-black screen, but without the reversed colors that you would see if you only selected the Switch to White on Black option. This is useful for color-blind people who also need increased contrast. However, when you select this setting, you are not able to work with color in applications such as image editors. Also, images that you save while the display is set to grayscale are not really grayscale; they appear in color when viewed in a full-color screen.

Use the Keypad to Control the Cursor

Y ou can use the Universal Access preferences to use the keyboard's numeric keypad to control the cursor on your screen instead of using the mouse. This is useful if you or one of the users on your computer find it difficult to control the mouse.

You can use this feature in conjunction with any of the other Universal Access options, such as the zoom or spoken items features. You can also enable this option for one of the users on your computer without affecting the control settings of the other users on the computer.

In addition to controlling the movement of the cursor, this option also allows you to use the numeric keypad to click an item. You can also use the keypad to click and hold an item so that you can select and drag items across the screen.

Enabling this feature does not preclude using the mouse to control the cursor in the default method. As a result, you are able to work on this user's account with the mouse, even if the user has selected the keypad control option.

① Click .

② Click System Preferences.

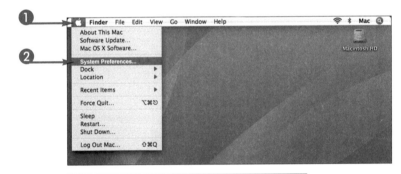

The System Preferences window appears.

③ Click Universal Access.

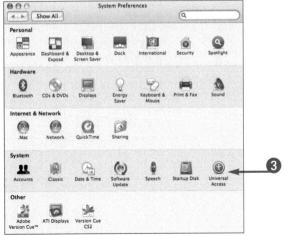

The Universal Access pane appears.

④ Click Mouse.

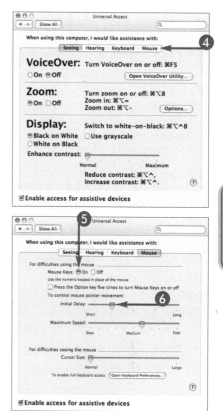

The Mouse pane appears.

⑤ Click the On option for Mouse Keys
(○ changes to ●).

⑥ Drag the Initial Delay slider to set the delay
between when you press a key and when the
mouse begins to move.

You can now use the keypad to control the
cursor.

**Can I create a shortcut for
turning the Mouse Keys feature
on and off?**

▼ Yes. In the Keyboard pane of the
Universal Access Preferences, check
the Press the Option key five times
to turn Mouse Keys on or off option
(□ changes to ☑). After you close
the Preferences window, you can
press the Option key five times in
succession to turn the Mouse Keys
feature on or off.

**Can I use the keypad to click an
item on the screen?**

▼ Yes. After you have moved the
pointer over an item you want to
click, press 5 on the numeric
keypad. You can also press 0 to
simulate pressing and holding the
mouse button, so you can drag
items using the keypad. When you
want to release the item, press 5.

Enable the
Spoken Interface

You can use the Mac OS X Speech preferences to enable your computer to read text aloud when you move the cursor over it. This is useful if you have trouble reading small text that appears on your computer's screen, in dialogs and buttons.

You can select a range of built-in synthesized voices, either male or female. You can choose fun-sounding ones, or simply a voice that sounds clearer to you. You can adjust the delay between when you move the cursor over text and when the computer speaks it. You can use a slider in the Default Voice pane of the Speech Preference window to change the rate at which the computer's voice speaks.

Mac OS X also comes with other speech options, such as automatically speaking alert text. This is useful if a background application requires your attention and you have the Dock hidden; normally, an alert triggers that application's icon to bounce in the Dock.

You can also choose to have the computer read highlighted text aloud at the touch of a button, rather than the text under the cursor. This serves as a more selective speech option, when you only want on-screen text to be spoken occasionally.

Enable the Spoken Interface

1 Click .

2 Click System Preferences.

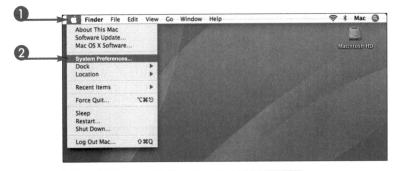

The System Preferences window appears.

3 Click Speech.

The Speech pane appears.

④ Click Text to Speech.

⑤ Click the Speak selected text when the key is pressed button (☐ changes to ☑).

⑥ Click Set Key.

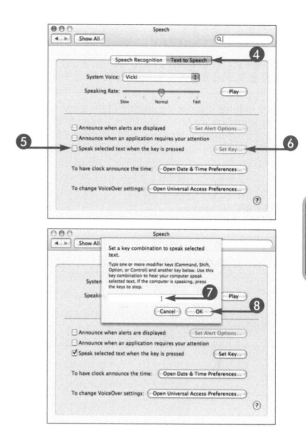

A dialog sheet appears.

⑦ Press the keys you want to set to tell the computer to speak selected text.

⑧ Click OK.

The computer will read highlighted text when you press the key combination.

Can I change the voice that is used by the computer to read selected text?

▼ Yes. In the Default Voice pane of the Speech Preferences window, select a new voice from the list. You can move the slider to change the rate at which the voice speaks. You can also preview the voice by clicking the Play button.

Can I change the voice that is used by the computer to speak alerts?

▼ Yes. You can select different alert voices from the Talking Alerts voice pull-down menu in the Talking Alerts section of the Spoken User Interface pane.

Will the computer read any text on the screen, including text in buttons and menus?

▼ No. With the Spoken User Interface options turned on, the computer speaks any text that you want it to if that text appears in the Finder, such as text that appears in menus and buttons. However, there are limitations. For example, this option does not work with graphical text, such as the content of PDFs and word-processing documents, or the contents of a Web page.

Elements of Automator

You can use Automator, Apple's new personal automation assistant, to create scripts that automate repetitive tasks, whether these tasks are simple or complex. Automator uses a graphical user interface (GUI), in which you can build a set of directions that your computer then uses to perform extensive operations. Once you create a script, or workflow, in Automator, you can launch it with a few clicks. It then proceeds through its programmed set of operations, rather than your having to perform them all yourself. You can also save the script with a specific name and have it placed automatically in the menu bar's Script menu. In addition, you can share workflows with friends and coworkers who have Mac OS X 10.4 or later, with Automator installed.

Although Automator produces programming code, you do not have to know or work with any code yourself. Instead,

you can drag actions, which represent the individual actions in a script, into the workflow pane. The actions are followed in order, passing along vital information as they are performed. You can specify various options for each action once you have dragged it into the workflow pane, thus further customizing your script. As a result, using Automator is more like building a flowchart than working with programming code.

Actions are organized into Libraries. By default, Automator contains an Applications folder in its Library list. In this folder is a list of applications, and you can click an application's name to see the actions that are associated with that application. Apple includes more than 100 actions, and third-party developers can also provide more actions that are specific to their applications or that make it easier for you to work in Mac OS X.

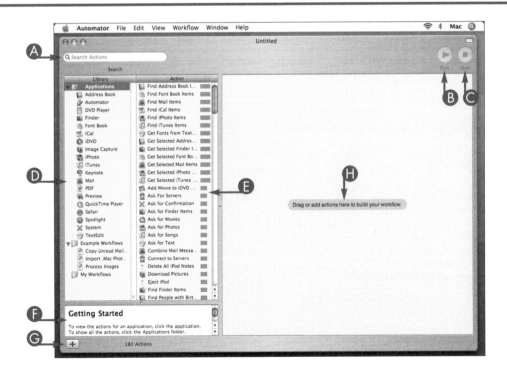

A Search Field

You can use the Automator search field to find an action within the Automator Library. This enables you to find the right action for the step that you want to include in your workflow. You can search by name or keyword. For example, if you search for the word "copy," the search field finds all of the actions that copy text, an image, or anything else. You can then choose the copy action that best suits what you want to do.

B Run Button

This button runs whatever actions you have placed in the workflow area. You can use the Run button to see what individual actions do, or to test your workflows. When you click the Run button, the actions that are placed in the workflow area begin working. As each action completes its task, a green check mark appears in the action's lower-left corner. Keep in mind that you do not have to save a workflow to run it.

C Stop Button

You can click this button to stop the currently active workflow from running, even if you have an incomplete workflow, or even just one action in the workflow area. If completed actions change a file or text, the file or text does not revert to its previous state after you press the Stop button. The Stop button appears grayed out when a workflow is not running.

D Library List

The Automator Library list shows all of the libraries that help to organize Automator actions. You can create new libraries and delete existing ones, although deleting a library deletes the actions that the library contains. By default, Automator organizes libraries into Applications, Example Workflows, and My Workflows. As its name indicates, the Applications library contains a list of applications; you can click an application's name to see the actions that are associated with it. The Example Workflows library contains workflows that were created by Apple; you can use these actions in their present form, or you can modify them to suit your needs. You can save the workflows that you create in the My Workflows library.

E Action List

The Action list shows a list of all actions in a selected library, or the actions that are associated with a selected application. The actions are listed in alphabetical order. You can drag an action from this list to the workflow pane to add the action to your workflow. If you select an existing workflow from the Example Workflows or My Workflows library, the Action list shows the actions that comprise the workflow, in the order in which they are enacted in the workflow.

F Description Pane

When you click an action, its name and description appear here. The description includes what kind of input the action requires and what kind of output it produces. For example, the Speak Text action requires text as input, and gives a result of text. This helps you to decide which actions to use, and in what way. Many actions have similar names but different purposes; the description pane can help you to distinguish between them.

G Add Button

You can click the Add button to add a new library to Automator's Library list. Automator creates a new folder in the Library list, and you can click the folder's name and enter a new name.

H Workflow Pane

The workflow pane is where you assemble your workflows. When you drag an action into the workflow pane, Automator displays the action's name, its sequence in the workflow, and more information about the action. You can click the turn arrow next to the action's name to display or hide the parameters for each action; if an action has options, you can click the turn arrow next to the word Options to see these options. On the bottom-right side of each action is the type of information that each action passes along to the next action, and on the upper-right side is the type of information that the action expects to receive from the previous action.

Add Actions
to a Workflow

Y ou can create workflows by selecting actions from the Action list and dragging them to the workflow pane. When you place actions in the sequence that you would like them to be enacted, you are creating a useful workflow out of individual actions.

Each action can pass along information to the next action, such as the name of a file or a personal contact. This enables complex interactions between data sets and applications.

Many actions have options attached to them, and so you can further customize what the action does. For example, you can tell an action not only to save an image, but also the file format in which you want to save the image.

You can make a workflow that performs a single action on multiple files, or multiple actions on a single file. Workflows can contain any number of actions, or as few as two actions. You can test a workflow before it is completed by clicking the Run button.

Add Actions to a Workflow

① Click an application icon in the Applications library.

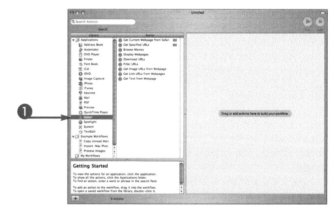

● The actions that are associated with that application appear in the Action list.

② Click to select an action.

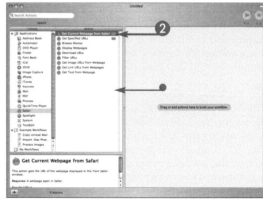

③ Drag the action to the workflow pane.

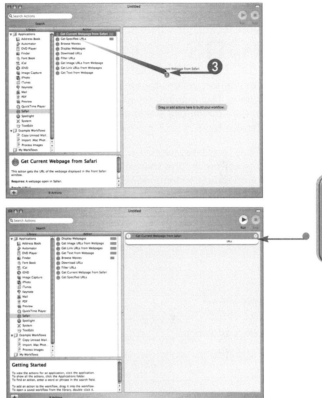

● Automator adds the action to the workflow.

Does Automator work by using AppleScript?

▼ No. AppleScript is a scripting language that was built into the Mac OS and that enables experienced scripters to automate many functions both in the OS and in applications. Actions in Automator are based on Xcode, which is Apple's own Integrated Development Environment (IDE). This means that Actions can be built in any language that Xcode understands, such as C or Java, and including AppleScript.

How can I find out what an action does?

▼ You can learn more about each action by using the description pane. When you select an action in the Action list, information about the action appears in the description pane. This tells you more about what the action does, as well as what kind of information the action requires for input and what kind of information it outputs.

Can I see whether an action has extra options?

▼ Yes. Some actions offer additional options that can affect how it runs, or how much user feedback it requires. To display an action's options, click the turn arrow next to the word Options in the action body when it is in the workflow pane.

Link
Actions

Y ou can connect actions together to form complex
workflows. This is useful because it allows you to
extend the power of a single action in order to
automate extensive tasks.

By linking actions to create a workflow, you can automate
almost any chain of procedures that you can normally
perform in the operating system. However, not all actions
can work together. If an action requires a particular type of
data, it has to follow an action that results in that type of

data. For example, you cannot place an action that requires
an image file after another action that results in text. If the
result and input types of two actions do not match, there
will be no connection arrow between them in the workflow
pane, and the input or result type shown in the actions may
appear red.

You can ensure that two actions can be linked by inspecting
them in the description pane. Click one action to show
what kinds of input and result it uses, and then click the
other action to see its input and result types.

Link Actions

① Click to select an Action.

② Drag the action to the workflow pane.

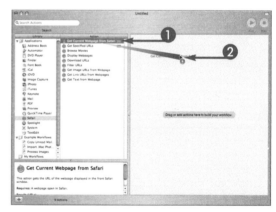

③ Select another action.

④ Drag it to the workflow pane.

The actions are linked.

If the Actions are incompatible, Automator
highlights the link in red.

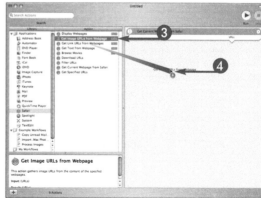

Search for Actions

Y ou can search through the Automator library of actions to find the right action with which to build your workflow. This is useful when you know what you want to do but do not know where the right action is placed within the Automator libraries.

Many actions are associated with a particular application, and these are stored in the Applications library in the Automator Library list. Many actions operate across many applications, or work system-wide, or perform tasks in Mac OS X's Finder. In addition, there may be actions installed by third-party applications, making it quicker to search for an action than to look through all of the Automator libraries.

Can I search for an action by describing what it does?

▼ Yes. In addition to searching for an action by using its name, or the name of the application with which it is associated, you can also search by describing what the action does. When you enter terms in the Automator search field, Automator looks through the information that you would see in the description pane.

Search for Actions

1 Type a search term.

● Automator displays relevant results.

As with the Spotlight feature in the Finder, Automator begins to display results as you type.

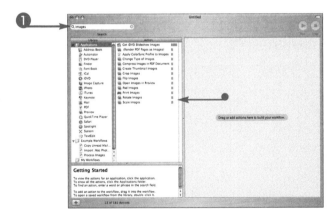

2 Click an action to select it.

● Information about the action appears in the description pane.

You can drag this action to the workflow pane.

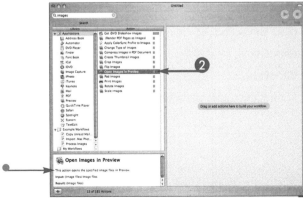

Copy an Action

You can copy an action in a workflow so that you can paste it in another place in the workflow. You can also copy groups of actions in a workflow and then paste them elsewhere in the workflow. This allows you to reuse strings of actions as modules of a workflow, or to reuse actions that you have customized.

When you copy an action, the action retains all of the changes that you have made, including any personalized text or changes to the action's options. For example, if you

enter "Dear Friends" in the Add Greeting feature of the Group Mailer action, and copy and paste that action, the pasted version retains the "Dear Friends" greeting, as well as any changes to the action's options.

You can also copy actions from one workflow to another. This allows you to reuse groups of actions, or to take a string of actions from a sample workflow in order to study how it works. You can copy actions and strings of actions from one workflow to another by selecting and dragging the action or actions.

Copy an Action

① Select the action that you want to copy.

② Click Edit.

③ Click Copy.

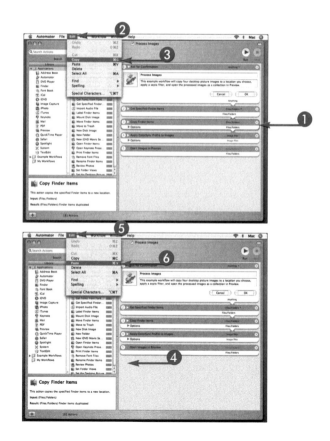

④ Click in the workflow where you want to place the action.

⑤ Click Edit.

⑥ Click Paste.

Automator copies the action to the selected position.

Delete an Action from a Workflow

Y ou can delete an action after you have placed it in a workflow, or you can delete an action from an existing workflow. This enables you to fix a mistake if you do not like the results when you add an action, and to modify existing workflows to make new workflows.

You can select multiple actions that you want to delete by holding down the Command key while clicking the actions. This is useful if you want to remove noncontiguous actions from a workflow. If the actions are contiguous, you can hold down the Shift key and click the first and last actions that you want to delete.

Can I exclude an action from a workflow test without having to delete the action?

▼ Yes. By disabling a particular action, you can test a workflow while skipping the action without having to delete it. To disable the action, press the Control key, then click the action's title bar. From the menu that appears, select Disable. To enable the action again, press the Control key, click the action's title bar, and select Enable.

Delete an Action from a Workflow

1 Select the action that you want to delete.

2 Click Delete.

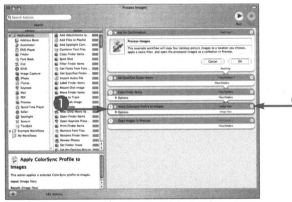

● Alternately, you can press the Control key, click the actions that you want to delete, click the title bar, and then click Delete from the pull-down list.

Automator deletes the action.

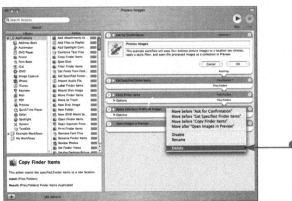

Save a Workflow as an Application

Once you have created a workflow in Automator, you can save it as an application. Saving a workflow as an application allows you to use the workflow in new ways, rather than having to open Automator, select the workflow, and then run it.

When you save a workflow as an application, you can double-click the workflow to launch Automator and run the workflow. This is faster than launching Automator and running the workflow from the application. You can also drag and drop files onto the workflow's icon to launch Automator and process the files.

After you open the saved workflow in Automator, you can make changes to the workflow. For example, you can change the content by adding, moving, or deleting actions, and you can also change which files or items the workflow affects. After you have made the changes, you can save the workflow again or rename it as a new workflow.

In addition, once you have saved a workflow as an application, you can share the workflow with other users. The recipient of the workflow must have Mac OS X 10.4 or later, with Automator installed.

Save a Workflow as an Application

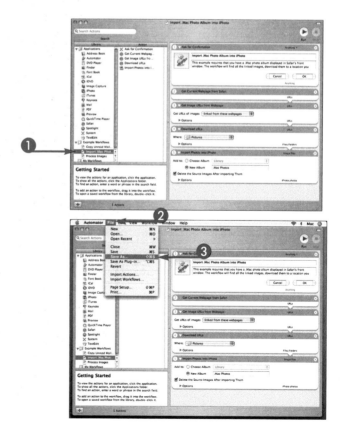

① Click to select a workflow in the Library list.

② Click File.

③ Click Save As.

190

The Save As pane appears.

④ Type a name for the saved workflow.

⑤ Click ⬦ and select a location.

⑥ Click ⬦ and select Application from the File Format menu.

⑦ Click Save.

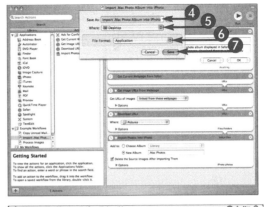

● Automator saves the workflow as an application.

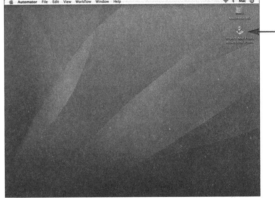

Can I make copies of a workflow that I have saved as an application?

▼ Yes. You can use the Duplicate command in the Finder to make copies of the workflow. Select the workflow that you saved as an application, click File, and then click Duplicate. Another version of the workflow with the word "copy" appended to its name appears in the same location as the original.

Can I delete the workflow that I saved as an application without affecting the original workflow in Automator?

▼ Yes. When you save a workflow as an application, the workflow from which you created it remains in the workflow pane in Automator. You can continue working with that workflow, even if you delete the version that you saved as an application. However, if you delete the workflow saved as an application and then quit Automator, you are asked to save the workflow.

Can I save a workflow as both a workflow and an application?

▼ Yes. When you save a workflow as workflow, it resides in the Library list in Automator. When you save the workflow as an application, it can reside anywhere on your computer.

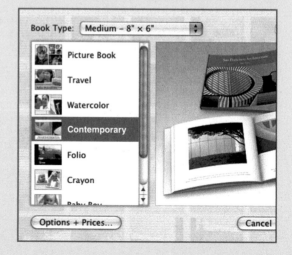

16 | Using iMovie HD

17 | Using iDVD to Make a DVD

Set Your System Sound Input Device

You can choose a variety of input devices to import audio into your Macintosh. These sound input devices can include your computer's built-in audio input, an external microphone, or a digital audio device. This is useful if you want to record sound so you can work with it in a sound-editing application, or if you want to issue voice commands to the system. Also, you can import audio from a tape deck or CD player so you can later use that sound when making a movie with iMovie or a slideshow in iPhoto. Most newer Mac OS computers accept both analog audio and digital audio input.

When configuring your choice of audio input device, you can also set the input level and monitor the input volume. This can help you to avoid distortion that may occur when input levels are too high, such as a screeching noise when high-frequency sounds are too loud. You can also raise the input level if you are using a microphone for voice commands and the computer does not recognize your words unless you shout.

Set Your System Sound Input Device

① Click the Apple menu (🍎).

② Click System Preferences.

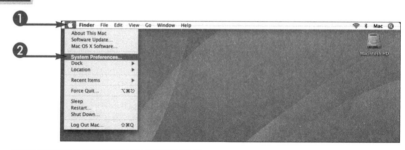

The System Preferences window appears.

③ Click Sound.

The Sound pane appears.

④ Click the Input tab to view its options.

⑤ Click the device that you want to use for sound input.

You may use the device that you selected to input sound.

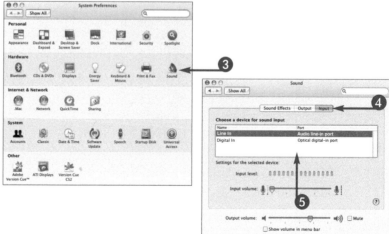

194

Set Your System Sound Output Device

Y ou can change your computer's sound output device by choosing your computer's built-in speakers, headphones, external speakers, or your own stereo setup. Most Macintosh computers allow a great deal of flexibility in how you can hear system alerts, music, audio conferencing, or movie audio tracks playing on your computer. This is useful if you want to switch between the convenience of the computer's internal speakers, the privacy of headphones, or the sonic fidelity of external speakers or stereo equipment.

When you plug in headphones or external speakers, your computer automatically shuts off its own speakers. This makes it more convenient to use headphones and eliminates the potential embarrassment of accidentally sharing all your music with family members or coworkers.

You can also use the Sound Preferences to change the balance and output volume. This can help you to avoid sound that is either too high or too low. The balance setting is useful for stereo output when you want to improve the listening experience. This becomes more important as you use better listening devices, such as good speakers or professional-quality headphones.

Set Your System Sound Output Device

① Click .

② Click System Preferences.

The System Preferences window appears.

③ Click Sound.

The Sound pane appears.

④ Click the Output tab to view its options.

⑤ Click an output device.

Your computer is set to play sound through the chosen device.

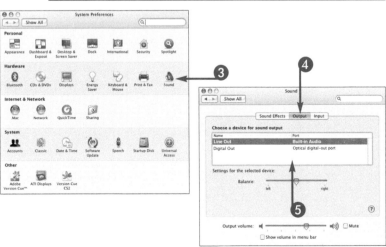

Transfer Video Clips with Image Capture

Many digital cameras can record video clips. You can use Image Capture to record and store video footage from your digital camera, if it is one that records movie clips, to your Mac. You can also use Apple's iSight Web camera with Image Capture to record and store video clips to your Mac. You can then import the footage of the clips into iMovie or iDVD and use them to create movies.

You can use iMovie to edit and reduce the file size of your video clips. This is useful when you want to share your video clips with other people through e-mail, or from your Web site by streaming or downloading the clip.

You can tell Image Capture to perform some actions automatically when you begin to transfer data. For example, it can place items in the folders that you specify. By default, Image Capture saves video clips to your Movies folder.

You can tell Image Capture to perform certain functions automatically. For example, Image Capture can launch or open another application, such as iPhoto, when you connect your digital camera. This is useful if you need to transfer single images or video clips to your computer as well as work with full projects in iMovie or iPhoto.

Transfer Video Clips with Image Capture

① Connect your digital camera to your computer.

   Image Capture launches automatically.

Note: Your camera may appear as a hard or removable drive on your desktop.

● If Image Capture does not automatically launch, double-click the application to launch.

② Click Download Some.

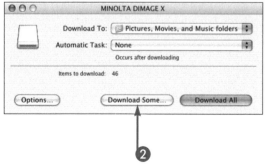

A window appears, displaying the available files on your digital camera.

③ Click to select the clips that you want to transfer.

④ Click Download.

Image Capture saves the selected clips to your hard drive.

How can I tell Image Capture to launch automatically when I connect my camera?

▼ In Image Capture's preferences, you can select Image Capture as the default application for transferring images. With Image Capture open, select the application's Preferences, and then click the Camera tab. Use the menu in the Camera pane to select Image Capture, and then close the Preferences window.

Can I choose another application to launch when I connect my camera?

▼ Yes. In the Image Capture preferences, select the Camera tab. In the Camera pane that appears, use the menu to select Other. An Open dialog appears. You can navigate to and select any application that you want to open automatically when you connect your camera.

Can I change the folder to which Image Capture saves my video files?

▼ Yes. You can change the location to which Image Capture saves files. In the Download To menu, select Other. An Open dialog appears; you can navigate to the target folder that you want, and then click OK. You can also choose to select Download Some or Download All. The Download Some option allows you to choose which files you want to transfer. The Download All option places all of the clips in the camera into the folder that you selected.

Download from a Digital Camera Using Image Capture or iPhoto

Y ou can download images from a digital camera to your computer. After downloading your images, you can print your photos, share photos through e-mail, on Web pages, or in photo albums that you transfer to recordable CDs or DVDs.

You can use Image Capture to download your photos directly to your computer. It places downloads into the Pictures folder of your user directory by default, although you can specify another location. Image Capture only transfers the images to your hard drive; it does not offer image-editing features, although you can use Image

Capture to delete pictures from a camera that is connected to your computer. Photos that you download through Image Capture can then be opened and edited in any image-editing application, such as Adobe Photoshop or iPhoto.

You can use iPhoto to import images from your camera to your computer and begin editing them directly. However, when you use iPhoto to import images, it places them into nested folders inside the iPhoto library. Unlike Image Capture, iPhoto automatically transfers all of the photos on your digital camera; it does not allow you to transfer only some of the images.

Download from a Digital Camera Using Image Capture

1 Connect your digital camera to your computer.

Image Capture launches automatically.

If Image Capture does not automatically launch, double-click the application icon to launch.

2 Click Download Some.

A window appears displaying the available files on your digital camera.

3 Click to select the images that you want to download.

4 Click Download.

Image Capture downloads the images that you selected to your hard drive.

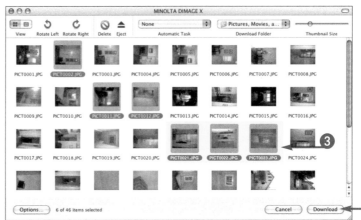

Download from a Digital Camera Using iPhoto

① Connect your digital camera to your computer.

● iPhoto launches automatically.

If iPhoto does not automatically launch, double-click the application icon to launch.

② Click Import in the iPhoto window.

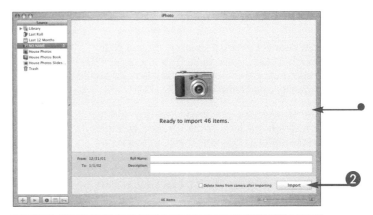

iPhoto imports all of the photos from the camera.

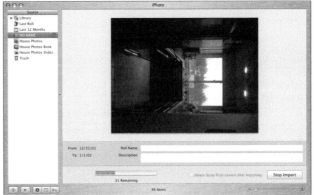

Can I cancel a photo transfer in iPhoto?

▼ Yes. You can stop iPhoto from importing photos from your camera at any time by clicking the Stop button in the main iPhoto window.

Why does nothing happen when I connect my camera?

▼ If your camera is in "sleep" mode, then your computer may not recognize it. Ensure that your camera is not set to sleep mode and connect it again.

Can I specify which default application will launch when I connect my digital camera to my computer?

▼ Yes. In Image Capture's Preferences, click the Camera tab. In the pane that appears, use the menu to select the application that you want to open when a camera is connected to your computer. You can specify Image Capture, iPhoto, or Other. If you select Other, an Open dialog appears; you can use this dialog to navigate to and select a different application.

Connect Speakers

Y ou can connect external speakers to your Mac. Although all Macs have built-in sound capabilities and built-in speakers, external speakers can provide better sound quality and stereo capabilities.

Most computer speakers are powered externally and connect with a stereo minijack. Some speakers connect through your computer's USB port; these speakers may draw power through the USB connection and so may not need an external power source. You can find ports for speakers on the back of most desktop Macs and on the side of most laptop Macs.

You can adjust the sound during audio playback in a number of ways. For example, you can use the volume keys on your keyboard to raise or lower the sound level, or mute the computer. You can also use the audio output volume control in the Sound Preferences window. Most speakers also have external volume controls.

As of this writing, Mac OS X does not support Dolby 5.1 surround sound. Individual applications, such as games or audio applications, for example iTunes, have different levels of support for stereo features.

Connect Speakers

① Plug the speakers into your computer.

② Click .

③ Click System Preferences.

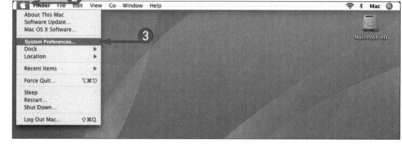

The System Preferences window appears.

④ Click Sound.

The Sound pane appears.

⑤ Click the Output tab to view its options.

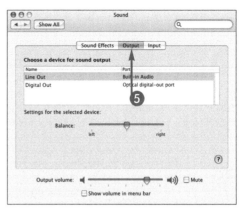

The Output pane appears.

⑥ Click to select the connected speakers.

● You can adjust the speaker balance and the output volume by dragging the slider.

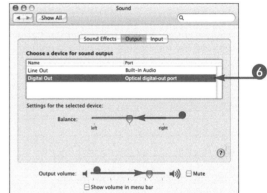

Can I play sound through the speakers and headphones at the same time?

▼ No. Plugging in headphones automatically mutes both external and built-in speakers. The computer assumes that you want to turn off the speakers if you are plugging in headphones.

Do I need to turn off my computer before attaching speakers or headphones?

▼ No. You do not need to shut down your computer to plug in or unplug external speakers or headphones. This is also true for microphones, telephone or S-video cables, or any USB equipment.

Can I change the speakers' volume using the keyboard volume keys without hearing the keys' sound effect?

▼ Yes. Normally, you hear a sound effect when you press any of the keyboard volume keys. If you do not want to hear this, such as when you are listening to music and do not want it interrupted, you can turn off this sound effect. In the Sound Preferences pane, click the Sound Effects tab. When the Sound Effects pane appears, deselect the Play feedback when volume keys are pressed option (☑ changes to ☐).

Scan Documents with Image Capture

You can use a scanner with Image Capture to scan a document or image to import to your Mac in digital form. Scanning inputs a digital image of a printed page into your computer. This is useful if you want to archive printed documents, make digital copies of photographs, or import articles to share with friends. You can also e-mail electronic versions of contracts and other documents that you have signed and then scanned, thus saving postage and faxing costs.

You can preview all of the items that you scan. After you scan an image, you can use this preview feature to crop the image before you create the final image and transfer it to the computer.

You can configure Image Capture to perform actions automatically when you scan images. These actions can include placing the images in a certain folder, changing image formats, and building a Web page from images transferred with Image Capture.

You can save scanned text documents as PDFs or in other image formats. You must have optical character recognition software if you want to convert your scanned text documents to editable text that you can import into a word-processing application.

① Connect or turn on your scanner.

● Image Capture launches automatically.

If Image Capture does not automatically launch, double-click the application icon to launch.

② Press the Scan button on your scanner.

● The scanned image previews in the window.

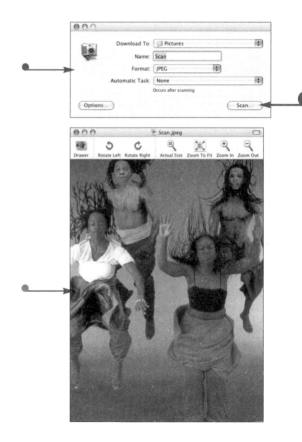

③ Click and drag the cursor over the area that you want to transfer.

Note: You must perform this step even if you want to transfer the entire image.

④ Click Scan.

Image Capture saves the image to your computer.

By default, Preview does not open.

In what file format does Image Capture save scanned documents?

▼ By default, Image Capture saves scanned files in TIFF format. Files in this format can be opened by any image-editing application. For more information about converting graphic files in Preview, see Chapter 6.

Can I change the default folder to which Image Capture saves files?

▼ Yes. Use the Folder menu in Image Capture's toolbar to select Pictures, Desktop, or Other. If you select Other, an Open dialog appears. Navigate to and open the folder to which you want Image Capture to save the image.

Can I change the application that opens the scanned image?

▼ Yes. Use the Application menu in Image Capture's toolbar to select Preview, None, or Other. If you select Other, an Open dialog appears. Navigate to and select the application in which you want to display the scanned image.

Set a Bookmark in DVD Player

You can create a bookmark when watching a DVD in DVD Player. DVD Player is an application that lets you watch DVD movies on your Mac. Bookmarking in DVD Player is similar to placing a bookmark in a book; you can return directly to the marked place at any time while you are watching the DVD. You can also return to the bookmark even after you have quit DVD Player and return to watching the movie later. If you have not set a bookmark manually, DVD Player creates one for you at the point where you quit the application.

This can be a more efficient way of returning to a DVD movie that you have not viewed in its entirety. Most DVD movies offer shortcuts to scenes, or chapters, but these may not match up with the spot you want to reach on the DVD.

You can create multiple bookmarks on a single DVD, as well as set bookmarks that are unique to different DVDs. This feature does not apply to DVDs that store data or to DVDs that cannot be opened in DVD Player. You can also delete bookmarks you no longer need.

Set a Bookmark in DVD Player

① In DVD Player, click Controls.

② Click New Bookmark.

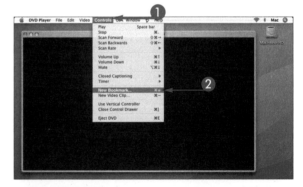

The New Bookmark window appears.

③ Type a name for the bookmark.

④ Click Add.

- The default name of the bookmark is the time in hours:minutes:seconds that appears in the movie.

Edit Bookmarks in DVD Player

You can manage multiple bookmarks in DVD Player to edit bookmark names or to delete bookmarks. Editing bookmarks is useful if you want to clear out a number of bookmarks that you have made while watching a movie for the first time, but do not need the bookmarks the next time you view the DVD. For information on how to create bookmarks in DVD Player, see "Set a Bookmark in DVD Player."

Editing bookmark names is also useful because of how DVD Player automatically names bookmarks. By default, DVD Player assigns names to bookmarks based on

what hour, minute, and second the bookmark appears in the movie, such as 01:42:35. You can replace the default name with a more meaningful one, such as "Exciting Fight Scene." This can help you navigate to favorite moments in a movie without having to remember when exactly they occurred.

You can also use the bookmark editing feature to create a virtual highlight reel from a movie. If you set up a series of bookmarks for favorite points in the movie, you can edit them with the names "Highlight 1" and so on, and let friends move from bookmark to bookmark, seeing the high points of the movie.

Edit Bookmarks in DVD Player

① In DVD Player, click Window.

② Click Bookmarks.

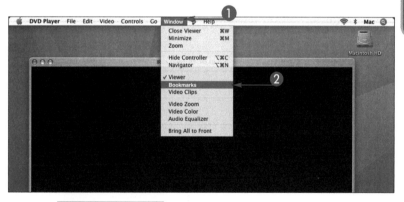

The Bookmark window appears.

③ Click a bookmark.

④ Click the Action button ( ).

⑤ Click Rename.

Note: To delete a bookmark, select Delete in Step **5**.

The Rename Bookmark dialog appears.

⑥ Type a new name for the bookmark.

⑦ Click OK.

The bookmark is renamed.

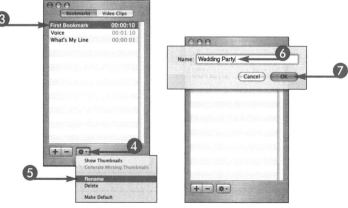

Turn On Subtitles in DVD Player

You can turn on subtitles in DVD Player to see captions in one of the languages offered in the DVD movie. Subtitles are text translations of the spoken words in a movie, often when the movie dialog is in a foreign language. Subtitles are useful if you prefer to watch a foreign movie with the original audio track, or if you want to listen in your language but see the dialog in another language.

Most DVDs come with various subtitle options. DVD Player cannot create subtitles for movies that do not have these options. The subtitles are burned onto the DVD in a track that is normally hidden if you do not turn subtitles on.

Not every word from the movie is duplicated in the subtitles. Because of the limited space available for subtitles, and the fact that people can only read so many words in a limited time, sometimes the subtitles offer truncated versions of the on-screen dialog.

To select the language in which the subtitles will appear, you can use DVD Player's own controls or the DVD's own interactive menu. Some DVDs do not offer subtitles. If this is the case, then DVD Player cannot offer subtitles for viewing.

Turn On Subtitles in DVD Player

1 While a movie is playing, click Controls.

2 Click Open Control Drawer.

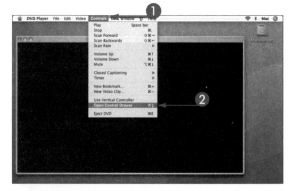

The Control Drawer appears in the DVD Controller.

3 Click the Title button.

4 Repeat Step **3** to select another language.

Subtitles now play over the video.

You can also change the default subtitle language in the DVD Player Preferences.

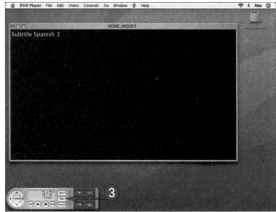

Enable Closed Captioning in DVD Player

You can configure DVD Player to display closed captioning whenever you mute the sound while watching a DVD. Closed captions give hearing-impaired viewers a way to follow along with the audio portion of a movie. The captions, which show the dialog of the movie, appear either over the video or in a separate window. This is useful if you regularly watch movies with closed captioning, or if you often have to mute the sound of your movie while you are watching it.

The closed captioning tracks are a built-in feature of the DVDs. If a DVD does not offer closed captioning options, then DVD Player cannot create the captions.

You can customize the look of the captions, including the color and transparency of the closed captioning box. This can help you see the captions more easily when they appear over the movie. To make these changes, open the DVD Player Preferences, and in the Windows pane, choose a color for the text, or a background color, or use the slider to set transparency levels for the closed captioning box. You can also use the pull-down menu to select a new font for the captions.

Enable Closed Captioning in DVD Player

① Click DVD Player.

② Click Preferences.

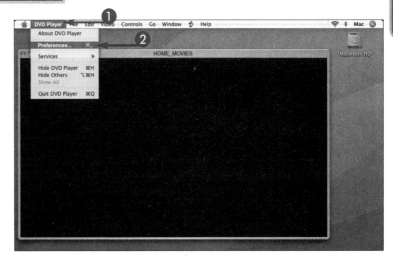

The DVD Player Preferences window appears.

③ Click the Show Closed Captioning check box when the DVD Player is muted (☐ changes to ☑).

④ Click OK.

Closed captions appear when you mute the DVD Player.

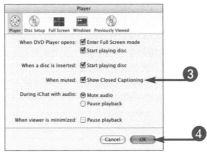

Choose the Right Audio Format and Bit Rate

You can record audio files in a variety of formats and at different bit rates. The format and bit rate that you choose affect the quality of the resulting file as well as its file size. Generally, there is a proportional relationship between file size and audio quality: the smaller the file size, the lower the audio quality. However, there are exceptions, and knowing what choice to make can affect the quality of your music library.

Audio File Formats

MP3

MPEG1 Audio Layer 3, or simply MP3, is the most common file format for digital music. MP3 can provide a compact file size and relatively good-quality music, shrinking an uncompressed music file to about one-tenth the original size while losing little fidelity. Keep in mind that MP3 is a *lossy* file format — some data is lost during compression. Regardless of the format to which you then convert an MP3 file, you never regain the lost data. Depending on the bit rate in which you choose to encode an MP3 format, you lose at least some data, which ultimately affects the quality of the music.

AAC

The Advanced Audio Coding, or AAC, format was recently developed especially for digital music. For example, AAC is the default format used for music at the iTunes Music Store. Because the AAC compression algorithm is more advanced than that for the MP3 format, AAC files lose less data and can sound better than MP3 files. For example, AAC files encoded at 96 Kbps can sound as good as MP3 files encoded at 128 Kbps. As a result, you can have a smaller file size with the same audio quality, or the same file size with better audio quality. Although the iPod works with AAC files, some handheld MP3 players are incompatible with AAC files.

AIFF and WAV

Audio Interchange File Format, or AIFF, files are uncompressed and are used for storing CD-quality sound. Because AIFF files are uncompressed, they can be quite large; however, this is a good format to store original versions of audio files because there is no loss of data. You can use AIFF files to convert to versions in other formats; when making a new version, you should always do so from the original, rather than from an already converted file.

WAVEform audio format (WAV) files use an uncompressed audio file format that is popular on Windows-based PCs. These files may require up to 10MB for each minute of music.

Apple Lossless

Apple Lossless is a virtually lossless audio file format that retains CD-quality fidelity. You can convert your Apple Lossless files to other formats, while preserving the original file. Apple Lossless files tend to sound better than MP3 files. However, Apple Lossless files, as with other lossless format files, are relatively large. Keep in mind that the Apple Lossless files only require about 5MB for each minute of music, making the Apple Lossless format more compact than AIFF or WAV.

Bit Rate Settings

Bit Rates

When converting music from one file format to another, the bit rate setting is what determines the overall quality and size of the resulting file. You can set the bit rate when you import the content of a CD to iTunes, or when you record original music. A bit rate is the average total of data that you record in one second of music. It is measured in kilobits per second, or Kbps. In iTunes, you can go to the application's Preferences and set the bit rate for AAC and MP3 recording. When you record to other audio file formats, the default bit rate is set to automatic. Although you can set all file formats to use custom bit rates if you have specific needs, this is generally not necessary. Keep in mind that a bit rate for one file format does not produce the same audio quality or file size as the same bit rate in another file format.

Constant and Variable Bit Rates

When you import music, you may see the terms *constant bit rate* and *variable bit rate*. *Constant bit rate* refers to a converter that applies the same bit rate throughout a song, so even silent passages increase the file size the same amount as the most complex parts of a song. *Variable bit rate* refers to the converter applying a different rate of encoding, depending on how much data are needed to accurately describe each part of a song. For example, the variable bit rate uses more bits for, and therefore assigns more data to, complex music than to simpler music, therefore saving more space if possible and providing a better-sounding result.

Converting Your Music

You can change the iTunes Preferences to encode your CDs in various file formats. The default file format is AAC, which is the same file format used for songs purchased at the iTunes Music Store. If you want to use a portable digital music player other than an iPod, then you should check its specifications; you may need to convert your favorite songs to MP3 format. If you are a stickler for audio quality, then the Apple Lossless format can provide you with the highest quality reproduction, although this requires a lot of hard drive space.

You can change the importing settings to fine-tune the sound quality of the music, too. Most people encode their music from CDs as MP3s at a bit rate of 128 Kbps, though some feel that this reduces the fidelity of the music slightly. Encoding the music in AAC format at 128 Kbps produces slightly better sound quality, though some digital music players, unlike the iPod, are not compatible with that file format. If you want to import your music at MP3s but desire the highest sound quality, you can set iTunes to import files at 192 Kbps. As always, the higher the bit rate, the larger the resulting imported file will be.

Share iTunes with Multiple Users

With iTunes 4.5 or later, you can share iTunes libraries between multiple users on one computer. If you have iTunes running, then other users who log on to their accounts can play music from your iTunes libraries or playlists.

Sharing iTunes between users does not involve copying these files from one computer or user to another. In fact, you cannot copy, alter, or burn another user's music to a CD. However, you can select and play any song in a library or playlist that is made available by other users. A user can password-protect his or her individual playlists from other

users, such as playlists that contain songs with explicit lyrics; you can also password-protect entire libraries. You can do this by selecting the Require password option in the iTunes Sharing Preferences.

To share libraries, you must ensure that iTunes is currently running in the user account that is sharing a library or playlist. This is just like one computer on a network running iTunes in order to share its library. You can also start a different song playing for each user account, although this may cause more confusion than enjoyment when all of the different songs are playing at once.

Share iTunes with Multiple Users

① Click iTunes.

② Click Preferences.

The Preferences dialog appears.

③ Click Sharing.

④ In the Sharing window, click Share my music
   (☐ changes to ☑).

⑤ Click an option to share your entire music
   library or a selected playlist (○ changes
   to ⦿).

⑥ Type the name that you want to appear in
   the iTunes Source list of other users that
   share your music.

⑦ Click OK.

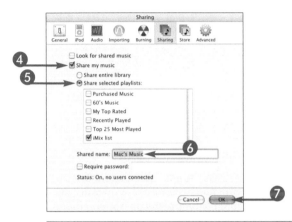

● Other account users are now able to see
  your music in their iTunes Source list.
  If you choose to protect your music with
  a password, then only users with the
  password can access your music.

If you cannot see your music, in Step **4**, select
the Look for shared music option in their
iTunes Preferences (☐ changes to ☑).

**In iTunes, can I play music in one user
account while burning a CD in another
account?**

▼ Yes. In iTunes versions 4.5 and later,
   you can switch to a new user and play
   music without disrupting the CD-burning
   process of another user. This is possible
   because iTunes now relies on a single,
   shared resource for music playback and
   recording. In previous versions of iTunes,
   if you switched user accounts while
   iTunes was actively burning a CD in
   another account, then iTunes would halt
   the burning of the CD.

**Why does the volume level seem to
change when I switch users while a
song is playing?**

▼ Each user account has its own settings,
   including the volume level. When you
   switch from one user to another, you
   move from one volume setting to
   another. Therefore, although the same
   music plays while you switch accounts,
   you may experience volume changes.
   You can adjust the iTunes volume level
   in the new account to equalize the
   volumes.

Share iTunes Libraries over a Network

You can share iTunes music libraries and playlists with other Macs on your local network. iTunes plays the songs that are hosted on the originating computer. If the network is not too busy, then the songs should play without a noticeable pause.

You can share MP3, AIFF, WAV, Apple Lossless, and AAC files, as well as streaming radio station links. However, you cannot share Audible.com content that was not purchased from the iTunes Music Store, or QuickTime sound files.

To share iTunes libraries over a network, all computers must have iTunes version 4.5 or later and be within the same

network subnet. In addition, the host computer must keep the iTunes application running. You can also restrict user access to your library or playlists by selecting the Require password option in the iTunes Sharing Preferences.

If the music was purchased from the Apple iTunes Music Store, then you can only authorize a certain number of computers to play these files. iTunes also prevents you from copying music files from one account to another. In addition, you are prohibited from burning another user's music to a CD or an iPod. You can visit the Apple Support Web site for more information.

Share iTunes Libraries over a Network

① On the computer or account from which you want to stream audio, click iTunes.

② Click Preferences.

The Preferences dialog appears.

③ Click Sharing.

④ In the Sharing window, click Share my music (☐ changes to ☑).

⑤ Click an option to share your entire music library or a selected playlist (○ changes to ⊙).

⑥ Type the name you want to appear in the iTunes Source list of other computers that share your music.

● If you want to restrict users who can share your music, select the Require password option.

⑦ Click OK.

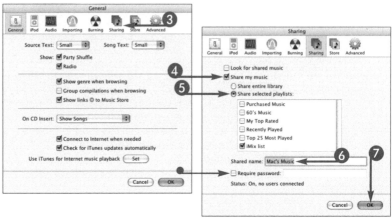

212

⑧ Repeat Steps **1** to **3**.

⑨ In the Sharing window, click Look for shared music (☐ changes to ☑).

⑩ Click OK.

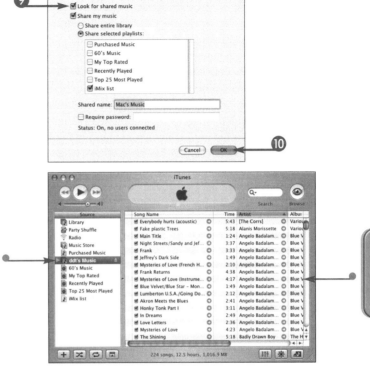

The name of the shared music library or playlist appears in the Source list of other computers on your network.

● Users can click the playlist name to see its contents and then click any song to play it.

With how many computers can I share my iTunes library?

▼ You can share your iTunes library with a maximum of five computers that are running iTunes 4.5 or later. This is due to licensing contracts with music that is sold through the iTunes Music Store, not because of technical limitations.

Can I only ever share with the same five computers?

▼ No. The rule about five computers only applies to five computers at a time. If one computer quits iTunes or shuts down, then you can share with another computer in its place. This is useful if you have an office or household with multiple computers sharing iTunes.

Can I make changes to another user's iTunes library?

▼ No. You cannot modify the library in another user's account. For example, you cannot delete, move, or add a song. You also cannot create or change playlists, although you can play any song you choose. You also cannot copy songs from a remote computer to your own.

Post and Share an iMix

You can post a custom playlist of your favorite songs to the iTunes Music Store. A custom playlist is called an *iMix*. Anyone viewing your iMix can give it a rating, refer it to their friends, and see all the iMixes that you have made. This is a good way to update friends on what you are listening to, as well as to see what your friends recommend. If you like a song on a friend's iMix, you can click to purchase it from the iTunes Music Store.

Visitors can also listen to a thirty-second preview of all of the songs that you have listed, just as they can for any song at the iTunes Music Store. Anyone viewing your iMix can then purchase each song with one click.

You can also update your iMix playlist by altering the playlist in the iTunes application and clicking one button. This allows you to create an iMix that reflects your daily listening habits.

If you have a .Mac or AOL account, or if you have registered to purchase music from the iTunes Music Store, then you can publish an iMix. There is no charge to publish an iMix.

Post and Share an iMix

① Click Add Playlist (+).

iTunes creates a new playlist.

② In the Source list, select the default playlist name, and type a name for your new playlist.

③ Click your Library in the Source list.

④ Press ⌘-click to select the songs that you want to share in your iMix.

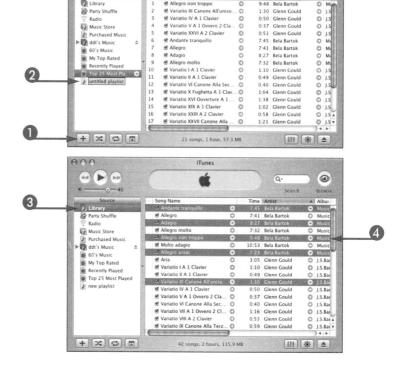

⑤ Click and drag the songs to your new playlist.

⑥ Click Publish (▣) to publish your playlist as an iMix online.

Note: *Clicking the Publish icon launches the iTunes Music Store. If you do not have a free account, which you need to publish an iMix, you are prompted to create one.*

You can view all of your published iMixes by logging in to the iTunes Music Store and clicking View Account.

Why do I not see all of the songs that I put on a playlist when I publish the list to the iTunes Music Store?

▼ Only songs that are currently available for sale at the iTunes Music Store can appear on your iMix list. As a result, many songs that you may have imported from CDs and that are not yet for sale at the iTunes Music Store do not appear.

Can I change the name and description of my iMix?

▼ Yes. To change the title or description of a published iMix, select the playlist's name in iTunes, click the arrow to the right of its name, and then type your changes. Click the arrow again to update the changes online.

How can I point friends to my iMix?

▼ After you have published your iMix, you receive an e-mail informing you that your iMix has been published. This e-mail contains a Web address that you can send to people; when they click it, iTunes displays the Web page that contains your iMix.

Use Party Shuffle

You can use the Party Shuffle feature in iTunes to create and play a dynamic playlist, which is a random selection of music from your library. You can create a queue of songs that, like a smart playlist, weighs songs by their ratings, or by how frequently you play them. What makes a Party Shuffle different from a normal playlist is that you can modify a Party Shuffle on the fly. You can use Party Shuffle to put together a soundtrack for a party, or for personal listening.

By default, the Party Shuffle feature automatically selects songs from your music library and plays them. You can then add or delete, or even reorder, what songs are in the queue, even as the music plays. For example, you can delete an upcoming song from the Party Shuffle list. This does not delete the song from your library.

You can also use Party Shuffle to make a dynamic playlist from selected playlists. This can be useful if, for example, you have spoken-word content in your main music library and you do not want these tracks to play when you are using iTunes to DJ a party.

① Click Party Shuffle.

   ● From your music library, a random song selection appears in the main iTunes window.

② Click ▦ and select the source from which you want to make a party shuffle.

③ Click ▦ and select the number of recently played songs that you want to display.

④ Click ▦ and select the number of upcoming songs that you want to display.

⑤ Click Play higher rated songs more often
(☐ changes to ☑).

iTunes forces the Party Shuffle feature to give
priority to songs that you have rated highly.

Note: If you do not assign ratings to songs, then
they are not considered to be highly rated.

● Alternatively, you can add a song to your
party shuffle or play a different selection
next by Control-clicking any song in any
playlist and selecting an option from the
pop-up menu.

**How does the Party Shuffle feature differ from
when I play my library or playlist with the
shuffle feature activated?**

▼ There are two basic differences. First, the Party
Shuffle feature takes into account play frequency,
so you do not hear the same song repeating
as much as you would with a random shuffle.
Second, you can make a dynamic playlist
created with Party Shuffle play your favorite
songs more often.

**Can I create a dynamic playlist from a shared
library over a network or from the library of
another user on the same computer?**

▼ No, you cannot select a shared library or playlist
that belongs to another user or another computer.

**Can I add a song to my dynamic playlist while
the party shuffle is playing?**

▼ Yes. You can add a song to the Party Shuffle list
whether it is currently playing or not by dragging
the song from another playlist or from the Library.
You can also Control-click any song in any playlist
or library to add it to the dynamic playlist.

Print a
CD Insert

You can use iTunes to design and print the front and back covers for a recorded CD. For example, if you are burning a copy of a commercial album, then iTunes can provide the original artwork from the album. If you are burning a mixed-music or MP3 CD, then iTunes automatically creates a mosaic of album covers. iTunes also automatically formats a list of songs on the CD. This feature works with any playlist, although it is best to use it in conjunction with a playlist that is designed to fit onto a single CD.

These CD inserts are automatically designed with crop and fold marks, so that you can fold and cut any size of printer paper to fit perfectly into a CD jewel case. You can also use any weight of paper, although a heavier stock with a gloss finish looks most professional.

The Themes include options such as using only the text of the song listings, a single album cover image, or a mosaic. You can also print any of these options in either color or black and white. The Theme options also include wrap-around covers for the CD jewel case, or single sides.

Print a CD Insert

① Select a playlist that you want to burn onto a CD.

② Click File.

③ Click Print.

The Print dialog appears.

④ Click the CD jewel case insert option
(○ changes to ⦿).

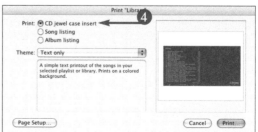

5 Click 🔹 and select a theme.

● A preview of your selected Theme appears in the window.

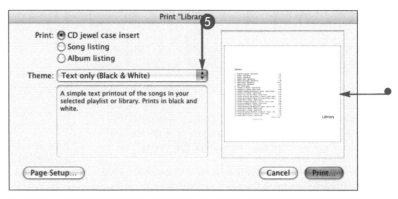

● You can click Page Setup to set specific options for your printer.

6 Click Print.

Your cover prints.

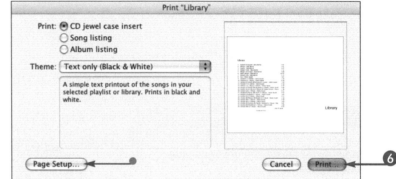

PART IV

Can I include my own artwork on a CD cover?

▼ Yes. Select a song in the main iTunes window, and then click Get Info. In the Info window that appears, click the Artwork tab; you can now drag an image into the artwork area, or click the Add button (⊞) to navigate to and select the image file you want. iTunes treats this artwork like any other album cover image. You should constrain your artwork to the size and proportions of a normal CD cover.

When I choose the Mosaic Theme, not all album covers appear in the preview or on the printed cover. Why does this happen?

▼ The Mosaic Theme gathers cover art from albums that are available at the iTunes Music Store. If you are trying to create CD cover art from a collection of songs that are not available at the iTunes Music Store, or songs that are original recordings, then iTunes cannot find and download cover art for those songs. As a result, your Mosaic Theme CD cover may seem a little empty.

Publish Libraries and Playlists to PDF

Y ou can use the Print command in iTunes to create custom-formatted printouts of your entire music library or individual playlists. You can also use this feature to create PDF files that you can use as a personal archive or to share with friends, even over the Web.

This feature can provide you with a clean and organized list of your albums and songs in an easily printable form, which saves you the trouble of manually typing song, artist, and album data in a spreadsheet or word-processing application.

You can also customize the printed list to sort all of the songs by title, by user rating, by dates played, or by the way that you have organized it in the iTunes main window. You can also simply organize them by album.

Once you have the list that you want in PDF format, you can print it out, as well as e-mail it to friends and upload it to your Web site. Keep in mind that multipage PDF files can be large compared to plain-text files, so you should check their file size before sending the e-mail.

Publish Libraries and Playlists to PDF

① Select your music library or the playlist that you want to publish.

② Click File.

③ Click Print.

You can also press ⌘-P to print a file.

The Print dialog appears.

④ Click the Song listing option to print a list of songs independent of their albums (○ changes to ◉).

● If you want to print out your list organized by albums, you can click the Album listing option (○ changes to ◉).

⑤ Click ▣ and select a Theme for printing your song list.

Selecting Custom as your Theme creates a listing that is organized in the same way that the songs are listed in iTunes.

⑥ Click Print to continue.

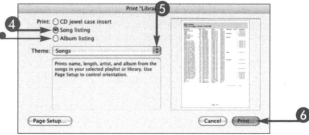

The Print dialog window appears.

⑦ Click PDF.

⑧ Select Save as PDF.

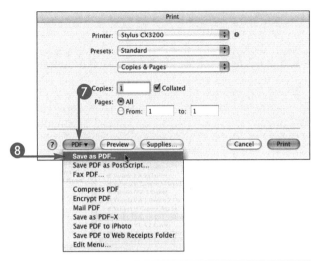

A standard dialog appears, asking where you want to save the resulting PDF file.

⑨ Click ▼ and select a location to save the PDF file.

The PDF file is created and saved to your specific location.

Note: By default, these files are named iTunes. You should give each file a more descriptive and unique name.

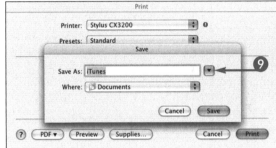

Can I include album cover art in this song or album list?

▼ No. This method is only for printing out a song list from a selected playlist. The resulting printed list is perfect for inserting into the back or inside cover of a CD jewel case. See the section "Print a CD Insert" for information on printing cover art.

Can I combine making a PDF of a song list with making a CD insert?

▼ No, you have to create the publishable song list and the CD cover insert separately. Although this requires an extra step, these two items normally fit in different places in a CD jewel case. See the section "Print a CD Insert" for information on printing cover art.

Can I save a song list as plain text?

▼ Yes. Select a playlist from your Library. Click File, and then click Export Song List. A dialog appears, asking you where you want to save the file, which is automatically given the name of your Library or playlist. You can save the file as plain text, Unicode, or XML.

Use Autofill to Place Music on an iPod Shuffle

You can use the Autofill feature of iTunes to automatically fill up an iPod Shuffle portable music player. The iPod Shuffle is a compact digital music player made by Apple; it holds only a few hundred songs, which is far less than most iTunes libraries. The Autofill feature makes it easy to transfer a random selection of songs without forcing you to choose all the individual songs.

You can tell the Autofill feature to transfer songs to the iPod Shuffle from your main Library or from a playlist you select.

By default, the songs are placed on the iPod Shuffle in the order they are displayed in the Library or playlist. However, you can tell iTunes to place the songs on the iPod Shuffle in random order.

When you use the Autofill feature, as many songs that fit on the iPod Shuffle are transferred. By default, these songs replace any ones previously on the iPod Shuffle. However, you can tell iTunes not to overwrite songs already on the iPod Shuffle. The Autofill feature will not overwrite other files, such as documents, already stored on the iPod Shuffle.

Use Autofill to Place Music on an iPod Shuffle

Note: Your iPod Shuffle must be properly connected to the computer.

① Click ⊞ and select a Library or a playlist from the Autofill pull-down menu.

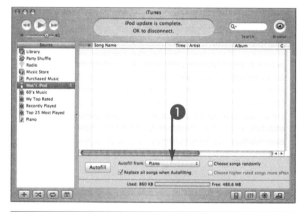

② Click the Autofill button.

③ To have iTunes transfer songs in a random order, click Choose songs randomly (☐ changes to ☑).

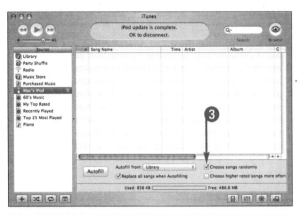

④ Click Autofill.

iTunes fills your iPod Shuffle.

Can I manually transfer songs from iTunes to the iPod Shuffle?

▼ Yes. To manually transfer songs from your iTunes music Library or from a playlist, select the songs and drag them to the iPod Shuffle icon in the Source list. You can drag them in any order but you cannot reorder them once they are transferred.

Can I manually delete songs from the iPod Shuffle?

▼ Yes. When the iPod Shuffle is connected to your computer, you can select the iPod Shuffle icon in the Source list. This displays the songs currently on the iPod Shuffle. You can then select a song and press the Delete key to delete it from the iPod Shuffle.

How many songs will an iPod Shuffle hold?

▼ There are two models of iPod Shuffle. One has a 512MB capacity. This should hold approximately 100 songs, depending on how long the songs are and at what bit rate they are encoded. The 1GB iPod Shuffle holds approximately twice that number of songs.

Set Up a Smart Album in iPhoto

Y ou can create Smart Albums in iPhoto to automatically include any photo that meets certain criteria that you set. This is a useful feature when you have hundreds or thousands of photos.

Smart Albums are similar to the Smart Playlists in iTunes. By defining criteria, you can tell iPhoto to display only images that meet these specifications. You can build your Smart Album by selecting any combination of keyword, date, filename, roll, title, album, my rating, description text, or comment.

Keep in mind that you have to assign much of the data manually. The names that digital cameras assign to photos

may not be very helpful to you when you are searching. Similarly, if you want to search for photos by the rating criterion, then you must first assign ratings to the photos.

One feature that makes Smart Albums such a powerful tool is that it updates as you import more photos that meet your search requirements. For example, if you set a Smart Album to include photos with comments that include the word birthday, then any new photo that you import with the word birthday in the comment field is automatically included in that Smart Album.

Set Up a Smart Album in iPhoto

1 Click File.

2 Click New Smart Album.

The Smart Album dialog appears.

3 Type a name for your Smart Album.

4 Click ⬦ and select the condition for the photos you want to include.

The default is Album, which allows you to limit the contents of your Smart Album.

5 Click the Add button (⊕).

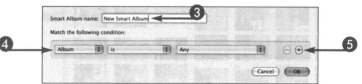

Additional criteria options appear in the dialog.

● You can click the Subtract button (⊟) to remove individual criteria.

● You can click ⬍ and select comments for the photos that you want to include.

⑥ Click OK.

⑦ Click the Smart Album's name in the Source list.

● As you add pictures to your Photo Library, your Smart Album updates its content automatically with pictures that meet its criteria.

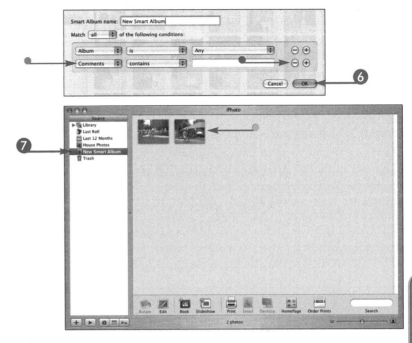

Can I change the criteria for an existing Smart Album?

▼ Yes. If you have an existing Smart Album and want to alter any of your settings, such as including a wider date range, then click the Smart Album's icon in the Album list. Click Photos and then click Show Info. You can type your changes in the Smart Album window that appears. Alternately, you can click the File menu and select Edit Smart Album while the Smart Album is selected in the Album list.

Can I create a Smart Album that searches for some, but not all, of the criteria that I have set?

▼ Yes. If you add multiple criteria when creating a Smart Album, you can tell iPhoto to match any or all of the conditions when performing a search. As a result, the Smart Album may contain all photos that meet each, rather than all, of the criteria. This is useful if you are looking for photos within a range of dates or if you want to combine photos from different events.

Make Batch
Changes to Photos

You can use the Batch Change feature in iPhoto to make the same change to certain criteria for any number of photos. This can save a lot of time if you want to change the names of groups of photos in your Library.

However, this feature is not a full-fledged batch editor that you find in professional applications such as Adobe Photoshop. For example, you cannot apply filters or change image sizes in iPhoto.

You can use the Batch Change command to revise the text labels or comments of any selected group of photos, or

alter the dates attached to that group of photos. This is especially handy when you import photos from a digital camera, because the photos are usually imported into iPhoto with long, generic names that are assigned by the camera.

Keep in mind that if you give a group of images the same comment through the Batch Change feature and then create a Smart Album with the comment as a criterion, then you end up with the same photos in your search results. To set Smart Album batching options, see the section "Set Up a Smart Album in iPhoto."

Make Batch Changes to Photos

① Press ⌘–click to select the photos you want to change.

② Click Photos.

③ Click Batch Change.

The Batch Change dialog appears.

④ Click ⊡ and select Title.

⑤ Click ⊡ and select Text.

● The lower part of the dialog window changes to include a text box where you can type a new title for your photos.

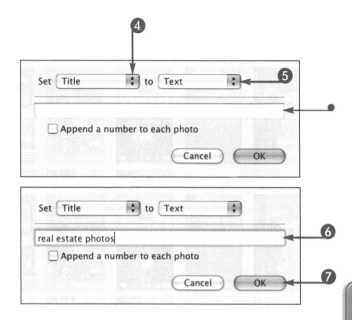

⑥ Type the title that you want to give to your photo selection.

⑦ Click OK.

The selected photos have the new title that you typed.

Can I use the Batch Change feature like I would use the find-and-replace feature in a word-processing program?

▼ No. You cannot use the Batch Change feature to search for the items you want to change. As a result, you must know which photos you want to change before you use the Batch Change feature.

Can I export keywords, dates, or ratings as metadata so that I can make a spreadsheet or list of photos showing these criteria?

▼ No. This appended information cannot be separated from the photos automatically. You can search through your photos by criteria using the Search field in the iPhoto main window.

Can I use the Batch Change feature to change other criteria?

▼ Yes. You can use it to change the Date or Comments fields for multiple-selected photos. In Step **4**, choose Date or Comments instead of Title. The resulting dialog window allows you to type data for either choice. When you click OK, these changes apply to all selected photos.

PART IV

Create a Slideshow

You can create a slideshow, which is a set selection of your photos saved in a ready-to-play slideshow format, from any album of photos. You can then name the slideshow and play it back at any time. This is a useful way to share a presentation of photos of a special event, such as a birthday or a vacation.

You can include individual photos in any number of slideshows. When you put a photo into a slideshow, it does not change the photo or remove it from the existing album, if you have stored it in an album, or from the iPhoto Library.

You can customize each slideshow with a music selection, transitions, and more. For more information on slideshow options, see the sections "Set Transitions for Your Slideshow," "Sync Music to a Slideshow," and "Add a Custom Ken Burns Effect to a Slideshow."

Even after you have created a slideshow, you can add new photos to it at any time. To do this, simply drag the photo from its original location onto the icon for the slideshow. iPhoto automatically imports this photo into its photo library.

Create a Slideshow

1 Select an album of photos.

2 Click File.

3 Click New Slideshow.

Note: You can rename the slideshow by selecting its name and entering a new one.

● A slideshow icon appears in the Source list.

● The iPhoto main pane changes to slideshow mode.

4 Drag photos into the desired order in the Photo Browser.

Your slideshow is ready to play.

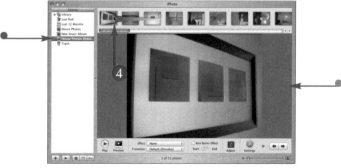

Display a Slideshow of Selected Photos

You can show a presentation of a selected group of photos without creating a new slideshow in your Source list. This is useful if you want to test how a group of photos will appear as a slideshow, or want to experiment with various slideshow settings, or only want to display this collection of photos together one time.

If you want to play the same slideshow later, you can create a slideshow from the photos you selected. For more information, see the section "Create a Slideshow."

You can adjust the settings for presenting the photos you have selected. This includes changing the transition used between photos, the duration of the transition, whether

the photos are shown in random order, how the photos are scaled, whether titles for the photos are displayed, whether and what music plays during the slideshow, and more.

When the slideshow plays, you can stop it by clicking the mouse button, pause it and restart it by pressing the Space key, and use the arrow keys to move through photos manually.

You can also edit the photos displayed in the slideshow, even if you do not save the slideshow.

Display a Slideshow of Selected Photos

① Select the photos you want to display as a slideshow.

Note: You can select noncontiguous photos by ⌘-clicking them.

② Click the Play button (▶) to display a slideshow of the selected photos.

The Slideshow Settings window appears.

③ Click Play.

The selected photos play as a slideshow.

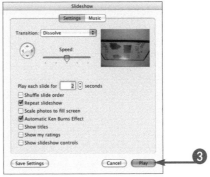

Fine-Tune Photos in a Slideshow

You can immediately present photos that you have imported into iPhoto as a slideshow to quickly check and fine-tune them. You can also make changes to photos as you download them from a digital camera. This means you can fine-tune photos in an album as you download them, without having to save them and then make changes. In previous versions of iPhoto, you had to exit the slideshow to make these edits.

You can use this feature to rotate the images in one direction or another, correctly orienting images that you

may have taken with the camera held sideways. In addition, you can set a star rating for each photo as it appears, which you can use in conjunction with the Smart Albums feature to instantly update a collection of top-rated photos.

You can also delete images as you view them in the slideshow. This can save storage space on both your camera and your computer. If you just want to watch the images as a slideshow, then you can hide the slideshow controls and let the series run automatically.

Fine-Tune Photos in a Slideshow

① Click Last Roll.

② Click ▶ to display a slideshow of the selected photos.

A Settings window appears.

③ Click Play.

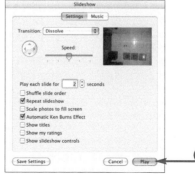

The slideshow begins.

④ Move the mouse cursor to display the slideshow control bar.

● You can make adjustments to change the photo orientation, for example, rotating the photo.

● You can click here to change a photo's rating anywhere from one to five stars.

iPhoto saves your photos automatically with the changes that you have made.

Can I use this feature to rename photo files as I import them?

▼ No. To do this, you must either name the photos individually in their iPhoto gallery or make a Batch Change.

How can I hide the slideshow control bar if I have set it to display all of the time?

▼ If you have not selected the Display slideshow controls option, then you can keep the slideshow control bar hidden by not moving the mouse. If you select that option, then you can return to the Slideshow options and deselect it.

Can I edit the content of my photos directly in a slideshow presentation?

▼ You can perform limited edits such as rotating and deleting photos. You can also assign star ratings to each photo as you view it. However, to edit content, or to save in a different file format, you can use an application such as iPhoto or Adobe Photoshop.

Set Transitions for Your Slideshow

You can use a variety of transitions for a slideshow of your photos as presented by iPhoto. These transitions include none, dissolve, cube, droplet, fades, various flips, push, reveal, twirl, and wipe. This can give a custom touch to your slideshow.

Some of these transitions utilize advanced graphics capabilities. As a result, some transitions may not play as well on older computers.

You can also set the speed of transitions and, in the case of some transitions, the direction. For example, you could

specify how rapidly a wipe moves across the screen and from which direction.

When you make these changes, they apply to the entire slideshow. You can change settings for individual slides by selecting the image in the photo browser at the top of the iPhoto window, and then clicking the Adjust button. When you do this, a translucent window appears and you can change settings, including transition type, speed, and direction, as well as the amount of time the slide is displayed. You can also undo the changes made to individual slides by clicking the Reset to Defaults button.

Set Transitions for Your Slideshow

① Select a slideshow.

② Click Settings.

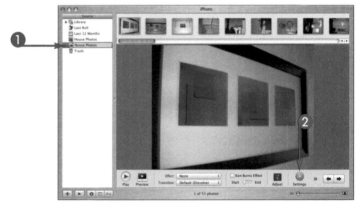

The Settings dialog appears.

③ Click ⊡ and select a transition.

④ Drag the slider to set the transition speed.

⑤ Click OK.

Your slideshow uses the selected transition.

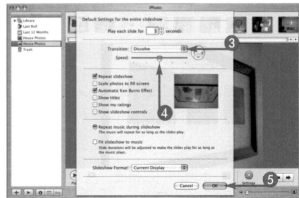

Change the Display Duration of a Slide

You can customize the duration in which all the slides in your slideshow display. This keeps each slide on your computer screen for a longer or shorter period of time. It is useful to increase slide duration if you have images you want viewers to see in more detail, and it is useful to shorten the duration if you want to create a more dynamic experience.

If you have created a custom Ken Burns pan-and-zoom effect for your slides, changing the duration the slides are presented also changes the speed of the effect. For more

information, see the section "Add a Custom Ken Burns Effect to a Slideshow."

Changing the settings for the duration of the slides changes how long all slides in the slideshow are displayed. Once this is set, you can also set how long individual slides are displayed if you want particular images to be presented longer or more quickly. You can do this by clicking the Adjust button when the desired slide is shown in the main iPhoto window and entering a custom duration in the translucent window that appears.

Change the Display Duration of a Slide

① Select a slideshow.

② Click Settings.

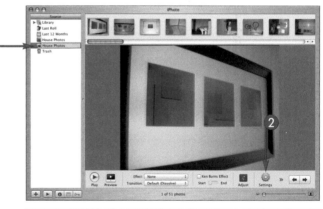

The Settings dialog appears.

③ Type the number of seconds the slides play.

④ Click OK.

The slide duration is set.

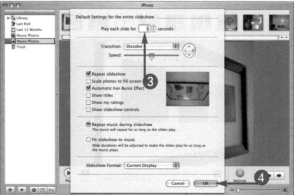

Sync Music
to a Slideshow

You can customize a slideshow so that it plays exactly as long as a favorite piece of music plays. This can create a total experience that can tell a story and avoid an uneven presentation, where the slideshow and the music do not end at the same time.

You can select any song from your iTunes library or a music file from the Sample Music folder included with iPhoto to play along with your slideshow. You can use the Music dialog to search for songs by entering the title or artist name in the dialog's search field. You can also sample the music by clicking the Play button.

iPhoto does not change the duration or speed of your selected music. Instead, it times the display of your slides so that the slideshow ends when the music does. Your settings for transitions, such as type, direction, and duration, are not affected. However, if you have only a few photos included in a slide show, some photos will repeat to fill up the duration of the music.

Sync Music to a Slideshow

① Click Settings.

The Settings pane appears.

② Click Fit slideshow to music
(○ changes to ⊙).

③ Click OK.

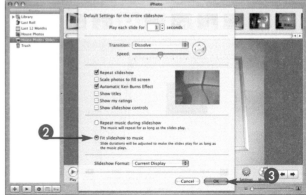

④ Click Music.

The Music dialog appears.

⑤ Select a Library.

⑥ Select a song.

⑦ Click OK.

Your slideshow syncs to the music selected.

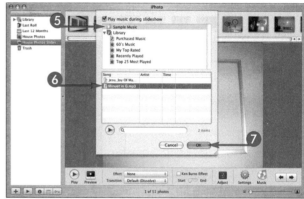

Can I set volume levels for the music that plays with my slideshow?

▼ No. The music that plays along with your slideshow plays at the volume level of the computer. To adjust volume as the slideshow plays, you can press the volume control keys on your computer's keyboard.

Can I use any music file for my slideshow?

▼ No. iPhoto allows you to choose from music that is stored in the iTunes Library or in iPhoto's Sample Music folder. You can move music files to these locations, but they must be in a format supported by iTunes. These include MP3, AAC, and Apple Lossless.

Can I preview the song?

▼ Yes. To preview a song, click the Play button in the Music pane once you have selected a song but before you click OK. This plays the song. To stop playing the song, click the Play button again. You can also preview the song along with the slideshow when you preview the slideshow as a whole.

Add a Custom Ken Burns Effect to a Slideshow

You can take advantage of a built-in iPhoto effect to reproduce the slow pan-and-zoom effect used by filmmaker Ken Burns in many of his popular documentaries. This can give your slideshow a sense of focusing on its subject and bringing them to life.

The effect involves some zooming into the image, and then panning around. The panning may incorporate some zooming as well. This can help highlight areas of the photo and then call a viewer's attention to the larger context of the photo.

You can create a custom Ken Burns effect for each slide in your slideshow. This allows you to be sure that the effect focuses on the subject of each photo and moves in the way you want it to move. The automatic option is not aware of the content of your photos, and so may not produce exactly the effect you would like.

You can also add an automatic Ken Burns effect when you create a slideshow. To do this, select the Automatic Ken Burns Effect option in the Slideshow settings dialog when you create the slideshow. For more information, see the section "Create a Slideshow."

Add a Custom Ken Burns Effect to a Slideshow

① Select a slideshow in the Source list.

② Select a photo in the photo browser.

③ Select Ken Burns Effect (☐ changes to ☑).

④ Click Start.

⑤ Move the Zoom slider to set the starting point for a zoom.

⑥ Click the main image and drag the photo to set the starting point for the pan.

⑦ Click End.

⑧ Repeat Steps **5** to **6** to set the end points for the zoom and pan.

The slide will play with the custom Ken Burns effect.

Can I choose how quickly or slowly the pan and zoom take place?

▼ Yes. You can adjust the speed of the pan and zoom effect, though not independently. Click the Settings button at the bottom of the main iPhoto window when your slideshow is open and desired slide is displayed. In the Settings pane that appears, change the number of seconds this slide is played. This changes the speed of the pan and zoom action together, in addition to how long the slide is displayed.

Can I preview the custom pan and zoom effect?

▼ Yes. Click the Preview button at the bottom of the main iPhoto window when the desired slide is displayed. This shows the slide with the custom effect. To return to iPhoto, press the Escape key.

Can I revise my custom effect?

▼ Yes. To make changes to your custom pan and zoom effect, repeat Steps **4** to **8**. You can then preview the slide to see if you like the changes you have made.

Share Your Photos over a Network

You can use iPhoto to share your Photo Library or albums over a home or business network so that other users can view all the images that you have taken and stored. This allows people not on the same computer to see your photos. This can save computer storage space if you have a family album that all family members want to share at home.

Other users can view your shared albums on their own Source lists if they select the Look for shared photos option in their iPhoto Preferences. This option is activated by default.

You can allow other computers to see your entire library or selected albums. When you do this, you can either protect all albums with a password, or share your images with everyone.

This is similar to how you can share music and playlists over a network with iTunes, except that when you share images through iPhoto, all users can copy, edit, or print their own versions of your photos. If you do not want this to happen with certain photos, then you should not include them in any shared albums.

Share Your Photos over a Network

① Click iPhoto.

② Click Preferences.

The Preferences dialog appears.

③ Click Sharing.

④ Click Share my photos (☐ changes to ☑).

⑤ Click an option to share either your entire photo library or only selected albums (◯ changes to ◉).

- To share only certain albums, click the albums you want to share from the list (☐ changes to ☑).

- To limit access to your photos, click Require password (☐ changes to ☑) and then type a password.

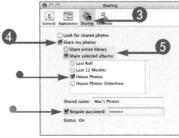

Publish Your Photos on .Mac

You can publish your photos and iPhoto albums at .Mac, Apple's Internet portal. The .Mac service allows you to share your personal and professional work with all users who have Internet access, whether they are on a Mac or a PC. If you want to show your photos only to friends, then you can protect your Web page with a password. You can also use iPhoto and .Mac to create an online slideshow, and other .Mac users can use your photos as a screensaver on their own computers, as long as they are currently connected to the Internet.

Using .Mac, you can place your photos into a variety of Web page templates, place captions, and edit layouts. You can also include your images from iPhoto in HTML-standard Web pages that you have created in other Web-page editors. You do not have to know how to make a Web page to create a slideshow with .Mac.

Although .Mac is a subscription service that requires an annual membership fee, a free 60-day membership is available. Full membership includes other services and features, such as virus protection, Web-based e-mail, and automatic file backup. For more information, you can go to www.mac.com.

Publish Your Photos on .Mac

1 In the Source list, click the album of photos that you want to share online.

2 Click HomePage.

If you do not have a .Mac account, you can sign up for one or open a trial account.

If you have a .Mac account, the HomePage publishing window appears.

3 Type a name for your online photo gallery.

4 Click to select a visual theme for your page.

5 Click Publish.

iPhoto automatically launches your Web browser and displays the published photo gallery page.

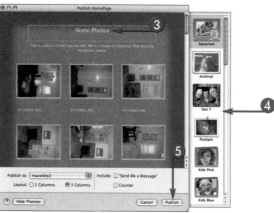

Preparing Slideshows in iPhoto

One way you can share your photos, or just enjoy them yourself, is to create a slideshow. For example, you can simply select an album, and play it as a slideshow in the iPhoto main window. You can add music soundtracks, use sophisticated transitions, display only certain albums, and use the slideshow as a screen saver. You can access all of these settings with one click of the Slideshow button in the main iPhoto window.

Organize into Albums

Although you can run a slideshow of your entire Photo Library, you may find it more enjoyable and efficient to organize photos by topic or context. For example, you can create a slideshow of a wedding, a family event, or even a house that you are trying to sell. You can always switch between albums, and even include the same photos in different albums and slideshows. You can also create Smart Folders, which are folders that automatically contain any photos that meet criteria, such as a keyword or a range of dates, that you set. This is useful if you want to keep albums based on topics, such as a family's birthday celebrations. For more information, see the section "Set Up a Smart Album in iPhoto."

Fine Tune Using a Slideshow

Although you can manage photos while watching a slideshow, you may want to fine-tune your photos before presenting them in a slideshow to others. For example, you can rotate them so that they are all properly oriented, eliminate red-eye effect in photos, crop photos that are out of balance, and correct the brightness and contrast if necessary. You may also want to scale photos so that they are all approximately the same size. For more information, see the section "Fine Tune Photos in a Slideshow."

Add a Soundtrack

You can add a soundtrack to any slideshow, to add drama or atmosphere to your photos. Experiment with different songs once you decide on the visual content of your slideshow. It is a good idea to pay attention to the tempo of the song in relation to the timing that you set for the slideshow, as each show has its own rhythm. You can tell iPhoto to time your slideshow to snyc with a particular piece of music. For more information, see the section "Sync Music to a Slideshow."

Use Duplicate Photos

Although you can use the same photo in more than one album, you can also display the same photo differently in each album. For example, you may want to have a photo in full color for one slideshow, but in black and white for another. Instead of importing that photo again, you can use the Duplicate command. You can then edit the duplicate and place the new version in a different slideshow.

Timing

You can set the amount of time that each photo in your slideshow appears on-screen, from one to 60 seconds. Experiment to see what works best for each album. A longer interval may be more effective for larger and more detailed photos, although too long a delay may result in a restless audience. You can either type the number of seconds in the text box or select the number of seconds from the pull-down menu. The Slideshow settings window provides a small preview of how the timing appears from one image to another. However, it only shows one transition, and so it does not give a full sense of how the timing affects the overall appearance of your slideshow. The number of seconds you enter in the Slideshow settings window specifies how long all the images in your slideshow appear on-screen. You can change the timing for individual images, so that one appears on the screen for one second, another for five, another for two. For more information, see the section "Change the Display Duration of a Slide."

Scale Your Photos

All of the photos that you take probably do not have the same proportions as your computer screen. By default, these photos appear on-screen surrounded by a black frame. If you want to avoid this effect, simply select the Scale photos to fit screen option. Keep in mind that this may result in parts of some photos being cropped. You should test this feature by viewing the slideshow before presenting it to others. If you want to edit the photos permanently, you can use the Batch Change feature of iPhoto to scale multiple photos at once. For more information, see the section "Make Batch Changes to Photos."

Display Titles

You can show titles along with images in your slideshow. Adding titles to your slideshow can improve the slideshow for the person viewing it by adding context and other information. To show the titles along with the images, select the Display titles option. This allows the name of each photo to appear on-screen.

Display Ratings

You can display the star ratings of each photo in your slideshow to highlight your favorite photos to viewers. This feature also works in conjunction with Smart Albums, so that you can create slideshows that contain photos with a specific rating or range of ratings, such as more than one star or less than four stars. To apply this feature from the Settings panel, simply select the Display my ratings option. You can change the ratings of photos as you watch them in a slideshow by moving the mouse to call up the slideshow controls and clicking on the star ratings area to change the rating for the displayed photo.

Print a Contact Sheet

You can use iPhoto to make and print a contact sheet. Contact sheets show thumbnails of all of the photos on one roll of film and are often used by photographers to provide a quick visual overview of the contents of a film roll.

You can use every photo from a roll or from one of your photo albums, or you can place thumbnails of selected photos from different rolls or albums on one page. You can also use contact sheets to print multiple copies of the same image, which you can use to make wallet-sized photos of friends or relatives. This works especially well when you print these images on photo-quality paper.

Keep in mind that the more images that you include in one contact sheet, the smaller each image must be. You can use the Save Paper option in iPhoto to automatically rotate each image in the same way, allowing you to fit more images onto one sheet of paper. However, if you have a mix of portrait and landscape photos on your roll and you click this option, then some images may not align properly.

Print a Contact Sheet

① Select the album of photos from which you want to make a contact sheet.

② Click File.

③ Click Print.

A Print dialog appears.

④ Click ▣ and select Contact Sheet.

⑤ Drag the Across slider to set the number of photos that you want to place on a page.

⑥ Click Print.

iPhoto prints out your contact sheet.

View Photos from a Specific Date

Y ou can use iPhoto's Calendar feature to look up and display photos from any day, week, or month. This allows you to better view your collected images, especially if you take many photographs at specific events.

You can only use this feature when you have an album or library selected in the Source list. If you do not select an album or library, all dates on the Calendar are dimmed and cannot be selected.

You can scroll between months or years, depending on which the Calendar is showing, using the up and down arrows in the Calendar title bar. You can view a photo from that date or month by clicking it.

Can I view photos taken on a particular day of the month?

▼ Yes. Click the View arrow, which is to the left of the year in the Calendar window, to switch between year- and month-view. You can then click a day of the month to see pictures from that day. You can scroll by month by clicking on the up and down arrows in the Calendar title bar.

View Photos from a Specific Date

① Select a library or album.

② Click the Calendar button (🖼️).

The Calendar appears.

③ Click a month to view photos from that month.

● The photos from that month appear.

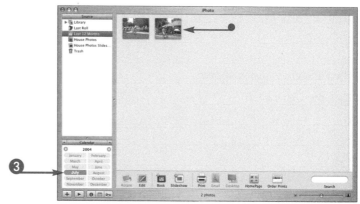

Open Photos for Editing in Another Application

You can open images stored in iPhoto with another application for more advanced editing opportunities. While iPhoto offers some basic image-editing features such as red-eye reduction, and brightness and contrast controls, a professional application such as Adobe Photoshop can provide far more extensive tools, such as filters and color curves. Once you have selected the image-editing application, you can double-click any image in iPhoto to open it in the chosen application.

One way to work with external applications and to remain organized is to have a separate folder for externally edited photos. When you work with a photo in another application, you can save the photo back to this folder inside the Photos folder in your user directory. For example, if you create a folder called Edited, then you can place this folder in the Albums folder, which is in the iPhoto Library folder. You can also save your externally edited photos to one folder, and then click and drag the photos into the iPhoto folder.

You can then use iPhoto to organize and present your entire image library, for example, in slideshows, while still using another application for editing and enhancing the photos.

Open Photos for Editing in Another Application

① Click iPhoto.

② Click Preferences.

The Preferences dialog appears.

③ Click the General tab.

④ Click Opens photo in (⊙ changes to ⊙).

⑤ Click Select Application.

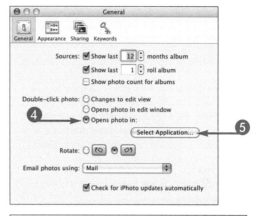

An Open dialog appears.

⑥ Select the image-editing application you want.

⑦ Click Open.

You can double-click an image to open it in the chosen application.

Can I change to a new application after I have chosen one?

▼ Yes. If you have chosen an application to open the photos stored in iPhoto, but then want to open the photos in another application when you double-click them, repeat Steps **1** to **5** but select the new application instead. Then click Open; you can then open your photos in that application by double-clicking the photos.

Can I specify multiple applications, so that some photos open in one and others in another application?

▼ No. When you set which application opens your photos when you double-click them, all photos open in that application. You cannot have some photos stored in iPhoto automatically open in one application and others in another application.

Can I see the edited versions of the photos in iPhoto?

▼ Yes. If you have edited an iPhoto image in another application and saved it with the same name and file format, all changes you have made are visible when you view the image in iPhoto. If you change the name or file format, you may see a new version in addition to the original.

Correct for Red-Eye

You can use iPhoto to edit photographs to eliminate red-eye. Red-eye is the result of a camera's flash reflecting off part of a person's eye, giving the eyes a reddish tint or glow. Red-eye reduction gives a more natural look to portraits taken with a flash.

iPhoto automatically corrects for the effect that causes red-eye. You do not need to understand advanced editing techniques or open the photo in another image-editing application. You can undo the red-eye reduction if the resulting changes to the photo are not to your liking.

MASTER IT

Can I revert to the original version of the photo after reducing red-eye?

▼ Yes. If you have not saved the photo after making the changes, you can click Edit and then click Undo Reduce Red-Eye. If you have saved the photo after reducing red-eye, you can click Photos and then click Revert to Original.

Correct for Red-Eye

① Select a photo.

② Click the Edit button.

The photo appears in the main iPhoto window.

Note: You may need to zoom in on a subject's eyes, using the zoom slider.

③ Click the Red-Eye button ().

The cursor changes to a crosshair.

④ Click in the center of each eye.

⑤ Click Done (Done).

Red-eye is reduced.

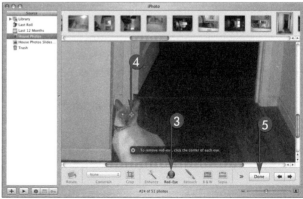

Straighten a Photo

Y ou can use iPhoto's editing capabilities to straighten a photo that appears crooked. This helps you make a photo look better, if it was taken with the camera not perfectly level.

If you straighten a photo, that photo will be straightened when it appears in every album and slideshow in which it is included. To experiment with changes through straightening, you can create a copy of the photo and test this tool on the copy.

This feature has certain hardware requirements. As a result, it is not available on computers based on a G3 or earlier processor. For more information on learning about your computer's hardware, see Chapter 26.

You can check the edited version of the photo against the original, before you have saved it, by pressing the Control key. This shows you the original and reverts to showing the edited version when the key is released.

Before you have saved the photo, you can undo changes by clicking Edit and selecting Undo Straighten. If you have saved the photo, you can click Photos and select Revert to Original.

Straighten a Photo

1 Select a photo.

2 Click the Edit button ( ).

The photo appears in the main iPhoto window.

3 Click the Adjust button ( ).

● The Adjust palette appears.

4 Drag the Straighten slider.

5 Click Done (Done).

The photo is straightened.

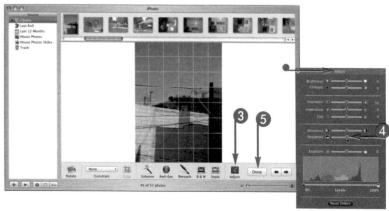

Retouch a Photo

Y ou can use iPhoto's retouching feature to cover up small defects, blemishes, and marks that may appear in a photo. This is useful if your subject has visual irregularities, or you want to make a person's portrait more flattering, or the photograph has some visual irregularities, such as a shiny spot.

Retouching works by blending data from the area surrounding the item you want to cover up. When you retouch a photo, you should use the retouch tool in short strokes over the area in question. If you use longer strokes,

iPhoto may sample data from a larger area, causing more visual irregularities than are covered by the retouching.

When you have retouched the photo, you can compare the new version to the original by holding down the Control key. You can undo changes by clicking Edit and then Undo Retouch, if you have not yet saved the changes. If you have saved the changes, you can click Photo and click Revert to Original to undo the changes. After you have saved the changes, these changes will affect all instances of the retouched image, whether the image is viewed in an album or a slideshow.

Retouch a Photo

① Select a photo.

② Click the Edit button (🖼).

The photo appears in the main iPhoto window.

③ Click the Retouch button (◥).

The cursor changes to a crosshair.

④ Place the cursor over the area you want to retouch and drag the cursor in short movements.

⑤ Click Done.

The photo is retouched.

Enhance a Photo

You can use iPhoto's editing capabilities to enhance the colors in a photograph. This is useful if a photo you have taken appears washed out, or too bright. This can be due to poor lighting or a poorly set camera, but these problems can be fixed in iPhoto.

You can allow iPhoto to automatically enhance the colors of a photograph. You can also manually adjust color parameters of the photograph. iPhoto allows you to change saturation, temperature, and tint controls, which determine how much color appears in the photo, how

bright these colors are, and how these colors are represented. This option is available only on computers equipped with a G4 processor or better. For more information on collecting information about your computer, see Chapter 26.

You can compare the original with your edited photo by holding down the Control key. If you do not like the changes, you can click Edit and then click Undo Enhance Photo before you have saved changes to the photo. If you have already saved changes to the image, click Photo and then click Revert to Original.

Enhance a Photo

① Select a photo.

② Click the Edit button (■).

The photo appears in the main iPhoto window.

③ Click the Enhance button (■).

● You can make manual changes by clicking the Adjust button instead and using the controls in the Adjust palette.

④ Click Done.

The photo is enhanced.

249

Prepare and Order a Photo Book

You can design a book of photos from an album in your iPhoto Library. These books use professionally designed themes included in iPhoto that present your photos in a ready-to-print book form. You can then order one or more copies of the printed book from Apple, though availability may be limited in some parts of the world.

You can let iPhoto arrange the photo placements in the book automatically, or you can lay out the book manually. Whether you place the photos or let iPhoto do it, you can write your own personal thoughts or messages, in any font, in available text areas in the book. You can also title the book and decide which photo will appear on the book's cover.

You can create and order a book in many sizes, from pocket-sized to 8.5 by 11 inches, in both hardcover and softcover. All books contain 20 glossy, acid-free pages, each of which can include one or more photos plus text. Once you are happy with the look of the book, you can order it online and have it shipped to you.

Prepare and Order a Photo Book

① Select the album or a collection of photos for your book.

② Click File.

③ Click New Book.

The Choose Theme pane appears.

④ Click ▣ and select a book type.

⑤ Select a theme.

You can click Options + Prices to view a Web page with pricing and ordering information.

⑥ Click Choose Theme.

The iPhoto dialog appears asking if you would like to manually or automatically lay out your book.

⑦ Click Automatically to let iPhoto lay out your book.

Note: *You can also use iPhoto's tools to lay out the book manually.*

Note: *You can manually drag photos and enter text to change an automatically laid out book.*

iPhoto presents the book.

⑧ Type your text to customize the book.

⑨ Click the Forward and Back arrows (◄ ►) to move through the book.

⑩ Click Buy Book (Buy Book).

Safari opens a Web page in which you can purchase the book.

Can I save an electronic version of my book?

▼ Yes. You can create an electronic version of the book you have designed, so that you can share it with friends who can view it on their computers. You can also print this copy of the book. Select the book in the Source list, click File, and then print. In the Print dialog that appears, click Save As PDF.

Can I change the name of the book in the Source list?

▼ Yes. To change the name of a book in the Source list, once you have created the book, select the book's title in the Source list and enter a new name. This name change is reflected in the name of the file if you save the book in electronic form.

What can I do if iPhoto displays a low-resolution warning?

▼ If you see a low-resolution warning, which looks like an international alert sign, this means that the photo placed is too low in resolution to avoid appearing jagged. You can place that photo on a page with more photos, reducing that image's size. You can also use the original version of the photo if the low-resolution alert shows up on a photo you previously cropped.

Elements of iMovie HD

Y ou can use iMovie HD to view, edit, organize, and arrange your video clips to create professional movies from your video collection. iMovie enables users to edit video, apply transitions and special effects to add professional quality, and select audio and photos for placement in their movie. You can even view items from your iPhoto and iTunes libraries, although you cannot make changes to these items in iMovie HD.

The main iMovie HD window contains most of the tools that you will use to create your movie. You can use this window to preview the elements that you want in your movie, and to view the movie as you work on it. iMovie HD uses the same aspect ratio as a television screen. When you shoot footage at a different aspect ratio, it appears in a letterbox format.

The iMovie HD Window

Ⓐ iMovie HD Monitor

You can preview clips in the Clip pane or Clip viewer and preview a movie in this viewing area concurrently as you edit. You can also monitor video as you record it with a digital camcorder or iSight.

Ⓑ Movie Clip Pane

You can organize clips that you have imported from a digital camera or your hard drive in the Clip pane. You can rearrange clips by dragging them. You can also change a clip name by double-clicking it and typing in a new name.

Ⓒ Scubber Bar

You can click and drag the playhead (▽) to move forward and backward in a clip or movie to view how transitions and effects appear between clips. You can also press the Forward and Back arrows on your keyboard to move frame by frame in a clip or movie. The number next to the playhead shows your position in the clip in a minutes:seconds:frames format.

ⓓ Clip and Timeline Viewer Button

You can use the Clip and Timeline viewers to compose your movie by placing clips and transitions in the order you want. The Clip and Timeline Viewer button toggles between showing the Clip viewer and the Timeline viewer. This button is located at the bottom of the main iMovie HD window. With the Clip viewer enabled, you can place and reorder clips; when the Timeline viewer is visible, you can add and edit audio and volume. For more information, see the section "Elements of the Clip Viewer and Timeline Viewer."

ⓔ Import/Edit Mode Switch

You can switch iMovie HD from editing movies to accepting video input from a digital camera, such as an iSight, by using the Mode Switch. When iMovie HD is accepting video input, the iMovie HD monitor acts as a live monitor, displaying what the camera is recording; it continues to offer live monitoring as you record. Edit mode is the default mode of iMovie HD, where you can construct, edit, and save your movie.

ⓕ Pane Buttons

You can select Pane buttons to access additional media elements and to create special effects, such as transitions and titles. Using the buttons, you can place new sets of tools in the pane area. These tools allow you to manage photos and audio clips, to create titles, transitions, and effects, and to export your movie to iDVD. When selected, these tools replace the Clip pane. You can return to any pane at any time without losing the changes that you have made.

ⓖ Disk Space Indicator

The Disk Space Indicator feature displays both a number and a visual indicator bar to show how much free disk space you have on your computer's hard drive. The less free space you have, the poorer iMovie HD's will perform. If the bar turns red, then you need to delete files to continue working in iMovie HD. It is a good idea to keep a minimum of 2GB free.

ⓗ iMovie HD Trash

You can drag video clips or audio tracks to the iMovie HD Trash in the Dock rather than use the Trash icon on your Desktop. You can restore items from the iMovie HD Trash as long as you have not emptied the items by using the Empty Trash command in iMovie HD's File menu.

PART IV

Elements of the Clip Viewer and Timeline Viewer

T he Clip viewer enables you to arrange your clips in the order in which you want them to appear in your movie. You can add clips to your arrangement to create a smooth transition. You can also reorder clips simply by dragging them to different locations. In addition, you can also view and reorder transitions.

In the Timeline viewer, you can add video effects and volume levels, and you can order and arrange audio tracks. You can also use the Timeline viewer to synchronize audio tracks to your video clips. This makes your movie appear more professional.

iMovie HD includes a wide arrangement of effects, such as titles and transitions that you can add, along with still images from your iPhoto library.

The Clip Viewer

Ⓐ Movie Clip

Displays the name of the clip that you have placed into your movie, as well as its title, duration, and order. All individual sections of video and still images that you import into iMovie HD are called clips. You may add multiple effects to these clips.

Ⓑ Transition Marker

Indicates where you have placed a transition between two clips, although it does not tell you what the transition is. Movie transitions visually merge two clips together in intriguing ways. You can use transitions between movie clips in the Timeline to change location, or to move through time as in day and night. You can also control the speed and length of a transition.

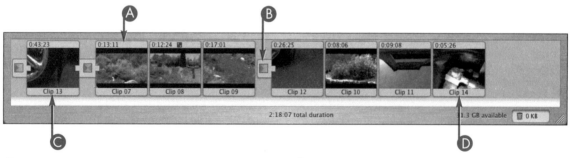

Ⓒ Opening Title

Gives your movie a distinctive name and sets the scene for your audience. For your opening title, you can choose from an extensive selection of text effects. You can also create music video titles.

Ⓓ Closing Title

Acknowledges everyone featured in your movie as well as those who have greatly assisted you in making this effort possible. You can create movie credits by selecting your fonts, size, speed, and pause effects.

The Timeline Viewer

Ⓔ Video Track

You can use this track to select clips to which you want to apply motion effects. You can import video clips from different sources to use in the movies you create in iMovie HD. After you import a video clip, you can preview it before adding it to the movie timeline.

Ⓕ Audio Tracks

You can insert and move audio clips here to match and complement your video clips. Timeline has two audio tracks. You can use these tracks to create background audio and music for your video, such as sound effects and or commentaries for your still frames. You can also turn off all audio in this track by deselecting the check box on the right.

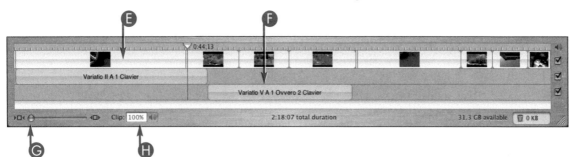

Ⓖ Zoom Slider

You can move this slider control to change the scale of the timeline. For example, you can scale it down to see many clips at once, or zoom in for fine timeline detail.

Ⓗ Edit Volume

You can increase or decrease the volume of a selected audio clip by using the Edit Volume slider.

Use Direct Trimming to Edit Clips and Sync Sound

You can use direct trimming to shorten or lengthen the part of an audio or video clip that you want to use in your iMovie HD. This nondestructive editing allows you to view the changes that you want to make, without affecting the original components. As a result, you can trim a clip without having to delete footage entirely.

Direct trimming makes it easier to synchronize audio and video clips, especially when you select the Timeline snapping option. Once you sync up the edges of the clips, you can finalize the edit.

Until you empty iMovie HD's Trash, you do not actually destroy the unused portion of each clip. In previous versions of iMovie HD, the only way to trim a clip was to delete the unwanted frames. To restore any of the deleted frames, you had to use the Restore Clip Media command, which would resurrect the original clip in its entirety. With direct trimming, the unwanted footage is only hidden, and not deleted, until you finalize the edit.

Even with direct trimming, you lose footage when you empty iMovie HD's Trash. If you empty the Trash and want any frames that you have trimmed, you must reimport the original video.

Use Direct Trimming to Edit Clips

① Click to select the clip that you want to trim.

A blue highlight appears around the clip.

② To trim from either end of the clip, position the cursor over the border of the clip until the cursor changes to ⊹ .

③ Drag the cursor towards the center of the clip to trim the clip.

You can play the clip in the iMovie HD monitor to review your edit.

Use Direct Trimming to Sync Sound

1. Click iMovie HD.

2. Click Preferences.

   The Preferences window appears.

3. Click Snap to items in Timeline
   (☐ changes to ☑).

4. Click ⊙ to close the Preferences
   window.

5. In the main iMovie HD window, click
   Audio (🔊).

   ● The Audio pane replaces the Clips
   pane.

6. Click a sound or music file.

7. Drag the selected sound or music file to
   the audio track on the Timeline.

   iMovie HD makes a popping sound to
   indicate that the clip has synchronized
   with the start of the video clip.

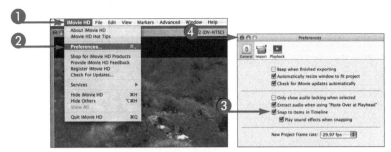

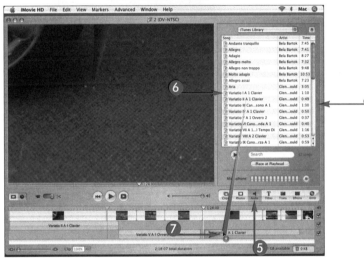

**How can I tell which clips have
been trimmed and which
have not?**

▼ You can distinguish between
these clips by comparing the
corners of the clips in the
Timeline. Trimmed or cropped
clips have straight corners, while
full clips have rounded corners.

**Can I move an audio clip from
the start of one video clip to
another?**

▼ Yes. To do so, just click and drag
the audio clip to where you
want it. You can also drag an
audio clip to begin in the
middle of a video clip or
anywhere else in the Timeline,
even with Timeline snapping
activated.

**Can I place a clip without
snapping it to something?**

▼ Yes. Even if you activate the
Timeline snapping option, which
automatically snaps clips in
place, you can Shift-drag the
playhead along the Timeline
without snapping it to another
element. Conversely, if Timeline
snapping is inactive, you can
Shift-drag a clip to snap it in
place.

Select Nonadjacent Clips

Y ou can select multiple clips in the Clip viewer, even if these clips are not next to each other. This eliminates the need to rearrange the order of clips in your movie if you want to delete nonadjacent scenes or create a preview from nonadjacent clips.

This also saves time if you want to create multiple, alternate versions of your movie. Because you can select nonadjacent clips, you do not have to arrange the order of one version, and then rearrange each individual clip to its new place in the alternate version of your movie.

MASTER IT

What else can I do with the selected clips?

▼ You can delete all of the selected clips or apply the same transition or effect to all of them. You can even paste all of the selected clips together to form a new movie.

Can I select adjacent and nonadjacent clips at the same time?

▼ Yes. You can select nonadjacent clips, and then select another clip that is connected to one of your selected clips.

Select Nonadjacent Clips

① Click Clip View (🔲).

The Clip viewer appears.

② Click the Clips button 🔲 to display your movie clips.

The Clip pane appears.

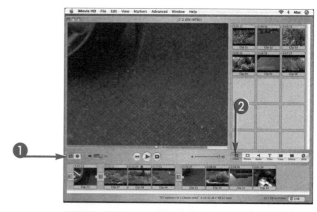

③ In the Clip viewer, click the first clip that you want to select.

You can ⌘-click each additional clip that you want to select.

You can continue to add more clips as long as you do not release the ⌘ key.

You can deselect a clip without losing your other selections by ⌘-clicking it.

Using Bookmarks to Mark Places in a Movie

You can use iMovie HD's Bookmarks feature just as a professional uses key frames in a high-end video-editing suite. Bookmarks can indicate precise locations in your movie. This helps you to quickly mark useful sections in your raw footage and speeds up your work if you use a clip multiple times.

You can also use bookmarks to mark places in audio tracks. For example, you can indicate where dramatic crescendos occur, or where there are quieter passages. You can delete bookmarks individually, or as a group when you no longer need them.

If I move a clip, do my bookmarks move with it?

▼ No. The bookmarks are attached to the Timeline, not to clips. As a result, if you move the first clip of your movie, perhaps to add empty space for titles, then all bookmarks in subsequent clips also need to be changed.

Can I drag my bookmarks to a new place in the Timeline?

▼ No. If you need to move a bookmark to another place in the Timeline, then you must delete the original bookmark and create a new one.

Using Bookmarks to Mark Places in a Movie

① Drag the Playhead (⬇) to the point in the Timeline where you want to place a bookmark.

② Click Markers.

③ Click Add Bookmark.

● A green diamond appears to indicate the bookmark position.

● You can navigate through assigned bookmarks by clicking Markers and selecting Next Bookmark or Previous Bookmark.

You have created bookmarks in your movie.

Share Clips

You can export selected clips from your movie. This is useful if you have a large movie and want to share only part of it, or share all of it over time on a clip-by-clip basis. You can also export small parts of your movie for inclusion on a Web page, in an e-mail, on a recordable DVD, or other options. Most viewers would rather see multiple and smaller clips than have to download a single, larger one.

You can use this feature to share clips with any QuickTime-equipped Mac or Windows-based PC. You can even share these clips with most PalmOS-based personal organizers and 3GP-compatible cell phones.

Will my clips be compressed differently, depending on the device to which I send them?

▼ Yes. iMovie HD automatically compresses your movies to a smaller size, depending on the target device. For example, iMovie chooses maximum compression when you send your clips to a Bluetooth-based device. The Sharing dialog tells you approximately how large the file will be before you send the clips.

Share Clips

① Press ⌘-click to select one or more continuous clips from the Timeline or Clip viewer.

Note: *This feature does not work if you select nonadjacent clips. You also cannot use this feature by selecting clips from the Clip pane.*

② Click File.

③ Click Share.

The Sharing dialog appears.

④ Click an option for how you want to share your movies.

⑤ Click Share selected clips only (☐ changes to ☑).

⑥ Click Share.

The selected clips will be compressed and shared according to the method you selected in the Sharing dialog.

Save Movies to Your .Mac Web Page

Y ou can put your movies on your .Mac Web page so that you can share clips and entire movies with others. You can do this without any knowledge of HTML and without having to find and manage server space.

When you use .Mac to host your movies, the footage is automatically compressed to 12 frames per second, at 240 pixels by 180 pixels, in QuickTime format at medium quality. Although this is not the highest quality that QuickTime can provide, this compression setting reduces download time. The movie automatically streams, so that viewers can start watching the movie before it downloads completely.

The .Mac site provides a variety of themes, such as Theatre, Projector, Drive-In, and Retro-TV, for the page on which you present your movie. You can also customize the page with your own titles and description.

Once you save your movie to the .Mac server, you receive an e-mail with the Web address of the page. You can then send this URL to friends and family with e-mail and a Web browser so that they can watch your movies.

You must have a .Mac account to use this service. For more information, you can go to www.mac.com.

Save Movies to Your .Mac Web Page

Note: If you do not have a .Mac account, then you can sign up for a free, limited-time trial account.

① Click File.

② Click Share.

The Sharing dialog appears.

③ Click HomePage.

④ Type the name of the clip or movie that you want to put on your Web page.

Note: The movie must have the .mov file extension.

⑤ Click Share.

iMovie HD automatically compresses your movie.

iMovie HD uploads your movie and directs your Web browser to the .Mac setup page.

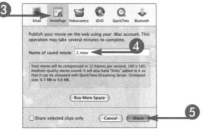

Use Your iSight with iMovie HD

You can record video footage directly into iMovie HD with an iSight Web camera. While the quality and resolution of the video and audio is not as high as that captured with a digital video camcorder, the cost is significantly lower.

The Import feature in iMovie HD automatically recognizes any iSight camera that you plug into your Mac, just as it would recognize any Firewire- or iLink-compatible digital video camcorder. Also, as with a digital video camcorder, iMovie HD's playback buttons can control the iSight, giving it pause and resume recording features.

The iSight is an auto focus camera with an f-2.8 lens and a focal depth from 50 millimeters to infinity. This makes it excellent for taking portrait movies but not as good for close-ups or outdoor events. However, despite these limitations, the iSight can help you create original movies for your friends and family.

The iSight also includes a built-in microphone. You can use it to capture audio along with video, or to record only sound that you later dub into an existing movie. However, it does not match the sound quality of dedicated directional or covered boom microphones. For higher audio quality, you can use an external microphone.

Use Your iSight with iMovie HD

① Connect your iSight to your Mac.

② Open the iSight shutter as directed in the iSight manual.

③ Move the Mode switch to the camera icon to switch iMovie HD to Camera mode.

④ Click here and select iSight in the pull-down menu.

Note: *Turning on your iSight may automatically launch iChat AV. If so, you can quit iChat.*

⑤ Click Record With iSight.

The iMovie HD monitor displays the video footage that you are recording.

⑥ Click Record With iSight again.

iMovie HD stops recording.

Apply a Transition to Multiple Clips

You can apply the same transition to multiple clips in iMovie HD. This is useful if you have a large movie, or you want to use a specific transition multiple times. For instance, you can always use a swirl effect to signal the beginning of a flashback, or a fadeout for the end of an interview sequence.

Although it is a good idea to use a variety of transitions — a jump cut provides a different dramatic effect from a fade in — basic transitions, such as fades, are generally used most often because they do not draw attention away from the movie's content. Experiment with various transitions to discover which is best for what application. You can also delete or change multiple transitions. This is useful if you want to change the tone of the movie. For example, you can change all fadeouts in a movie to cuts to black; this gives a more startling effect to the ends of scenes. If this does not work, you can use the multiple transition change technique to rescind the changes.

Apply a Transition to Multiple Clips

① Click the first clip to which you want to apply the transition.

② Hold the Shift key and click the last clip to select it.

iMovie HD highlights a range of clips in blue.

Note: *You can select noncontiguous clips by holding down the ⌘ key instead of the Shift key.*

③ Select a transition in the Transitions Pane.

④ Click Apply.

iMovie HD applies the same transition to all of the selected clips.

To delete multiple clips, you can follow Steps **1** and **2**, and then press Delete.

Build a Movie Automatically
with Magic iMovie

Y ou can use iMovie HD's Make a Magic iMovie
feature to automatically create a full-fledged movie
from any video recorded on a video camera that
features FireWire connectivity. Making a Magic iMovie is
useful if you have shot footage of an event with a digital
video camera and want to present the footage you have,
but do not want to go through the iMovie editing process
yourself. Your digital video camera must include a FireWire
interface for you to use this feature of iMovie HD.

The Make a Magic iMovie feature imports your video
directly from the video camera and turns the footage into a
movie you can save, share with friends, and import to
iDVD. You are not able to make edits, such as changing the
order of scenes or trimming scenes, when you use the Make
a Magic iMovie feature.

You can tell the Make a Magic iMovie feature the name of
your movie, and to place transitions between the scenes
imported from your video camera. You can also include
music in your Magic iMovie. For more information, see the
section "Add Music to a Magic iMovie."

Build a Movie Automatically with Magic iMovie

① Turn on your video camera and set it to VTR,
also called Play or VDR.

② Connect the camera to your computer with a
FireWire cable.

③ Click File.

④ Select Make a Magic iMovie.

The Magic iMovie settings pane appears.

⑤ Type a name for your movie.

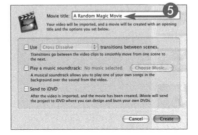

⑥ To have iMovie HD place transitions between scenes, click the Use selection (☐ changes to ☑).

⑦ Click ⬛ and select which transition iMovie HD uses.

⑧ Click Create.

iMovie HD creates a Magic iMovie automatically from your raw footage.

Can I edit the order of the scenes in my Magic iMovie?

▼ No. The Make a Magic iMovie feature takes the clips in your video camera and automatically creates a movie from them in that order. However, once you have allowed iMovie HD to make a Magic iMovie for you, you can edit it in iMovie HD as you would any other project.

Can I use the Make a Magic iMovie feature if I use a video camera that is not a standard definition digital camcorder (DV)?

▼ Yes. You can use nonstandard format digital video cameras with the Make a Magic iMovie feature. You can select your camera's format from the Video format option in the Magic iMovie settings pane.

Can I use more than one kind of transition in a Magic iMovie?

▼ Yes. You can choose Random in Step 7; this inserts a random choice of transition between each scene. The choice of transitions is automatic; however, you cannot specify which transition appears when.

Add Music to a Magic iMovie

You can use iMovie HD's Make a Magic iMovie feature to add music to your iMovie. This creates a soundtrack for the movie, which can help create a mood that augments the experience of watching the video clips.

You can choose to use any piece of music in your iTunes Library, or use one or more tracks from an audio CD that you have placed in your computer's optical disk drive. If your video is shorter than the song you have chosen, the song ends at the end of your movie. If you have a longer

movie and have selected multiple songs, the songs play one after the other with this order repeating until the movie is over. The music selection pane in the Make a Magic iMovie feature displays each song's length in minutes and seconds, helping you to choose songs that fit the length of your movie.

You can also set whether the music plays softly or loudly underneath the audio of your movie. If you do not want your movie to use the sound captured with the video, you can tell iMovie HD to use the music only.

Add Music to a Magic iMovie

1 Click File.

2 Click Make a Magic iMovie.

The Magic iMovie settings pane appears.

3 Click Play a music soundtrack (☐ changes to ☑).

4 Click Choose Music.

The Choose Music window appears.

5 Click ⬛ and select the source of the music for your movie.

6 Press ⌘-click to select your audio tracks.

7 Drag your audio tracks into the Music in your movie section.

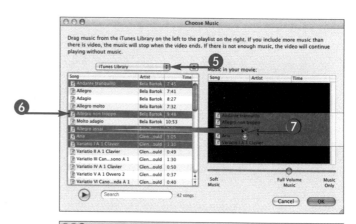

8 Drag the songs into your desired order.

9 Drag the slider to set the music level.

10 Click OK.

Your Magic iMovie plays with a music soundtrack.

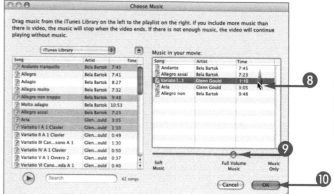

Can I preview songs before I put them in my movie?

▼ Yes. You can select any song in the song list and then click the Play button. This plays the song so that you can preview it and decide if you want to use it as a soundtrack for your movie.

Can I preview a song while watching the Magic Movie play?

▼ No. The process of creating your Magic Movie includes selecting the music for its soundtrack, if you want one. If you have created a Magic iMovie and you decide you do not like the music you chose, you can delete the Magic iMovie and start again as long as you have not erased or taped over the footage in your video camera.

Can I replace with music the audio that I shot along with the video?

▼ Yes. You can choose to have the music soundtrack replace, rather than play along with, the audio recorded along with the video footage. In Step **8**, move the slider to the Music Only position. The movie will feature only your selected music when the movie plays.

Select a Still Image to Add to Your iMovie

You can place a still image into your movie. This image can be a photograph, a PDF, or other illustration. This can enable you to show a map or a drawing in your movie, or use a still photograph for more emotional impact. You can even import snapshots taken by your Webcam, such as Apple's iSight camera.

The imported images appear in the iMovie HD clips pane. You can then incorporate them into your movie as you would a regular video clip. You can move the image's placement in the movie, add transitions, add sound, and more.

Can I create a still image from a frame of one of my movie clips?

▼ Yes. You can create a still image from a frame in one of your movie clips; you can then use the still image in your movie. To create the still image, select a clip, position the playhead so that iMovie HD presents the image you want to use, click Edit, and then select Create Still Frame. The still image appears in the Clips pane.

Select a Still Image to Add to Your iMovie

① Click File.

② Select Import.

An open dialog appears.

③ Select the image.

④ Click Open.

The still image appears in the Clips pane.

You can use the image just as you would use a clip.

Record a Voiceover for Your iMovie

If you have a microphone attached to your computer, or a built-in microphone, you can record a voice track to add to your movie. You can also use your video camera to record the audio. This allows you to add a narration or commentary track to your movie.

To insure that your voice is recorded properly, check that your external or internal microphone is properly selected as the sound input device in the System Preferences. For more information on selecting an input device, see Chapter 13.

MASTER IT

Can I adjust the recording volume of my microphone?

▼ Yes. You can adjust the recording level of your microphone, whether it is an internal or external one, by changing the input volume in the System Preferences. To do this, open the System Preferences, select Sound, click the Input tab, and click the input level meter.

Record a Voiceover for Your iMovie

① Click the Audio button (□).

The Audio pane appears.

② Click the Record button and begin speaking.

Note: *The input meter should be yellow while you are speaking — if it turns red, you are speaking too loudly.*

③ Click the Record button to stop recording.

● Your recorded voice track appears as the first audio clip in the timeline viewer. You can drag this audio clip to sync with any video clip in your movie.

Elements
of iDVD

T he main iDVD window is where you develop and preview a custom DVD movie presentation. You can also use iMovie clips, still photos, audio files, and saved images to create a professional-looking menu that allows viewers to navigate through your final presentation. When you are finished, you can burn the movie to DVD, if you have a Macintosh equipped with a SuperDrive.

A iDVD Menu

You can create an iDVD menu for your DVD presentation. You can drag pictures, movies, and audio files to this area to customize the appearance of your menu. Depending on which theme you choose, the layout of menu items may change.

B Drop Zone

You can drag pictures or movie loops that play as part of the DVD menu to themes with drop zone areas.

C Customize Button

You can click the Customize button to open the Customize drawer, which gives you access to the tools that you need to create a custom DVD.

D Folder Button

You can click the Folder button to make a submenu button on your DVD menu. This creates another customizable level of menus on your DVD.

E Slideshow Button

You can click the Slideshow button to add it to your DVD menu.

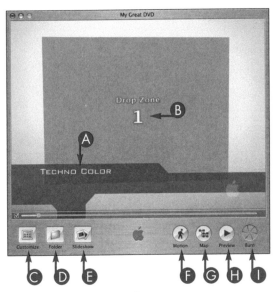

F Motion Button

You can click the Motion button to turn the motion and sound of your DVD menu on and off.

G Map Button

You can click the Map button to view a map of the DVD's organization. The map displays the structure of folders, menus, and movie clips.

I Burn Button

You can burn your project to DVD with two clicks of this button. The first click enables the process, and the second click begins the DVD-burning process.

H Preview Button

You can click the Preview button to preview your DVD. You can control the playback of the DVD and navigate its menus with a DVD player remote control window, which appears automatically.

Elements of the Themes Pane

You can open the Customize drawer and choose the Themes pane to select a theme for your DVD. This pane allows you to see and preview any available theme, which forms the basic template for the images, menu structure, and button placement on the menu of your DVD.

A Pane Selection Buttons

You can select a Themes pane using the Pane Selection buttons. When you choose the theme you want to use, you can then use these buttons to select other tools for changing settings or for managing your digital media and monitoring their status.

B Theme Sets

You can use this pull-down menu to view either selected sets of themes for you to preview, or all available themes at once. When you add themes, they appear in this list; if you place new themes into an existing folder, they appear in the theme list when you select that folder from this menu. There are initially no items in the Favorites list. This list contains themes that you have customized and saved as a Favorite in the Settings pane.

C Themes List

You can display thumbnail previews of the themes that are available from the folder you select in the theme sets pull-down menu. You can select any theme by clicking its thumbnail, and the theme appears in the main iDVD window. You can then begin the process of customizing your DVD menu.

Elements of the Settings Pane

You can open the Customize drawer and choose the Settings pane to select a theme for your DVD. This pane allows you to change and customize the overall appearance and sound of your DVD. For example, you can also use this pane to customize the choice of fonts and colors of the menu text, add video and sound to the DVD menu background, and change the appearance of the menu buttons.

Ⓐ Background Image/Movie Well

You can drag movie clips or still images here to set them as the background of your DVD menu.

Ⓑ Audio Well

You can drag audio files here to set them as the background music for your DVD menu.

Ⓒ Transition Menu

You can use the Transition pull-down menu to specify the transition you want when you click a DVD menu button. For some transitions, you can use the arrows to the right of the pull-down menu to set the direction from which the transition starts.

Ⓓ Duration Slider

You can use the Duration slider to control the amount of each background movie or audio clip that plays in a loop. You can include up to a total of 15 minutes of video in the DVD menu. This control also applies to any video that appears in menu buttons.

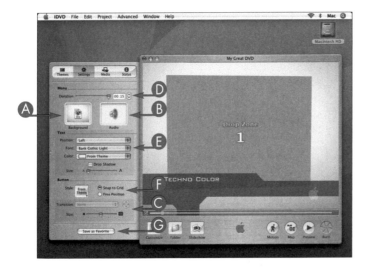

Ⓖ Save as Favorite

You can use the Save as Favorite pull-down menu to save your result after customizing a theme. This completed theme appears in the Favorites list in the Themes pane.

Ⓕ Button Controls

You can use the Button controls to set the position, shape, and size of the buttons on your DVD menu. Different shape options are available, based on the theme that you choose.

Ⓔ Text Controls

You can customize the text in your DVD menus, titles, and buttons. The text controls include settings for font, color, size, and alignment, which you can set in the Position pull-down menu.

Elements of the Media Pane

Y ou can easily find your movie, photo, and audio files in the Media pane and use them to customize your DVD menu. The Media pane allows you to access finished projects from iMovie, songs that you have catalogued in iTunes, and all of your iPhoto albums. From this pane, you can drag all of these media to the main window of iDVD and make your project unique.

Ⓐ Media Menu

You can use this pull-down menu to navigate to the folders that contain your movies, photos, and audio files. Selecting Audio displays all of your iTunes playlists from which you can select songs. Selecting Photos displays your iPhotos albums. Selecting Movies opens your iMovie project files. If you have made subfolders in any of these folders, then you can open them, as well.

Ⓑ Folders List

This list displays the contents of your selection in the Media menu. You can change iDVD's Preferences to tell iDVD to look for movie files in locations other than the iMovie Movies folder.

Ⓒ Items List

When you select Movies in the Media menu, you can click and drag any movie from here to the main window in order to create a movie button. You can also drag photos to the main window to place the photos in the featured section of the DVD menu. In addition, you can drag audio clips to create a soundtrack for your DVD menu.

Ⓓ Search Field

You can type text in this field to search for a specific file by name. This is useful if you have many files and do not want to scroll through a long list, or if you have any files in subfolders. The search returns the results as you type, so you may not need to type the full filename. The search is limited to the type of file that you choose in the Media menu. For example, the search finds only movie files when you select Movies in the Media menu.

Elements of
the Status Pane

You can monitor the current state of your overall DVD project and the files that you have used to create it with the Status pane. For example, this pane shows you how much remaining space is available on a recordable DVD, and how much of a recordable

DVD you have filled with particular types of media. The Status pane also displays how many menus you presently have, as well as how many you can place into your DVD menu. In addition, it shows you how you have placed audio and slideshow tracks, and what assets you have used on your project.

Ⓐ DVD Capacity

This meter shows you how much space you have used up, in relation to the space that is available on a recordable DVD.

Ⓑ Motion Menus

This meter displays the remaining available time that you can use for video and audio loops in the menu backgrounds and motion buttons. You can use up to 15 minutes of looping audio and video.

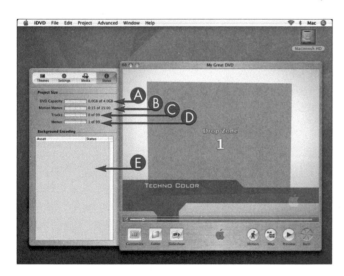

Ⓒ Tracks

The Tracks meter shows you how many audio tracks and slideshows you have used on your DVD. You can use up to 99 tracks and slideshows.

Ⓓ Menus

This meter displays how many submenus you have used and how many remain. You can use up to 99 submenus when creating the menu structure for your DVD.

Ⓔ Asset List

This lists the names of the movies that you have used in your iDVD project. The Status area on the right shows whether or not the movies have been encoded; all movies must be encoded before you can burn your project to DVD. All files are encoded automatically when you click iDVD's Burn button.

Pick a Movie to Open a DVD

Y ou can use iDVD 4 and later to create a DVD that automatically plays when it is inserted into a DVD player. This helps you to build a DVD that immediately plays a movie, without requiring viewers to click any buttons; this may be less likely to confuse novice viewers who may find a menu screen confusing.

You can use any movie clip that you have created in iMovie as your opening to your DVD. This movie can include titles, special effects, and sound, and leads to the DVD menu and all of the viewing options.

Can I create a DVD that contains only a movie that plays automatically?

▼ Yes. You can use any movie that you have created as an automatically playing movie, as long as it fits within the storage space of a recordable DVD and is in the right file format.

Can I replace or delete a movie that I have dragged to the AutoPlay tile?

▼ Yes. To do this, simply drag a new movie to the AutoPlay tile. If you want to delete the autoplaying movie, then drag it from the iDVD Map screen. This does not delete the original file.

Pick a Movie to Open a DVD

① Click Customize to open the Customize drawer.

② Click Media to display the Media pane.

③ Click Map to display the DVD menu map.

④ Click ⊟ and select Movies from the pull-down menu.

⑤ Drag the movie that you want to play at the start of the DVD to the AutoPlay tile in the Map diagram.

The movie is set to play automatically at the start of your DVD.

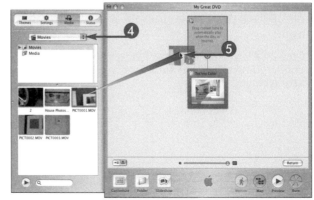

Pick a Slideshow to Open a DVD

You can use iDVD to create a DVD that automatically opens and plays a slideshow when it is inserted into a DVD player. This slideshow does not require viewers to click any buttons or navigate any menus, although you can use the slideshow to lead into your regular DVD menu.

You can create slideshows from a collection of images, including your favorite iPhoto albums. As with iPhoto, you can control the display duration for each image and add various transitions between photos. You can also choose to display on-screen controls so that viewers can move forward and backward between photos.

These slideshows can also feature background music. You can include any music from iTunes or other audio files to play as the photos appear. The slideshow and music can loop until the viewer clicks the screen to move to the DVD menu, or it can play once and then display the custom DVD menu that you have created.

Keep in mind that iDVD does not automatically scale the resolution of the photos that you have chosen. If you include low-resolution images, they may appear blocky or blurry on a TV screen.

Pick a Slideshow to Open a DVD

① Click Customize to open the Customize drawer.

② Click Media to display the Media pane.

③ Click Map to reveal the DVD menu map.

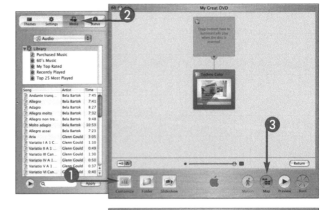

④ Click 🔽 and select Photos from the pull-down menu.

⑤ Drag an iPhoto album or select individual photo thumbnails to the AutoPlay tile in the Map window.

⑥ Double-click the AutoPlay tile in the Map window to change the main window to the slideshow interface.

⑦ Click ⊡ and select a slide duration between photos from the pull-down menu.

⑧ Click Transition ⊡ and select a transition effect from the pull-down menu.

You can also drag an audio file to the Audio Well to add background music to the slideshow.

The slideshow is set to play automatically at the start of your DVD.

PART IV

Can I make the opening slideshow loop?

▼ Yes. You can tell iDVD to make the opening slideshow loop, or play over and over again, rather than playing once and stopping. Click the project icon, which is the top left icon in the map view, and click Advanced, and then select Loop Slideshow. When your DVD plays, the slideshow will start again from its beginning once it has finished.

Can I add music to the opening slideshow?

▼ Yes. You can double-click the autoplay icon, which opens your selected slideshow in the slideshow editor. You can then drag a music file from the Media pane into the slideshow editor's audio well. The music will play when the slideshow plays.

Can I remove a slideshow from my DVD once I have put it into the project?

▼ Yes. You can remove slideshows from your project, so that the movie begins with a different slideshow or another media element. To remove the slideshow, drag the slideshow icon out of the project icon in the Map view window.

Create and Style Text Boxes
on a Menu Screen

You can use text in iDVD to add labels and messages to your DVD menus and interim screens. You can then customize the font, style, size, and color of the text. For example, you can add a label to a button that takes the viewer to a slideshow or movie of a ski trip.

You can then add text to the screen that frames the slideshow or movie preview. This text can include information about when and where the trip took place. If you want, you can

even add personalized messages for each copy of the DVD that you burn for friends or family, although you would have to revise the text and save the project for each customization.

If you want to change the appearance of the text on an entire page, iDVD allows you to do this quickly and easily. When you click one text object, and then click Select All from the Edit menu, you can then change the font, style, size, or color of all of the text on a page of your DVD menu.

Create and Style Text Boxes on a Menu Screen

① Click in an open area of the Menu screen.

② Click Project.

③ Click Add Text.

As an alternative, you can press ⌘-K.

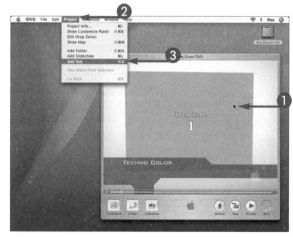

The words *Click to edit* appear on the screen.

④ Double-click the text to select it and type your new text.

⑤ Position the cursor on the edge of the text box until it looks like a hand.

⑥ Drag the text box to place it where you want it.

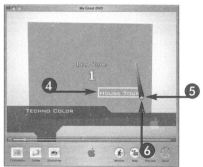

7 Click Customize to open the Customize drawer if it is not already open.

8 Click Settings to switch to the Settings pane.

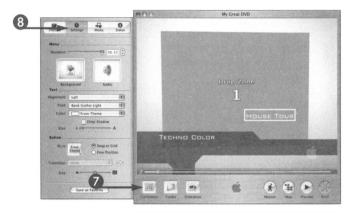

9 With the text selected, select the alignment, font, and color options that you want to apply.

- You can add a drop shadow to your text by clicking Drop Shadow (☐ changes to ☑).

10 Drag the slider to increase or decrease the size of the text.

- Your text appears with your selected styles.

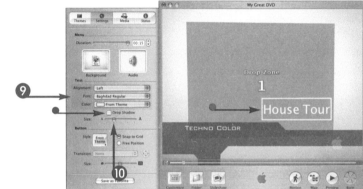

Can I place text over a preview movie?

▼ No. You can place text over the area on a menu where a preview movie would go, although this text replaces the preview movie. You cannot have both. If you create a still image clip with text titles in iMovie, you can edit that clip into your preview movie. For more information on adding a still image to your iMovie, see Chapter 16.

What does the From Theme option in the Color pull-down menu do?

▼ Each preset Theme is designed with a certain set of button shapes, layouts, and colors. Although you can choose any color for your text, the From Theme option chooses colors that are consistent with your selected theme. These colors are chosen to match well with other colors in the Theme when the DVD is viewed on a television screen.

Can I control kerning and leading?

▼ No. iDVD does not support either user-defined kerning, which is spacing between letters, or leading, which is spacing between lines. You can experiment with fonts and the placement of text boxes to achieve your desired layout, however.

Create and Style
Text Boxes on Buttons

You can use text in iDVD to add labels to your DVD menu buttons. These buttons are used to show viewers where to click to select movies, folders of photos, slideshows, and submenus. The text can help viewers distinguish which buttons lead to which elements of your DVD better.

Each time you add a movie or folder to your iDVD project, the application automatically creates a new button with a label that contains the name of the movie file or folder. If

you have clear and unique names for all of your movie clips, such as My Desert Trip and My Birthday, and you are satisfied with the appearance of the text in the Theme that you have selected for your DVD, then you may not need to change the text.

However, if your movie and photo files have labels such as Movie_1, then you can change the name to make it clearer for your viewers. For instance, you can name a movie clip Birthday and another one Car Wash. You can also customize the font, size, style, and color of the text.

Create and Style Text Boxes on Buttons

① Click Customize to open the Customize drawer.

② Double-click the text to select it and type your new text.

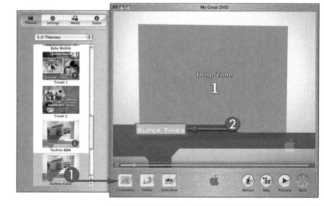

③ Click Settings to open the Settings pane.

④ Click ▦ and select Right, Center, or Left to change the text alignment on the button.

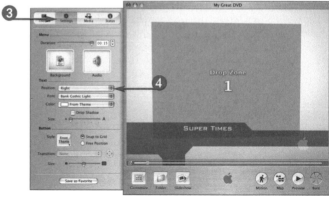

⑤ Click ▦ and select the font option from the pull-down menu.

⑥ To change the text color, click ▦ and select a color from the pull-down menu.

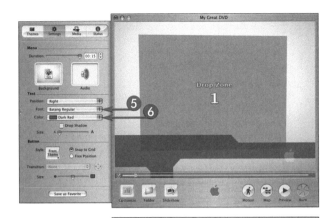

⑦ Drag the Size slider to increase or decrease the size of the button text.

● Your button appears with your selected styles.

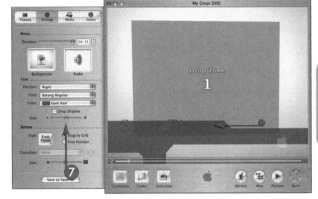

Can I make a style or formatting change to just one button on a menu screen?

▼ No. When you change the text on one button, the text on the other buttons reflects the same changes. For example, if you align the text on one button to the right, then the text on all of the buttons also aligns to the right.

When I try to select the text on a button, sometimes a movie starts playing. Why does this happen?

▼ The buttons are active even when you edit them. If you click too quickly when you try to select the button text, then you may signal to iDVD that you want to go to the scene or menu screen to which the button is supposed to send you. Try clicking the text once, pausing, and then clicking it once again, rather than double-clicking quickly.

Can I make a button without any text on it?

▼ Yes. If you want to create a button on your DVD that has no label, you can select No Text from the Position menu in the Settings pane. However, this can result in an invisible button if the color of the button is set to From Theme.

Create Menu Transitions

You can add special effects transitions to your DVD movie for when viewers move from one menu screen to another. Special effects can occur when a user clicks a button on the main menu page to view a movie, to move from one menu to another menu, or from a menu to a slideshow. For example, you can specify a dissolve to a movie when you click the DVD menu button for that clip.

By default, menus do not use transitions. You must choose and set a transition for your DVD. This choice applies to your entire DVD; you cannot mix transitions or apply a

different transition to different buttons. When you choose a transition, you should preview the entire DVD to see whether it plays well throughout the DVD.

Some transitions can move from one direction to another. If the transition that you choose has directionality, the default is from right to left, although you can change this to left to right, top to bottom, or bottom to top. The more transitions that you include, and the more involved they are, the longer it takes to burn your DVD.

You cannot set a transition to play when coming back to a menu from a slideshow or a movie. In addition, you cannot include any audio background for the transitions.

Create Menu Transitions

① Click Customize to open the Customize drawer.

② Click Settings to open the Settings pane.

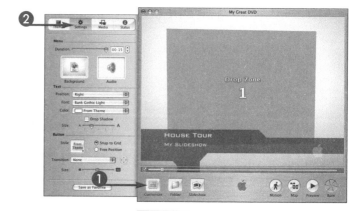

③ Click the button to which you want to attach a transition.

④ Click 🔃 and select a transition from the pull-down menu.

● If you can choose the direction of the transition, then one of the arrow buttons is highlighted. You can click to choose the direction in which you want the transition to move.

⑤ Click Preview to view the transition.

Create a Full-Motion Movie Background

Y ou can insert a movie clip into the background of your DVD menus to give your DVD a more dynamic appearance. This background movie plays behind other elements of the DVD menu when you play the DVD. This feature also allows you to include a movie with a custom audio track, which can be useful if you want to record an introduction or verbal instructions. However, when choosing your background movie, keep in mind that it will loop, so you should not choose anything that may become annoying upon repetition.

Some Themes have drop zones, which are areas that are designed to contain and show pictures or movies. You can recognize them because they display the phrase Drag photos or movies here. An example of this is the curtained stage area in the Kids Theater One Theme that is used in the iDVD tutorial. In these Themes, your movie only appears within the drop zone. In other themes without specific drop zones, your movie may be shown as the entire background of the DVD menu.

Create a Full-Motion Movie Background

1 Click Customize to open the Customize drawer.

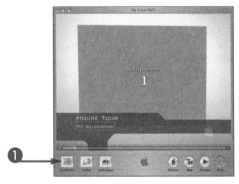

2 Click Settings to display the Settings pane.

3 Drag a movie file to the Background Well.

4 Drag the Duration slider to set how long the movie plays before it loops.

The movie appears as the background in the main iDVD window.

● You can toggle the movie on and off by clicking Motion.

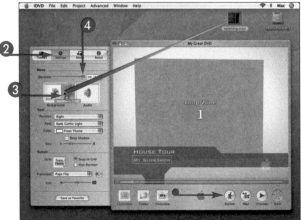

Optimize Quality and Performance Options

You can choose one of two ways to encode your project before you burn it to a recordable DVD. This process converts your video to the file format that is read by DVD players. The first option, Best Quality, gives you the highest fidelity results. However, this quality requires a longer encoding and burning time. The second option, Best Performance, encodes and burns your DVD project more quickly, but at a slightly lower fidelity. You can use Best Performance for projects that total less than 60 minutes in length, while you can use Best Quality for any length project.

Setting Performance Options

You can tell iDVD to encode your DVD and the elements that compose it at different levels of quality. The higher quality setting will produce better-looking and better-sounding results, but take longer to process. To select an encoding option for your DVD, open the iDVD Preferences and click the General icon. You can then select either the Best Quality or Best Performance setting.

Best Quality or Best Performance

As the name suggests, the Best Quality setting is for recording the highest fidelity DVD. However, this means that the encoding and burning process takes much longer, especially on older or slower Macs. You can choose the Best Performance option to reduce encoding and burning time if you prefer to save time rather than have a top-quality result. Keep in mind that you cannot choose the Best Performance option if your DVD contains more than 60 minutes of video.

Background Encoding

If you select the Best Performance setting, then you can check the Enable background encoding option in the iDVD Preferences. This allows iDVD to begin to encode all of your media items as soon as you drag them into the project. As you build your DVD, iDVD prepares files in the background. You must not burn your DVD until the Status pane shows that all assets have been encoded. You cannot use background encoding with the High Quality setting because iDVD chooses how it compresses and encodes content based on the total amount of content; the more content you add, the more compressed the content must be.

Quality in Relation to Content Time

Because recordable DVDs can contain only so much content, iDVD has to compress your movies and audio to fit the DVD. In general, using the Best Quality setting provides a better result than using Best Performance; however, the length of your DVD also affects the result. For example, a two-hour DVD encoded with the Best Quality option may look and sound similar to a one-hour DVD encoded with the Best Performance option.

Supported Media

You can use almost all QuickTime media except for MPEG and QuickTime VR movies, and Flash tracks. You can also use photos from iPhoto and Adobe Photoshop, as well as AAC, MP3, and AIFF audio files. In addition, you can use bitmapped graphics and vector images that have been translated to bitmapped format.

Quality of Source Material

The old adage, garbage in, garbage out, applies to the movies that you use and the appearance of your final DVD movie. For example, when you use low-quality QuickTime movies, such as clips from the Web, and video transferred from VHS tapes, these do not produce a high-fidelity result on your DVD. For best results, use video taken with a digital video camcorder and edited in iMovie or other video-editing software.

Time to Encode

The time it takes to produce a DVD depends on the speed of your optical drive, your computer, the amount and quality of content, and the complexity of transitions. If you have a spare recordable DVD, then you should test how long it takes to burn the two-and-a-half minute tutorial project that is included with iDVD.

Checking Content Time

Knowing how much content you have in a project is key, so that you do not end up having to delete content to fit your project onto one recordable disk. You can use the DVD Capacity meter in the Status pane of the Customize drawer to monitor how much content you have already dedicated to your DVD.

Changing Quality Settings for Multiple DVD Versions

Some recordable disks allow you to burn content in multiple sessions; that is, you can record some data to the disk, and then later add data. If you have already burned a DVD with one quality setting and you have deleted some media items, then you can select Delete Encoded Assets from the Advanced menu. This removes the previously encoded assets from your project file and allows you to choose a different encoding option.

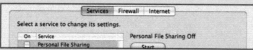

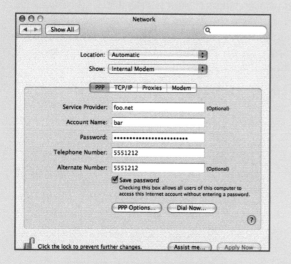

PART V

MANAGING NETWORKING: LOCAL AND REMOTE

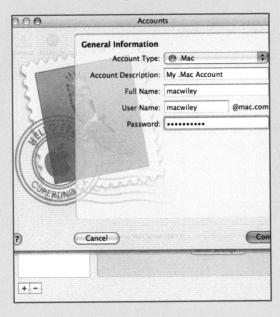

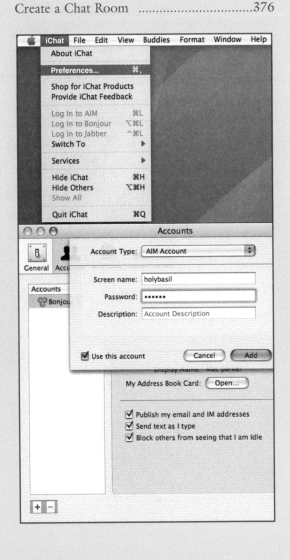

Enable Network Access to Your Public Folder

You can use the Sharing pane of the System Preferences window to enable other computers on your local network, such as on a shared AirPort connection or a wired network, to access your Public folder. This is useful for sharing documents, notes, photos, or other digital files, and is similar to setting up a shared folder between users on the same computer.

By default, your Public folder has read-only permissions. This means that other users can view and copy the contents of your Public folder although they cannot make changes to

the files in this folder, nor can they add items to it. However, Public folder contains a Drop Box folder to which they can add items. The Public folder is located in your home directory.

The Public folder is different from the Shared folder. The Shared folder is for sharing items between users on the same computer; it is located in the Users folder, and has read and write permissions by default. This means that other users can read and copy files from the folder, as well as make changes to items and add items to that folder.

Enable Network Access to Your Public Folder

① Click the Apple menu (🍎).

② Click System Preferences.

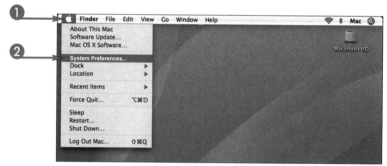

The System Preferences window appears.

③ Click Sharing.

The Sharing pane appears.

4 Click Services.

● The Services pane appears.

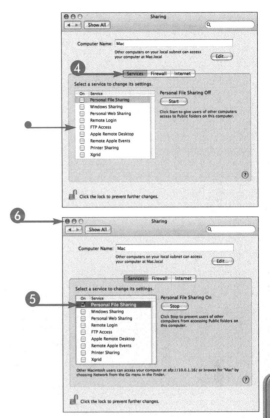

5 Click Personal File Sharing (changes to ☑).

Selecting the Personal File Sharing check box automatically starts up file sharing.

6 Click ◉ to close the Preferences window.

What if the Service options are grayed out?

▼ If the options in the Service pane are grayed out and you cannot make changes, check to see whether the Lock icon at the bottom of the pane is closed. If it is, then the message "Click the lock to make changes" appears next to it. You can click the Lock icon and type your Administrator password to enable changes to the Sharing options.

Can I change permissions to either my Public or Drop Box folders?

▼ Yes. You can change the permissions for any of the folders that other users on the network can see. For more information about changing permissions, see Chapter 3.

Will turning on network access to my Public folder prohibit other users on my computer from accessing the folder?

▼ No. Other users on the same computer still have the same level of access to your Public and Drop Box folders. However, if you make changes to the permission levels of these folders, then these changes also affect the access level of users on the same computer.

Connect to a Public Folder over a Network

You can connect to the Public folder of another computer on your local wired or wireless network, as long as that computer has Personal File Sharing turned on. This option is located in the Sharing section of the System Preferences. Connecting to the Public folder of another user is useful if you regularly share files such as documents, images, and movies. Although these types of files can also be e-mailed, large files can take longer to transfer by e-mail and put a strain on size-limited mailboxes.

When you connect to a computer, you gain access to that computer's Public folder. By default, this folder has read-only permissions, which means that you can view and copy the items in the Public folder, but you can neither place items into that folder nor make changes to any items that it contains. However, if you copy an item to your own user directory, then you can make any changes to the item, provided the item has not been locked or had its permissions set to read only. For more information on permissions, see Chapter 3.

Connect to a Public Folder over a Network

① Click Go.

② Click Connect to Server.

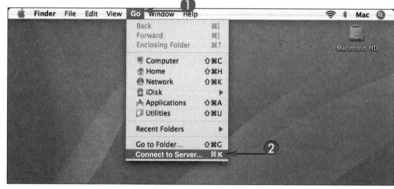

The Connect to Server window appears.

③ Click Browse.

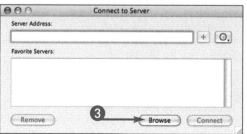

A new Finder window appears.

④ Click the Network icon in the Sidebar if it is not already selected.

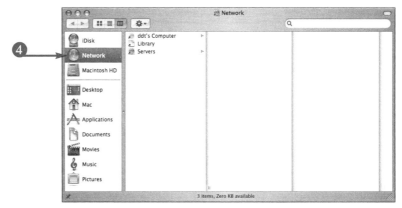

Icons appear for the available servers.

⑤ Double-click the icon for the computer to which you want to connect, or click its icon and then click the Connect button if the window is in Column view

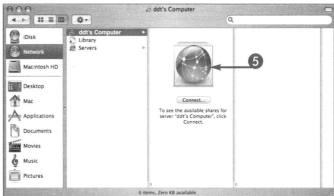

Will I have access to the Public folders for all users on the target computer?

▼ If the target computer is configured with multiple accounts, then you can press Shift and select multiple accounts on the target computer. You will then see icons for the target computer mount in the Sidebar of your Finder windows, and you will then be able to access the Public folders of all the selected user accounts.

How many computers can connect to my computer to access its Public folder?

▼ Mac OS X allows up to ten users to connect to your computer at once via the Personal File Sharing option in the Sharing Preferences. If you require more simultaneous connections, you can upgrade to Mac OS X Server.

continued

Connect to a Public Folder over a Network *(Continued)*

I f you want to transfer an item, such as a photo or document, to that user, then you can place it into the Drop Box folder. This folder resides inside the Public folder and has write-only permissions, which means that you can place items into it, but not view or make changes to the contents of the folder.

Turning on Mac OS X's built-in firewall does not hamper access to Public folders. A firewall is a piece of software that prevents some specific forms of communication over a network. The purpose of a firewall in a networked environment is to prevent malicious exploits, such as viruses, from reaching your computer, and to prevent personal information, such as your network address, from being discovered by untrustworthy parties.

You can turn on or off Mac OS X's firewall through the Sharing section of the System Preferences. The sharing services that you have selected, such as Personal File Sharing, are automatically accepted from being blocked by the firewall. For more information, see the section "Turn On Your Computer's Firewall."

Connect to a Public Folder over a Network *(continued)*

A Connect dialog appears.

⑥ Click the Guest option (◯ changes to ◉).

⑦ Click Connect.

The target computer's icon appears in the Sidebar.

⑧ Click OK.

⑨ Click the target computer icon.

- The contents of the target computer's Public folder appear in the Finder window.

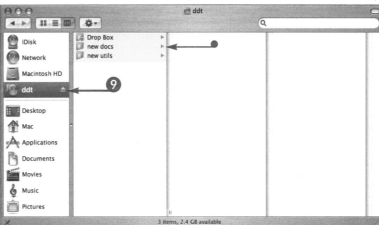

Can I be prevented from connecting to one user on a target computer if another user has turned on File Sharing?

▼ No, at least not through the File Sharing option. Once an Administrator opens File Sharing for the computer, the Public folders of all users on that computer are accessible to all other computers. You can change permissions on Public folders to the no access setting, which prevents other users, whether local or remote, from being able to open or drop items into these folders.

Can I place an item in the Drop Box of one user so that it is available to all users on that computer?

▼ No. Placing an item in one user's Drop Box only makes the item available to that user. If you want to send a file to all users on a computer, then you have to connect to each user and put the item in their Drop Box.

PART V

Use Go and the Finder to Connect to Servers

You can use either the Go menu or the Network icon in the Sidebar of a Finder window to locate and connect to remote computers or servers on a local network or the Internet. This is a convenient way to work with other users and other computers.

Once you connect to a server or remote computer, you can add its icon to the Sidebar. The icon remains in the Sidebar even when you are not connected to that computer, and you can reconnect by clicking the icon. You can disconnect

from the server or computer by clicking the Eject button next to the icon in the Sidebar.

You can also add your username and password for the server or remote computer to your keychain by checking the Add Password to Keychain option when you enter your username and password. The next time you connect, you do not need to enter the information again. However, this means that anyone who can access your user account is also able to access all of your servers and remote computers without having to enter a password.

Use Go to Connect to Servers

1 Click Go.

2 Click Network.

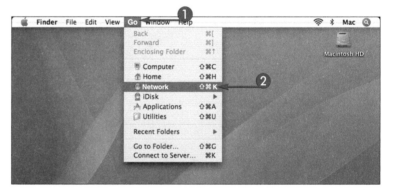

A Finder window appears, displaying available servers.

3 Double-click the target server's icon.

Note: *You may be prompted to enter a username and password.*

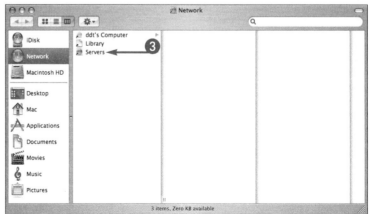

Use the Finder to Connect to Servers

1 Click the Network icon in a Finder window.

The right pane of the Finder window displays the available servers.

2 Double-click the target server's icon.

Note: *You may be prompted to enter a username and password.*

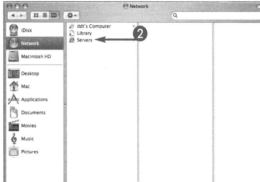

PART V

Can I connect to any computer or server?

▼ No. You can connect to Macs on your local network only if they have turned on Personal File Sharing, and Windows-based PCs only if they have turned on Window Sharing. Each computer Administrator may also restrict access to users they have registered and to whom they have assigned passwords. You can also connect to file servers on the Internet if you have their IP or host name, and to AFP, SMB, FTP, and WebDAV servers.

Can I find servers in different network areas or workgroups?

▼ Yes. If the network Administrator has allowed access to servers or network areas, then you can find servers in different network areas. You can navigate through the Finder window that displays available servers as though the network areas were directories on your local computer.

Can I change my username and password for remote servers?

▼ Depending on the level of security at the remote server, to change your username or password, you may need to contact the Administrator of the server or remote computer. If you do not need this authorization, you can click the Action button in the login window and select the Change Password option.

Share a Printer on a Network

Y ou can share a printer with other computers on your local network. This can save a great deal of resources, as you do not have to connect a printer to each computer on a network, and can save time in that you do not have to have a printer physically connected to each computer in order to print a document from that computer.

Once you enable and configure shared printers and have a printer list, you can print from any device on the list. This is

true whether the displayed printers are directly connected to your computer or whether you connect to them over your network. In the same way, all users on the network who enable shared printing can print to every printer, including the one connected to your computer.

All users on your local network — which is your IP subnet — who have enabled sharing, are able to see all networked printers directly in the Print dialogs of all their applications. However, changing the default printer requires you to makes changes in the Printer Setup Utility.

Share a Printer on a Network

① Click .

② Click System Preferences.

The System Preferences window appears.

③ Click Sharing.

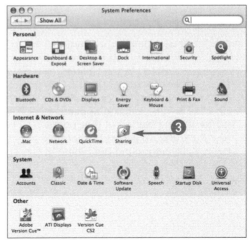

The Sharing pane appears.

④ Click Services.

● The Services pane appears.

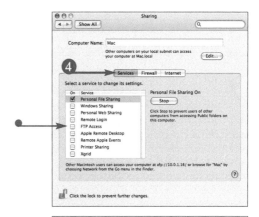

⑤ Click the Printer Sharing option (☐ changes to ☑).

● Printer Sharing starts up, and other users on the network can access all printers to which you have access.

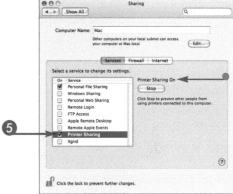

Is there a way that I can allow other users to know where to find the actual printers that they are using remotely?

▼ Yes. You can let other users know the physical location of networked printers. Launch the Printer Setup Utility, which is located in the Utilities folder. Then click View and click Show Printer List. When the list appears, select a printer, click the Printer's menu, and click Show Info. A dialog appears in which you can type a description of that printer's location. All users are able to access this location description and can therefore find out where their document has printed.

Do I need to configure a print server if I am running shared printers?

▼ No. You do not need a print server, which is a host computer dedicated to managing print queues as well as the files being spooled for printing. When you use Printer Sharing to let Mac OS X and Windows computers share a printer on the network subnet, your computer hosts the printer queue. As a result, the files being spooled for printing are stored on your hard drive. If you have problems with the print queue, then you should ensure that you have sufficient available hard disk space.

Turn On Your Computer's Firewall

You can increase your Mac's level of security by enabling the built-in firewall in Mac OS X. The firewall blocks unauthorized and possibly unwanted network traffic on certain ports; these types of communication are often used to compromise the security of remote computers by installing viruses or Trojan horses, or by enabling remote access to the computer.

You can select which ports the firewall blocks. A port is an interface for communicating with a computer application over a network. Network ports are usually numbered and assigned to specific services, such as serving Web pages or

sharing a printer. Therefore, closing specific ports determines which services are prevented from being shared. In the case of specifying which services are allowed by your firewall, you need to select those services that you want to share while the firewall is turned on; these ports remain open.

You can make these selections in the Firewall pane of the Sharing Preferences window. The services that you can share while still protecting your computer with a firewall include Personal File Sharing, iTunes Music Sharing, Printer Sharing, and iChat over Rendezvous.

Turn On Your Computer's Firewall

① Click .

② Click System Preferences.

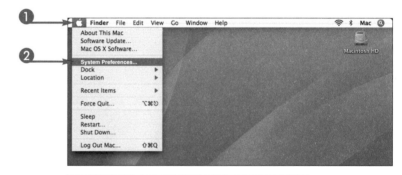

The System Preferences window appears.

③ Click Sharing.

The Sharing pane appears.

④ Click Firewall.

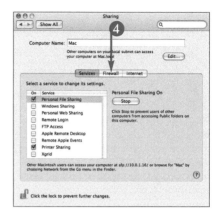

The Firewall pane appears.

⑤ Click the services you want to share
(☐ changes to ☑).

Firewall protection is turned off for the
services you select.

⑥ Click Start.

The firewall is enabled.

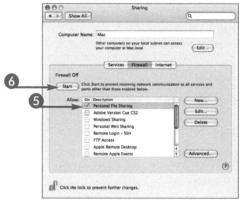

**Why am I unable to change the access
option for some of the services in the
Firewall pane of the Sharing Preferences
window?**

▼ If you select a service that you want to
share in the Sharing pane of the Sharing
Preferences window, that option is
automatically selected in the Firewall pane.
To make a change to the availability of
these services, deselect the option in the
Sharing pane. There are other services that
are not assigned access in the Sharing
pane, such as iTunes Music Sharing. You
can change their accessibility through your
firewall in the Firewall pane of the Sharing
Preferences window.

**Can I keep my computer secure while
allowing some shared services?**

▼ Yes. If you need to share a service
temporarily, you can turn this service on
and then off when it is no longer needed.
You can also turn on your firewall and
allow this service, and turn the service off
when it is not required. There are some
services that are less secure than others.
For example, turning on iTunes Music
Sharing allows less access to your
computer than turning on Remote Login
or FTP Access. If you are not familiar with a
service, do not turn it on.

Check Your Network Connection Statistics

You can use Network Utility to monitor the statistics of your active network connection. You can use Network Utility to determine whether your AirPort wireless connection is working, whether your Ethernet connection to a wired network is secure, whether you can contact another computer on your network, how many data packets are being sent and received, and addresses for hardware devices.

You can monitor network connections to determine the cause of network problems, such as why a connection appears to be slow. You can also use this information in conjunction with the System Profiler to identify hardware

problems, such as when a network card is damaged or inactive.

You can also use the Traceroute feature of Network Utility to see the steps over various servers your computer takes to connect with a Web site or other computer. This can help you discover how well you are connected to a network, or what might be the cause of apparent slowdowns in your Web browsing.

Network Utility's Ping feature allows you to send a test message, or ping, to another computer. If the computer responds to the ping, your connection to that computer is good.

Check Your Network Connection Statistics

① Launch Network Utility.

Note: *Network Utility is located in the Utilities folder, which is in the Applications folder.*

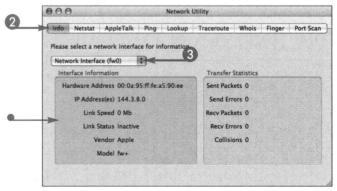

The Network Utility interface appears.

② Click Info.

③ Click ⊞ and select a network connection from the pull-down menu.

An AirPort connection may be listed as an Ethernet interface.

● Information about your network connection appears, updating in real time.

Look Up User Information

Y ou can use Network Utility's Finger feature to look up and display information about users on a server or Web site to which you are connected. This is useful if you are working on a network and want to see who is registered on the system as well as who has access to various network services.

The Finger feature provides a list of information about a user, provided this user has entered the data into its account file. These data can include mail status, username, idle time, and login shell. You can also use the Finger

feature to determine if a user is currently logged on to his or her account.

However, though the Finger protocol was widely used, service providers currently do not offer Finger service. For the Finger feature to work, a server must run a particular program that responds to a remote computer's Finger request. If the server does not have installed or is not running that program, the Finger request will be refused and no data will be returned.

Look Up User Information

1 Launch Network Utility.

Note: *Network Utility is located in the Utilities folder, which is in the Applications folder.*

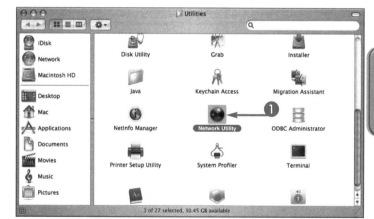

The Network Utility interface appears.

2 Click Finger.

The Finger pane appears.

3 Type a username.

4 Type the domain address.

5 Click Finger.

● Information appears about the user.

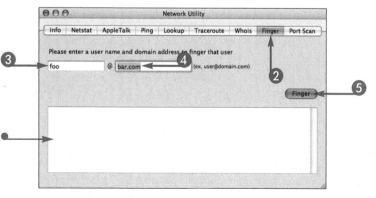

Configure
a Modem

You can connect to the Internet or other networks through a telephone modem. A modem is a device that translates digital information from the computer into audio signals that can be transferred across regular phone lines. A modem at the receiving end then translates the audio back into digital information.

Most desktop and laptop Macs come with built-in modems. You can connect any regular telephone line into the modem port to make your connection.

A modem does not transfer data at the same speed as high-speed connections, such as digital subscriber lines

(DSL) or cable modems. Most modems transfer data at 28.8 to 56 kilobits per second (Kbps), while DSL and cable connections can transfer data at rates of up to 1.5 megabits per second (Mbps).

When you set up your Mac for the first time, the Mac OS X Setup Assistant helps you to configure many features of your computer, including the modem settings. Whether you use the Setup Assistant or the Network Preferences, you need to know information from your Internet Service Provider (ISP), such as their access telephone number, your username, and your password.

Configure a Modem

① Click the Apple menu (🍎).

② Click System Preferences.

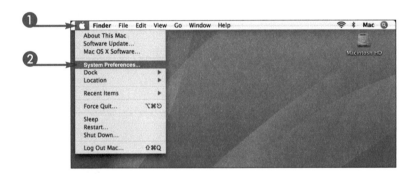

The System Preferences window appears.

③ Click Network.

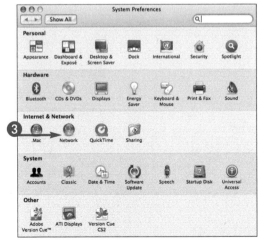

The Network pane appears.

4️⃣ Click 🔽 and select Internal Modem from the pull-down menu.

The Internal Modem pane appears.

5️⃣ Type the information provided by your ISP.

6️⃣ Click Apply Now.

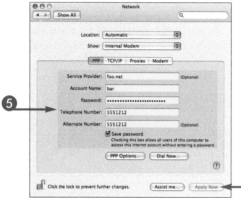

Can I use the Network Setup Assistant at any time, or only when I first start up a new computer?

▼ You can use the Setup Assistant at any time, although the Setup Assistant does launch the first time you start a new computer. You can launch the Setup Assistant at any time by clicking the Assist me button at the bottom of the Network Preferences pane. The Setup Assistant guides you through the configuration process.

What information do I need from my ISP to set up my connection?

▼ Your ISP supplies you with an account username and password, both of which you can select. For security, it is best to have a password that is a combination of letters and numbers, and not something obvious such as your or your pet's name, or a birthday. You also need the dialup telephone number for your ISP, and whether the connection uses the TCP/IP or PPP protocols. It may be the case that your TCP/IP settings will be based on your PPP settings.

Connect with a Modem Using Internet Connect

You can easily connect to the Internet with either an internal or external modem, using the Internet Connect utility. This enables you to get online or offline without having to reconfigure any System Preferences or to re-enter your modem information.

The Internet Connect utility helps you to connect to the Internet. It is useful to connect your modem to the Internet; most modems do not stay connected when your computer is sleeping or turned off. You can also use the Internet Connect utility to get online with other types of connections, though those are usually of the always-on type. The Internet Connect window displays a graphical representation of the signal strength of your connection, so that you can quickly and easily monitor the quality of your network.

You can launch Internet Connect by double-clicking it in the Utilities folder, which is in the Applications folder. However, to connect and disconnect more quickly, you can keep the Internet Connect window minimized in the Dock for quick access.

Internet Connect can also help you to configure Bluetooth devices, such as wireless keyboards and mice. You can also use Internet Connect to access the Internet through a Bluetooth modem.

Connect with a Modem Using Internet Connect

① In the Applications Folder, double-click Internet Connect.

The main Internet Connect window appears.

② Click Internal Modem.

The Internal Modem options pane appears.

③ Click 🔃 and select a configuration from the pull-down menu.

Note: For information on how to make a configuration, see the section "Configure a Modem."

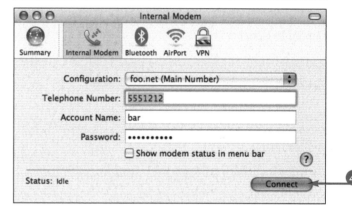

The configuration pane appears.

④ Click Connect.

Your modem dials in and connects to your ISP.

What if I am using a phone line that requires me to dial a number for an outside line?

▼ If you are using a phone line that requires you to dial a number to access an outside line, then you can type that number, followed by a comma, before the ISP's dialup connection number. The comma signals the modem to pause for one second, which gives the phone time to register a dial tone after dialing the access number. If the line needs more time, then you can add extra commas.

Can I add configurations?

▼ Yes. Select Edit Configurations from the Configuration pull-down menu in Step **3**. A pane appears that allows you to type a telephone number, account username, and password, as well as other options. You can change the name by typing a new name in the Description field. Once you are done, click OK to make this setup available from the Configuration pull-down menu. To add more configurations, you can click the Plus button below the Cofigurations list. You can have one configuration for when you are at home, and another for travelling.

Show Modem Status in the Menu Bar

You can configure Mac OS X to show the status of your modem in the Finder's menu bar. This allows you to connect, disconnect, and monitor how the modem is functioning without opening any applications or utilities. It also allows you to check whether your modem is connected or not with one glance.

You can click the Modem Status icon in the menu bar and select Connect from the pull-down menu. If the modem is connected, then you can choose to disconnect. This saves you the step of locating the Internet Connect utility and double-clicking it to launch it.

You cannot use the Modem Status icon to create new modem configurations or to change existing ones. To do this, you need to open the Internet Connect utility, which is located in the Applications folder on your hard drive. For more information on the Internet Utility, see the section "Configure a Modem."

Adding the modem status icon to your Menu bar may result in other icons in the Menu bar shifting their location. This does not alter their functionality, however.

Show Modem Status in the Menu Bar

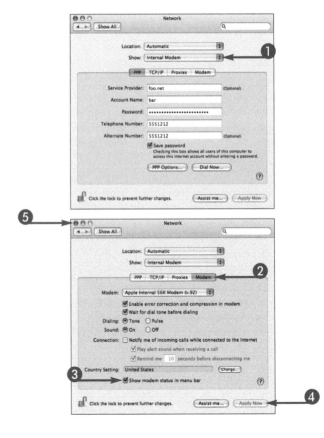

① In the Network Preferences window, click ⬍ and select your modem from the Show pull-down menu.

② Click Modem.

The Modem pane appears.

③ Click Show modem status in menu bar (☐ changes to ☑).

④ Click Apply Now.

⑤ Click ⬤ to close the Preferences window.

A Modem Status icon appears in the Finder menu bar.

Turn Off Modem Sounds

You can turn off the sounds that the modem makes when it connects to a network. This is useful if you work in a shared office space, or simply do not like hearing the clicks and beeps that the modem makes when it dials for a connection. You can also turn the modem sounds back on at any time.

Although the noises may seem random, they can indicate where problems arise when you are establishing a dialup connection. For example, listening to the sounds can tell

you whether the modem is finding a dial tone, whether it is able to dial a number, or whether it is receiving a busy signal on the other end.

If you have trouble connecting with your modem, listening to the modem sounds can help you gather information that can help you solve the problem. If the problem is due to the line to your ISP being busy, you can hear a busy signal. If there is another problem on the phone line, you may be able to hear the message identifying it.

Turn Off Modem Sounds

① In the Network Preferences window, click ⬆ and select your modem from the Show pull-down menu.

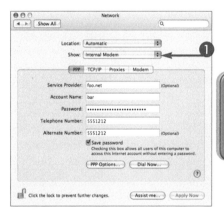

② Click Modem.

The Modem pane appears.

③ Click the Sound Off option (○ changes to ◉).

The modem sounds are turned off.

Choose a Cable or DSL Internet Service

When you use either a cable modem or a digital subscriber line (DSL) to connect to the Internet, you can receive and send data at a much greater speed than that provided by your computer's modem. Your computer modem transfers data to and from your computer at rates ranging from 28.8 to 56 kilobits per second (kbps), while a cable modem and DSL connection can transfer data at rates of up to 1.5 megabits per second (Mbps).

The actual rate, or throughput, depends on many variables, including what type of service to which you subscribe. The quality of your phone line is a factor in DSL throughput speeds, and how many other people in your area also using the service affects access speed on a cable modem. Keep in mind that even a slow DSL or cable connection can still offer much higher access speeds than a modem does.

Both cable modems and DSL connections also have a much lower *latency* than telephone modems. Latency is a measure of how long it takes a packet of data to travel from your computer to the server and then back to your computer. Low latency is important for high bandwidth Internet use, such as voice communications and online gaming.

Cable Modem

If you have cable TV, then cable modems can transfer data to your computer over the same coaxial cable that connects to your television. The actual cable modem is a box that connects to the cable that runs into your house. You can then connect both your television and your computer to the cable — the computer through a cable modem — to receive both cable TV and a high-speed Internet connection. Check with your local cable TV provider for details on pricing and services available.

One potential advantage of cable modems over DSL is peak performance. Cable modems can theoretically transfer data at up to 30 megabits per second (Mbps), while most DSL connections transfer data at up to 10 Mbps. However, your actual top speed depends on your service plan, and real-life bandwidth for both types of service is about the same.

Another potential advantage for cable modem service is simplicity. Most cable TV companies include high-speed Internet access as part of a package deal. This can result in a quick installation, and keep your monthly billing simple.

One of the main drawbacks of using a cable modem is that it is a shared service. A *cable node* connects the cable system's network to all of the coaxial cables in a neighborhood. A single cable node can connect up to 1,000 people. The more people that access the Internet at once, the slower the Internet connection is for each person who is accessing the Internet.

Another drawback is that in a shared structure, other users on the same cable node can theoretically access your computer. Each node, in effect, acts as a local network. Because Mac OS X ships with all sharing settings turned off by default, your Mac is fairly secure. However, if you create a local network at home, then you may be opening up your computer for sharing across a cable node.

DSL Internet Connection

A DSL connection uses your existing telephone lines. In fact, you can use your existing telephone line for both regular calls and your high-speed Internet connection at the same time. Similar to a cable modem, you need to pay a service provider to set up your DSL line and use a DSL modem to connect from the phone line to your Mac.

The DSL modem uses an internal signal splitter that allows voices to transfer at their normal frequency, while separating out the high-frequency data signal. As a result, you can use both your phone and your DSL connection simultaneously. You can even run a fax machine on the phone line while using the DSL portion to connect to the Internet.

Many telephone companies offer DSL service for a monthly fee. This may or may not include the price of the actual DSL modem and installation fees. However, some independent DSL service providers may offer competitive rates and more personalized service. In fact, some companies may be able to provide DSL service without the need of a dedicated phone line, which can reduce your monthly costs. Regulations vary from region to region; you may need to maintain a regular line from the local telephone company in order to receive DSL service.

A DSL connection can offer more security than a cable modem connection, especially if you run a home network and do not want to turn on a firewall. Also, because you do not share your DSL line as you would with a cable modem connection, you do not see a reduction in service when other people in your neighborhood are online.

One drawback to having a DSL connection is that you must be within a particular range of the provider's public exchange or central office to receive good quality service. Also, because the connection relies on the existing copper cables of a typical telephone infrastructure, the quality of service may degrade the farther away you are from the provider's public exchange or central office.

The DSL service is always on, which means that you do not need to connect to the Internet as you do with a telephone modem. Also, like cable, a DSL connection may have an asymmetrical service plan, where the upload speed is not as high as the download speed. For most people this is not a problem, as most of their interaction with the Internet consists of downloading data. If you are planning to run a server, whether to publish Web pages, run a game server, or establish an e-mail service, you should ask about higher upload speeds. In addition, you may need to check the Terms of Service with your service provider, because your plan may restrict you to a set limit of uploading and downloading.

Configure a High-Speed Connection

You can connect to the Internet or other networks through a high-speed connection such as a cable modem or DSL. Both of these services take digital information from the computer and send it across either a cable or telephone connection to a server or a remote computer, and then send information back. Both types of services provide faster access to the Internet than telephone modems do, so you can browse Web sites and send e-mails more quickly.

Both cable and DSL modems connect to your Mac through the Ethernet port. This allows for a better transfer rate than

through the modem port. While a telephone modem provides a connection speed of 28.8 to 56 kilobits per second (Kbps), most cable modems or DSL connections can download data at up to 1.5 megabits per second (Mbps).

When you set up your Mac for the first time, the Mac OS X Setup Assistant helps you to configure many features of your computer, including the connection settings. Whether you use the Network Setup Assistant or the Network Preferences, you need some information from your Internet Service Provider (ISP), such as their access telephone number (if using a telephone or DSL modem), your username, and your password.

Configure a High-Speed Connection

1 Click the Apple icon (🍎).

2 Click System Preferences.

The System Preferences window appears.

3 Click Network.

The Network pane appears.

④ Click and select Built-in Ethernet from the Show pull-down menu.

The Ethernet pane appears.

⑤ Type the information provided by your ISP.

⑥ Click Apply Now.

Your connection is activated.

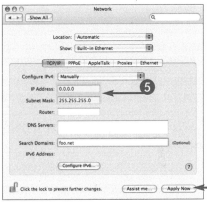

Can I use the Network Setup Assistant to configure any kind of Internet connection?

▼ Yes. You can launch the Setup Assistant at any time, not just when you start up a new computer, to help you configure a new kind of Internet connection. You can do this by clicking the Assist me button at the bottom of the Network Preferences pane. This will step you through the process.

What information do I need from my ISP to set up my high-speed connection?

▼ Your ISP supplies you with an account username and password, both of which you can select. For security, it is best to have a password that is a combination of letters and numbers, and not something obvious such as your pet's name, or a birthday. You also need to know whether to configure TCP/IP manually and your IP address if you are configuring manually. If you connect through your ISP using the DHCP protocol, most of this information will be supplied automatically.

PART V

Configure an AirPort Base Station

You can use an AirPort Base Station, which is a networking accessory that you can plug into a phone line or cable or DSL modem to create a wireless network. All Macs within range that are equipped with AirPort wireless card can use the AirPort Base Station to connect with the Internet wirelessly. Window-based PCs equipped with wireless capability, often called Wi-Fi, can also connect. This is useful if you need to use computers that are away from telephone or cable modem jacks, or if you want to move your laptop computer while remaining connected to the network.

You can protect your wireless network from unauthorized users by assigning password protection to the network. For more information, see the section "Connect to an AirPort Network." Many things affect the range of an AirPort Base Station. Thick walls can block the AirPort signal within your house, and wireless telephones can interfere with the wireless signal. In addition, the orientation of your laptop or desktop computer can affect its reception. If this is of concern to you, many third party vendors sell antennas for AirPort Base Stations, which can increase the effective signal distance.

To configure the AirPort Base Station, you must know the settings from your Internet Service Provider (ISP). Check with your provider for more information.

Configure an AirPort Base Station

① In the Utilities folder, double-click AirPort Setup Assistant.

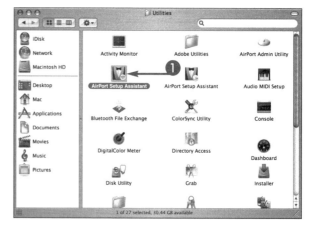

The main AirPort Setup Assistant window appears.

② Click Set up an AirPort Base Station (◯ changes to ◉).

③ Click Continue.

④ Follow the on-screen instructions and type the information given to you by your ISP.

When you are finished, the AirPort Base Station is configured to provide wireless Internet access.

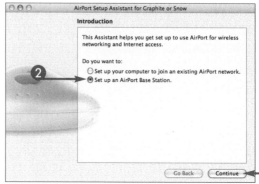

Name an
AirPort Network

You can assign a name to an AirPort wireless network using the AirPort Admin Utility, which is located in the Utilities folder. This is useful if you live or work in an area where there are multiple wireless networks, or you work on a large network.

When you first turn on the AirPort connection on your computer, you are presented with a list of possible networks to join from a pull-down menu that appears when you click the AirPort icon in the menu bar. You can

select any listed network to join if you see multiple networks listed. However, other people may protect their networks with a password.

When you name your network, you can keep track of which network you have joined; this is useful because different networks may have access to different items, such as printers. You can also name your AirPort Base Station. This is useful if you have to troubleshoot different Base Stations on a larger network. You can also add contact and location information to each AirPort Base Station.

Name an AirPort Network

① In the AirPort Admin Utility main window, click an AirPort network.

② Click Configure.

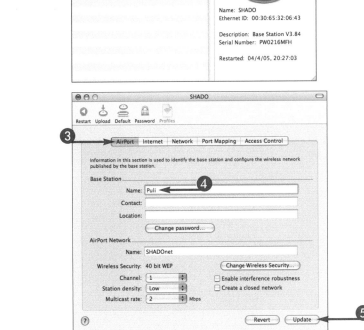

The configuration window appears.

③ Click AirPort.

④ Type a new name.

⑤ Click Update.

The AirPort network name is changed.

PART V

Connect to an AirPort Network

If you have an AirPort card or other wireless networking card installed in your Mac, then you can connect wirelessly to the Internet and local networks. This enables you to browse the Web, send e-mail, and connect with other computers without having to plug in cables or configure any network settings.

If you are trying to connect to an AirPort network that is protected by a password, then you are prompted to enter the password before being allowed to join the network. If

you do not know the password, then you can cancel the attempt to join the network and join another network.

You can use the Internet Connect utility to connect to the Internet. The Internet Connect window displays a graphical representation of the signal strength of your connection, so that you can easily monitor the quality of your network.

You can keep the Internet Connect window minimized in the Dock for quick access. This allows you to connect and disconnect more quickly than if you have to access Internet Connect in the Utilities folder.

Connect to an AirPort Network

1 Click the AirPort menu (📶).

2 Click Turn AirPort On.

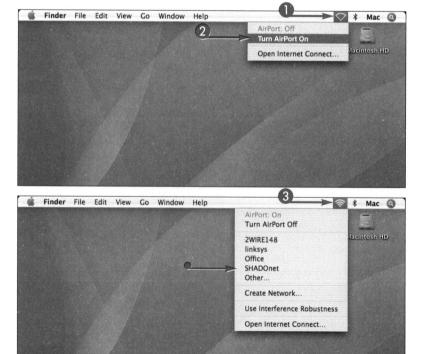

3 Click 📶 again.

● A list of available AirPort networks appears.

④ Click a network.

⑤ If the network is password-protected, then type the password.

⑥ Click OK.

If the network is not protected, you are not prompted for a password.

What if I cannot see an AirPort icon in the Finder menu bar?

▼ If you cannot see the AirPort icon in the Finder menu bar, then you need to activate it. Click and then click System Preferences. When the System Preferences window appears, click Network. In the Network pane, select AirPort from the Show pull-down menu. In the pane below, click the Show AirPort status in menu bar option (☐ changes to ☑). When you close the window, the AirPort icon appears in the Finder menu bar.

How can I maximize signal quality in a wireless connection?

▼ Various items in offices and homes can interfere with your wireless network signal. For example, solid doors, walls, cordless phones, and microwave ovens can either block the wireless signal or partially jam it with their own signal. If you experience interference despite being in close range to an AirPort Base Station, then you can select the Use Interface Robustness option by clicking the AirPort icon in the Finder menu bar. A check mark appears next to the option (☑).

PART V

Elements of Safari

Y ou can use Safari — the default Mac OS X Web browser created by Apple — to peruse any page of information posted to the Web. Web pages can include text, pictures, sound, and video.

Web pages also include links, called hyperlinks. Hyperlinks usually look like underlined or highlighted text, although images can also serve as links. When you click a link, it generally takes you to another Web page.

The Safari interface consists of a standard window, containing minimize and close buttons, a variety of toolbars, and the main pane, in which the Web page appears. You can customize the interface of Safari to make surfing the Web even easier.

You must be connected to the Internet to view Web pages. However, you can use Safari to view many other types of files that you store locally on your computer, such as Web-ready image files, text files, and HTML files.

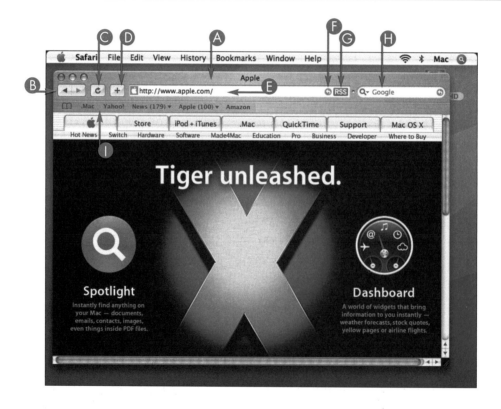

A Title Bar

You can grab the title bar to move the Safari window on the screen. In this, Safari's title bar is similar to a Finder window's title bar; it also features window control buttons to close, minimize, and expand the window. In addition, Safari's title bar displays the title of the Web page that you are currently viewing. If you have not enabled the Status Bar, this is the only place you can grab to move the Safari window.

B Back/Forward Buttons

You can use these buttons to navigate through Web pages that you have recently visited. When you click the Back button, you return to a page that you have previously viewed. You can also click the Forward button to view previously viewed pages; however, this button is enabled only if you have already moved back at least one page. You can click and hold either button to display a pull-down menu that shows a list of previously visited pages; you can scroll down this menu to select a page to jump to immediately.

C Stop/Reload Button

While a Web page is loading, you can click the Stop button to halt the process. This is useful if a page is failing to load or is loading improperly. While the page is loading, the button looks like an X; clicking this stops the page from loading. After the page has loaded, the button features the icon seen here. After the page has completely loaded in Safari, you can click the Reload button; then Safari asks the remote server to send the Web page again. This is useful if the page has not downloaded correctly. Reloading the page also updates it if there has been any change to its content in the time since you originally loaded the page. Sometimes Safari will show you a page cached in its memory. To force a full reload, press the Shift key while clicking the Reload button.

D Add Bookmark Button

When a Web page has loaded, you can click the Add Bookmark button to add the page to your list of bookmarks. When you click the Add Bookmark button, a dialog appears that allows you to name the bookmark; by default, the bookmark name is the title of the Web page. You can rename the bookmark if the title of all pages of the Web site is the same, so that you do not end up with the same title denoting different pages in your Bookmarks list. You can also specify whether the bookmark is stored in the Bookmarks bar or the Bookmarks menu. For more information about the Bookmarks bar, see the section "Hide the Bookmarks Bar."

E Address Field

You can type the Web address, also called a Uniform Resource Locator (URL), of any Web page that you want to visit, in the Address field. After you type the URL and press Return on your keyboard, Safari displays that page. The Address field also displays the URL of the current page, even if you arrived at this page by choosing a bookmark or clicking a link on another Web page. The Address field also shows a small icon, called a favicon, to the left of the URL. Web sites can create custom icons that also appear next to the name of the site in your Bookmarks menu. Not all sites have them and they add no functionality other than as a quick visual reference when you browse your Bookmarks menu.

F SnapBack

Clicking the SnapBack button (🔲) returns you to the SnapBack page. This is the default Web page that Safari first displays when you launch the program. You can change the SnapBack setting by clicking the History menu and selecting the Mark Page for SnapBack option. Then, you can later click the SnapBack button to return to that Web page immediately, as long as you have not changed windows in Safari.

G RSS Feeds

Some Web sites provide their content in Real Simple Syndication (RSS) format, which Safari 2.0 supports. When you view the RSS feed from a Web page, for example from the Web site of a newspaper, you see the headlines and a summary of the top articles. You can then click a link to see the complete article. You can organize RSS feeds by category and click the category in the Bookmarks bar. You can then select individual Web sites or their RSS feeds to view. The number shows how many new articles have appeared since your last viewing.

H Google Search

You can search the Web using the Google search engine. Start by typing terms in this window and pressing Return on your keyboard. Safari displays a Google Web page with the results of your search.

I Bookmarks Bar

You can store your favorite bookmarks in the Bookmarks bar. This allows you to access these Web pages with one click. You can add URLs to the Bookmarks bar using the Add Bookmarks button. You can remove bookmarks by dragging the Web page's name above the Bookmarks bar. You can also rearrange the order of bookmarks by dragging them left or right.

Customize Safari's Buttons

Y ou can customize the button bar in Safari's interface by choosing which buttons appear and which do not. This useful feature allows you to see only the buttons that you use most often, while hiding the rest.

You can also decide where each button appears in the Address bar. When you have the Customize Address Bar sheet open, you can drag any Address bar item to move it; other items in the Address bar move out of the way automatically. You cannot drag Address bar items when the Customize Address Bar sheet is not open.

The buttons that you can show or hide include the Forward and Back navigation buttons, the Home button that sends you to your Web browser's home page, AutoFill that completes forms using data from your Address Book or previously filled forms on Web pages, Text Size that makes the text on the Web pages larger or smaller, Stop/Reload, Add Bookmark, Print, Google Search, the Address window, and Report Bug that sends a bug report to Apple when you find that something has gone wrong.

Customize Safari's Buttons

① Click View.

② Click Customize Address Bar.

The Customize Address Bar sheet appears.

③ Click the button you want to appear in the Address bar.

④ Drag the button to the desired location on the Address bar.

To make the button disappear, you can drag the button out of the Address bar when the Customize Address Bar sheet is open.

Show Safari's Status Bar

You can enable the Status bar in Safari. This is useful because the Status bar shows you the target for a link on a Web page without your having to click the link. For example, you can see if a link will take you to a new Web site or open a new window.

The Status bar appears at the bottom of the Safari window. It displays the target of a link when you hover the cursor over the link. The target information disappears when you move the cursor away from the link. You can also click and hold the cursor on the Status bar to drag the Safari window.

By default, the Status bar is not displayed in Safari. This can save you room onscreen if you have a small monitor and want to extend the main Safari window as far down on the screen as possible. However, without the Status bar visible, the only place you can use to drag a Safari window on the screen is the Title bar.

Show Safari's Status Bar

① Click View.

② Click Show Status Bar.

● The Status bar appears at the bottom of the Safari window.

A check mark appears next to the Status bar menu item if the Status bar is already visible.

Hide the Bookmarks Bar

You can customize Safari's interface to hide the Bookmarks bar. This simplifies the interface and takes up less screen space. However, you can still use the Bookmarks menu to access your favorite Web sites.

The Bookmarks bar appears between Safari's Address bar and the main window, where the Web pages display. It lists the bookmarks you have placed in it, along with names of RSS categories and, in parentheses, the number of new news items available. If you have more bookmarks than space in the Bookmarks bar, arrows appear on the right of the bar; you can click these arrows to access more of your bookmarks. You can click and drag any bookmark in the Bookmark bar to move it to any position.

Hiding this bar erases that space and allows you to see more of the Web pages you have opened in Safari and reduces the amount of scrolling you need to do to view the entire contents of the Web page. You can choose to show the Bookmarks bar again at any time.

Hide the Bookmarks Bar

① Click View.

② Click Hide Bookmarks Bar.

● The Bookmarks bar disappears.

To display the Bookmarks bar, you can deselect the Bookmarks bar option in the View menu.

Hide the Address Bar

You can customize Safari's interface so that the Address bar is not visible. This gives you more screen space for viewing Web pages, but it also means that you are not able to type a new Web address or use any of the navigation buttons. You also will not have access to the buttons that normally appear in the Address bar, such as Back, Forward, and the Google search field.

When you hide the Address bar, the Safari window automatically resizes so that the dimensions of the window do not change. Instead, the window displays more of the Web page. When you enable the Address bar again, you will see less of the displayed Web page.

You may want to do this if you are using Safari as a presentation tool, or showing a single Web page, and you do not want viewers to leave that page. However, you can still use the Bookmarks menu or, if it is visible, the Bookmarks bar, to go to a different Web page.

Hide the Address Bar

1 Click View.

2 Click Hide Address Bar.

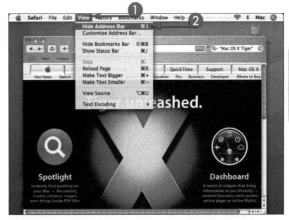

● The Address bar disappears.

To show the Address bar again, you can select the Address Bar option in the View menu.

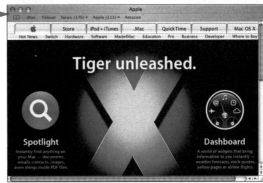

Enable Tabbed Browsing

You can use tabbed browsing in Safari to view multiple Web pages in one Safari window. This is a useful way to display multiple Web pages at once without having to take up screen space by opening multiple Safari windows.

The tab bars appear below the Bookmarks bar. Each tab displays the title of the Web page that appears in the tab. Clicking the tab bar opens the content of that tab in the main Safari window. Each tab bar also contains a Close button. Clicking this Close button closes only that tab.

If you close the main Safari window, then you also close all of the tabbed contents.

As you open more tabs, the size of individual tab bars shrinks. If the tab bars become too small to display the titles of their Web pages, then you can open a new Safari window with additional tabs.

Opening too many tabs can slow down older computers or computers with less RAM. To browse more efficiently, it is a good idea to close tabs when you are done with them.

Enable Tabbed Browsing

① Click Safari.

② Click Preferences.

The Preferences window appears.

③ Click Tabs.

The Tabs pane appears.

④ Click Enable Tabbed Browsing
(☐ changes to ☑).

⑤ Click ◉ to close the Preferences window.

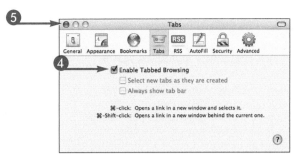

⑥ Press ⌘-T.

● A new tab appears.

Can I open a link from a Web page in a new tab?

▼ Yes. You can ⌘-click a link in a Web page to open the target page in a new tab. You can also Control-click to display a pull-down menu, from which you can select Open Link in New Tab.

Can Safari immediately display the Web page that I open in a new tab?

▼ Yes. In the Tabs pane of the Safari Preferences window, click the Select new tabs as they are created option (☐ changes to ☑). When you open a Web page in a new tab, Safari switches from the tab that you are currently viewing to the new tab. If you do not check this option, the tab loads in the background. You can open that tab by clicking its tab bar.

Can I open a bookmark in a new tab?

▼ Not if you are selecting a bookmark from the Bookmark menu or the Bookmarks bar. Bookmarks open in the current tab. However, you can create a new tab by pressing ⌘-T and then selecting a bookmark. You can also press and hold ⌘ and click a bookmark in the Bookmark bar or the Bookmark menu.

Enable and Disable Cookies

You can tell Safari to accept or reject cookies. Web sites often use cookies to log in registered users, to track which pages a visitor has previously accessed, and to enable you to purchase items from a commerce site. You can set Safari to reject all cookies in order to maintain some anonymity as you browse the Web, or enable cookies to access Web sites that require them.

Cookies are small files that Web sites send to your Web browser. They help to identify individual users and what they have done on the issuing Web site. Cookies generally do not pose a security risk on their own. However, if you share

your computer account with other users, then you may want to disable cookies to prevent these users from accessing your accounts on cookie-enabled, registration-only Web sites.

You can maintain greater security even when browsing with cookies, by setting Safari to accept cookies only from the Web sites that you choose to visit. Many Web sites host advertising or links to other Web sites that send cookies in order to track the number of successful ad views. By choosing this option, you can access your favorite sites without giving away information to others.

Enable Cookies

① Click Safari.

② Click Preferences.

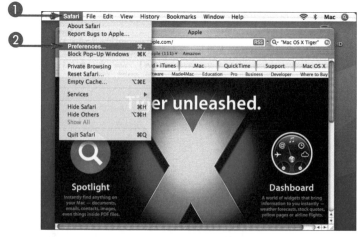

The Preferences window appears.

③ Click Security.

The Security pane appears.

④ Click the Always option for Accept Cookies (○ changes to ◉).

Your browser accepts cookies.

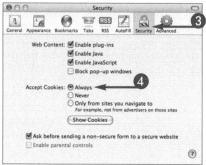

Disable Cookies

① Click Safari.

② Click Preferences.

The Preferences window appears.

③ Click Security.

The Security pane appears.

④ Click the Never option for Accept Cookies
(○ changes to ●).

Your browser will not accept cookies.

**Does disabling cookies in Safari affect any
other applications?**

▼ Yes. If you turn off cookies completely,
then other applications that require access
to these cookies, such as Sherlock, may be
affected. If you find that disabling cookies
affects other applications, then you can use
Safari's Preferences to turn cookies back on
while you use the other applications, and
then disable the cookies again in Safari
when you are done.

**Can I see what cookies Safari has accepted,
and get rid of the ones that I do not want?**

▼ Yes. To see what cookies you have accepted
when browsing the Web with Safari, open the
Safari Preferences, click the Security icon, and
then click the Show Cookies button. A window
appears, listing all of the cookies that Safari
has accepted. You can then examine the
contents of the cookies, such as the server
from which they originated. You can select an
individual cookie and delete it by clicking the
Remove button. You can also delete all cookies
by clicking the Remove All button. However,
you may need to re-register for membership
sites after doing so.

Elements of the Bookmarks Library

You can use Safari's Bookmarks Library to organize your collected bookmarks of Web pages, including the ones that you have saved in the Bookmarks bar and the Bookmark menu. This gives you one interface for managing all of the saved locations that you have visited and want to visit again.

You can access the Bookmarks Library by clicking the icon at the left side of the Bookmarks bar; the Bookmarks Library appears in the main pane of the Safari window. Clicking the icon again returns you to the last Web page

that you viewed. If you do not have the Bookmarks bar visible, then you can access the Bookmarks Library by clicking the Bookmark menu and selecting Show All Bookmarks.

The Bookmarks Library also allows you to view items in the Address Book, Rendezvous, and History collections. The Rendezvous collection discovers and shows the Web addresses of printers, Web cams, and other devices on your local network. The History folder keeps track of Web sites that you have visited in the past, and organizes them by date.

A Bookmarks Library Icon

You can access the Bookmarks Library by clicking this icon. The Library appears in the main pane of the Safari window, temporarily replacing the displayed Web page. You can return to the last Web page viewed by clicking this icon again or by clicking the Back button. The Bookmarks Library icon cannot be dragged off the Bookmarks bar and deleted as other icons can. If you hide the Bookmarks bar, you can access the Bookmarks library by clicking the Bookmarks menu and selecting Show All Bookmarks.

B Collections Column

This column displays your bookmark collection folders. You can use the default folders, or create your own, to organize your bookmarks as you would folders in the Finder. The Bookmarks bar and Bookmark menu collections show what Bookmarks you have saved in the Bookmarks bar and the Bookmarks menu, respectively. You can edit the contents of the Bookmarks bar and the Bookmark menu by clicking their collections; the contents appear in the Bookmarks column. You can also reorganize the collections by dragging them into any order. You can also reduce or enlarge the width of the Collections Column by dragging the vertical line that divides it from the main pane of the Bookmarks window.

C Collections Folder

You can use folders to organize your bookmarks, just as you can use folders in the Finder to organize files and applications. By default, Safari comes with a variety of collection folders, but you can delete them and add your own. Deleting a folder also deletes the contents of the folder. You can rename existing collections by selecting the collection's name and typing a new one, just as you would for a folder in the Finder. You can also drag a collection folder to the Desktop to save or share the bookmarks or drag a folder up or down to reorganize the list of folders.

D Add Collection Button

You can click this button to add a new collection folder to the Collections column. This is useful if you want to reorganize your bookmarks. You can also make duplicates of a bookmark and place the duplicates in different folders. For example, you could place the bookmark to a news site in a News collection folder, as well as a Daily collection folder. The new collection folder appears with the name Untitled Folder. You can then select the folder name and type a new name. To delete a collection folder, you can select it and press Delete.

E Bookmarks Column

This is where the contents of your bookmark collection folders appear when you click the collection's icon in the Collection column. Also, if you click the History icon in the Collection column, this is where your history of visited sites, organized by day, appears. You can rearrange bookmarks by clicking and dragging them within a collection folder. You can also double-click a bookmark to open it in Safari or press Delete with that bookmark selected to delete it.

F Add Bookmark Folder Button

You can add a new bookmark folder in the Bookmarks column by clicking this button. You can also rename existing folders by selecting the collection's name and typing a new one, just as you would for a folder in the Finder. Using folders inside bookmark collections is a useful way to organize large collections of bookmarks. When you click the Bookmarks menu, you see an arrow next to a folder you have created, signifying that there are more bookmarks to be displayed when you scroll down to that folder. You can remove a folder from the Bookmarks window by selecting the folder and pressing Delete.

G RSS Count

This number, which appears in parentheses after the Bookmarks bar and folders, shows you how many new items are available in the RSS feeds for the sites you have placed in the Bookmarks bar and folders. This can alert you when new news appears.

PART V

Move a Bookmark

Y ou can move a bookmark into any collection, from the Bookmarks bar to the Bookmark menu, or vice versa. This is a useful tool in helping you to organize your bookmarks.

When you create a bookmark, a dialog allows you to place the bookmark in the Bookmarks bar, the Bookmark menu, or a collection. However, if you want to reorganize your bookmarks, or if you placed the bookmark incorrectly, then you can move the bookmark to a better location, or to a new collection. You can also move a copy of the bookmark

if you want to be able to access the saved Web page from more than one place.

Where you place a bookmark is not important, as long as you can access it easily. This is why it is useful to be able to move bookmarks. You may at first place a bookmark in the Bookmark bar, but then decide that you do not want to have the Bookmark bar visible, or you find you have too many bookmarks in the Bookmarks bar. Instead of making a new bookmark in a new place, you can move an existing bookmark.

Move a Bookmark

① Click a bookmark in the Bookmark column.

② Drag the bookmark to the target collection in the Collections column.

You can hold down the Option key while dragging the icon to place a copy of it in the target collection.

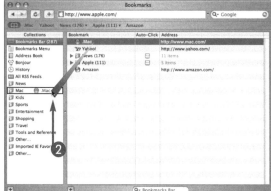

Delete a Bookmark

Y ou can easily delete bookmarks from the Bookmarks bar, Bookmark menu, or a collection. This is useful if a Web site becomes defunct, or if you no longer want to visit it, or you want to reduce your collection of bookmarks.

Once you delete a bookmark, it is no longer accessible in the Bookmarks Library. However, you can click the History collection in the Library to open the Web site and bookmark it again. There is a time limit in this, though, as the History collection only remembers sites you have viewed within the past few days. The site will be

unavailable if you have cleared the History list or if you have enabled Private Browsing. For more on Private Browsing, see the section "Enable Private Browsing in Safari."

You can also delete duplicate bookmarks if you have the same bookmark in more than one place — for example, if you have a site in both the Bookmarks bar and in the Bookmarks menu. Deleting the copy does not affect the original, and deleting the original does not affect the copy. This is not the same as with regular files in the Finder, where an alias becomes useless if you delete the original.

Delete a Bookmark

① Click a bookmark in the Bookmarks column.

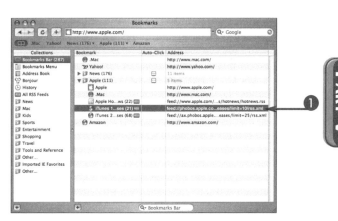

② Press Delete.

● Safari deletes the bookmark.

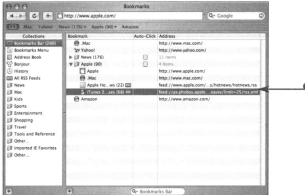

Drag Images from Safari

You can download most images that appear on Web pages by dragging the images to your Desktop. This is useful if you want to save a single image rather than saving the entire Web page.

Once you drag the image to your Desktop, you can rename it and edit it, just like any other file on your hard disk. You can also open it in an image-editing application and save it in a different file format. Keep in mind that most images on the Web are copyrighted intellectual property, and

therefore are not available for reuse without a licensing agreement. This may also include personal use.

Many images on Web pages have long and nondescriptive names; if your Desktop is set to arrange items by name, the downloaded image may not appear where you think it should. In addition, many images on Web pages are not downloadable. For example, you may not be able to download a Flash animation by dragging, or see all of an animated image without specialized software.

Drag Images from Safari

① Click and hold an image.

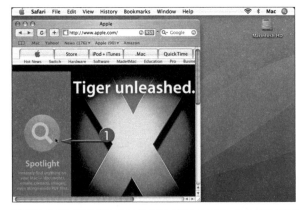

② Drag the image to your Desktop.

● The image file's icon appears on your Desktop.

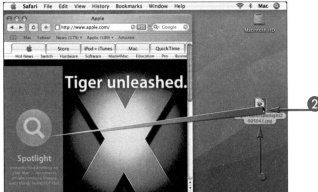

Copy Text from Safari to TextEdit

You can copy text from Web pages and save it in TextEdit so that you can read it later, print it out, or e-mail it to a friend. This is useful if you need to read the content of a Web site while you are away from the computer, or if text on the Web page is hard to read due to text size or low legibility between the text and the page's background.

In addition, after you have saved the text from a Web page, you can edit it or comment upon it. However, most content on Web pages is copyrighted, so be careful before reproducing or sharing content from Web pages.

You can use any text editor or word processor other than TextEdit to save text taken from a Web page; all Macintoshes ship with TextEdit for free. You can also drag the text that you have selected on the Web page to the Desktop, where it is saved as a clipping. You can read and share clippings, or copy their contents to a word-processing application.

Copy Text from Safari to TextEdit

1 Select text on a Web page.

2 Press ⌘-C.

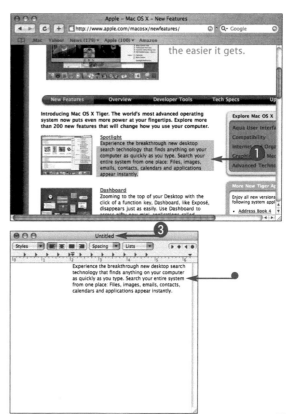

3 Open a new file in TextEdit.

4 Press ⌘-V.

● The text appears in the TextEdit window.

Add an RSS Feed to Safari

Y ou can take advantage of Real Simple Syndication feeds, which are specially formatted news feeds created by news and other Web sites. These feeds push to you updates and top stories; when you have bookmarked a feed, Safari will notify you when there is new content from the feed. This saves you the trouble of repeatedly checking Web sites to see if the content has updated, or the possibility of missing when news breaks.

You do not need to know if a Web site offers an RSS feed; Safari discovers this for you automatically. If a site you visit offers the option of an RSS feed, Safari displays an RSS icon in the right side of the Address field. You can click the RSS icon and Safari will display the RSS feed from that Web site. You can click the RSS icon again to return to the normal Web page.

You can bookmark both the normal Web site and the RSS feed from that site. If you bookmark the RSS feed, Safari notifies you when new news items are available on that feed.

Add an RSS Feed to Safari

Note: When you visit a Web site with an RSS feed available, the RSS icon is visible.

① Click the RSS icon.

The RSS feed page appears.

② Click the Add Bookmark button.

③ Type a name for the bookmark.

④ Click 🔽 and select the bookmark's location.

⑤ Click Add.

The RSS feed is bookmarked.

Search RSS Feeds

Safari allows you to search your bookmarked RSS feeds by URL, name of the feed, and by its parent. A feed's parent is defined by Safari as the collection or folder within a collection within which you placed the feed's bookmark. This is useful when you want to find a feed but cannot remember where you have bookmarked it, or if you want to browse bookmarked RSS feeds either by name or by category.

You can search for words in the parent, which can help you narrow your search. For example, if you have a Sports collection folder, you can search all your RSS bookmarks for Sports; this should narrow the results to RSS feeds related to sports.

The search feature is powered by Spotlight, which means that it will start returning results as soon as you begin entering text. For more information on Spotlight, see Chapter 1.

Search RSS Feeds

① In the Bookmarks window, click All RSS Feeds.

Note: *To open the Bookmarks window, see the section "Elements of the Bookmark Library."*

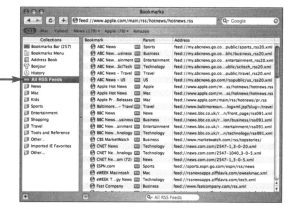

② Type the search parameter.

● Results appear above.

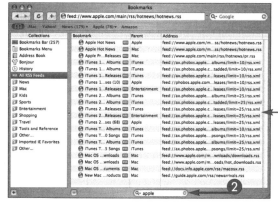

Enable Private Browsing in Safari

You can enable Private Browsing in Safari. This feature helps protect your identity and personal information when you are browsing the Internet from other people who share your computer. Private Browsing also protects your personal information if you use Safari on a public terminal, such as a computer in a coffeehouse or other public place.

When Private Browsing is on, what Web pages you have viewed are not added to Safari's History. In addition, any downloaded items are automatically removed from Safari's Downloads window; AutoFill information, such as names and passwords, are not saved; and the words entered into the Google search field are not saved.

Private Browsing does not disable the Back and Forward buttons, so you can still move back and forth between pages you have viewed. However, if you close the browser window, you cannot use these buttons to go back to previously viewed pages. This makes it easier to share a computer; rather than having to clear Safari's history and cache, as well as quit and reopen the application, you can simply close a browser window and be secure that all your personal information is safe.

Enable Private Browsing in Safari

1 Click Safari.

2 Click Private Browsing.

An alert window appears.

3 Click OK.

● The History window remains cleared.

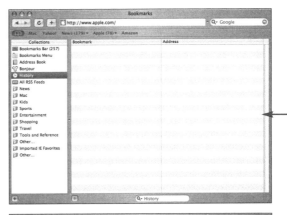

● The Downloads window automatically clears itself after you download items.

PART V

Can I still access Web sites that require cookies when I have enabled Private Browsing?

▼ Yes. Private Browsing precludes Safari from saving AutoFill information as well as placing items in the cache and History. However, it does allow the use of cookies as set in Safari's Preferences. This means that you can still access various Web-based e-mail services and other cookie-enabled Web sites even while using Private Browsing. For more information about cookies, see the section "Enable and Disable Cookies."

Can I disable Private Browsing easily?

▼ Yes. To return to regular browsing, so that the History feature is enabled, along with the AutoFill function, you can simply click the Safari menu and select Private Browsing so that this option is unchecked. You cannot go back and find the history of Web pages browsed while Private Browsing was on, but Safari begins tracking pages viewed as soon as Private Browsing is turned off.

Save Archives
of Web Pages

You can use Safari to save archives of Web pages you have loaded. This is useful if you want to save the contents and layout of a Web page you have visited, complete with layout and images. The archived Web pages also include active links, so that you can click the displayed archived page and Safari takes you to the linked page on the Web.

The saved Web page appears as a file with the Safari icon and the word Archive. This distinguishes it visually from a standard Safari document icon, which does not have the word Archive.

You can share these archived Web pages with anyone who has Safari. They can double-click the archived site icon and the entire page, complete with images and links, appears in their browser. However, these archived Web pages may have large file sizes, as they contain both the layout information and the images on the page.

You can also use the archived page as you would a live Web page. You can view the HTML source code, copy the images, and anything you would do with a regular Web page.

Save Archives of Web Pages

Note: *Have the page you want to save loaded in Safari.*

① Click File.

② Click Save As.

A Save dialog appears.

③ Click ◆ and navigate to the desired location for saving.

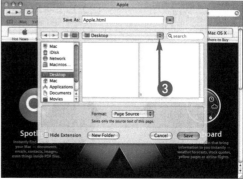

④ Click Format ⬍ and select Web Archive.

⑤ Click Save.

● The page saves in Archive format.

You can double-click the Web Archive to open it in Safari. Safari will display a local file path rather than a URL.

PART V

Can I save just one frame of a Web page composed of multiple frames?	Can I save archives of all Web pages?
▼ Yes. You can save just one frame of a multiframe Web page; this is useful with pages that have frames for navigation or pages that place ads in frames. Press the Control key and click the frame you want to save. When a contextual menu appears, select Save Frame As. Follow Step **3** and following in the task above.	▼ No. Some Web pages are designed to prevent people from saving items, such as images, or the entire content of the Web page. Some pages may present information or images in Macromedia Flash format, which you cannot archive; others use dynamically generated pages that build the page content from a remote database.

Set Up an E-Mail Account

You can set up and configure Mail to access any existing e-mail accounts so that you can use Mail to send, receive, and manage your e-mail correspondence. This provides you with a central application from which you can handle all of your e-mail.

The first time that you launch Mail, it asks you for the information that it needs to access your account. You must have an e-mail account with an ISP and you must know your username, account name, password, the sending and receiving mail server names, and what kind of account it is. For example, it can be from a .Mac account, or it may use the POP, IMAP, or Exchange protocols.

You can also set up new accounts for Mail to check, even after you have gone through the initial configuration. This allows you to check multiple e-mail accounts. You still need to know all of the information listed above for each new account.

If you make a mistake when you set up your account, or you have changed account information such as your password, then you can change these settings in Mail to update the account information. You can also delete accounts that you no longer use.

Set Up an E-Mail Account

① Click Mail.

② Click Preferences.

The Preferences window appears.

③ Click Accounts.

The Account Information pane appears.

④ Click Add (⊞).

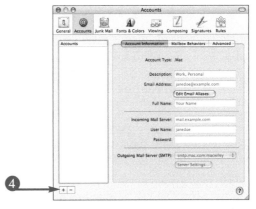

A configuration pane appears.

⑤ Enter your account information.

The Account Information data will appear in the Accounts list.

⑥ Click Continue

Note: *Mail configures access with the specified remote e-mail server.*

Note: *You may receive a message asking you to confirm the process. If so, click Continue.*

Mail is configured to receive your e-mail.

How can I find out the information that I need to configure my account?

▼ Your account information is available from your ISP, or from your company's technical support department if your e-mail account is supplied by your company.

How can I delete an account?

▼ You can delete an account by opening the Mail Preferences and then clicking the Account Information tab. In the Accounts column, select the name of the account that you want to delete. Then click the Remove Account button (⊟).

What are the different types of e-mail accounts?

▼ A .Mac account is an e-mail account that Apple provides as part of its .Mac service. A Post Office Protocol (POP) account is used by some ISPs; it holds all of your messages on a server until you connect to your account, at which point all items are transferred to your computer. An Internet Message Access Protocol (IMAP) account allows you to view your messages, but leaves them on the server. This allows you to access your messages from more than one computer.

Get Mail on a Secure Connection

You can access your e-mail over a secure connection to your mail server if your ISP offers this service. This gives you increased security to prevent other users from gaining access to your e-mails and attached documents. It will not preclude others from sending you spam or other unwanted e-mail messages, however.

This does not mean that anyone can automatically gain access to your e-mail account if you have not configured a secure connection; your account is still protected by your password. However, a secure connection guards against intrusions by skilled malicious parties.

These secure connections use the Secure Sockets Layer (SSL) protocol. This open-standard protocol is designed to offer protection to users of e-mail servers. If your mail server does not support the SSL protocol, then you will receive an "Unable to connect" error message. For more information about whether your ISP supports a SSL connection, contact your ISP's technical support.

You can change back from a secure connection at any time. This is useful if you have been having trouble connecting to your ISP.

Get Mail on a Secure Connection

① Click Mail.

② Click Preferences.

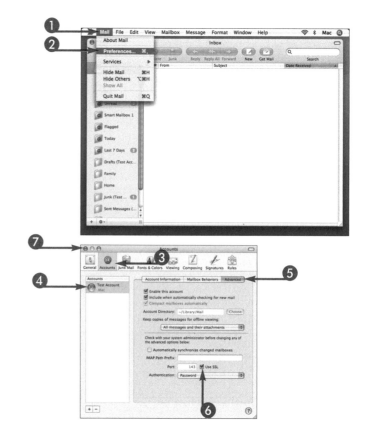

The Preferences window appears.

③ Click Accounts.

④ Click an account.

⑤ Click Advanced.

The Advanced options pane appears.

⑥ Click the Use SSL option (☐ changes to ☑).

⑦ Click ◉ to close the Preferences window.

Note: *You should only change the port number if your Network Administrator tells you to.*

Import E-Mail from Other Applications

Y ou can import e-mail messages into Mail from other e-mail clients. This allows you to migrate from another e-mail application to Mail, as well as to manage accounts that you may access from a number of e-mail clients in one place.

Your imported e-mails are stored in a mailbox called Import, which is located in the On My Mac area of the mailbox list. You can create new mailboxes and drag the imported messages into them. Mail does not import empty mailboxes.

This is useful if you have been using another e-mail client other than Mail, but want to move to Mail. The importing process may not save all your folder structures from the other e-mail application, so you may have to create new mailboxes in Mail and sort your imported messages manually.

You cannot import e-mail messages and mailboxes directly from an e-mail account you access via a Web interface, such as Yahoo! Mail. However, you may be able to access the e-mails directly from Mail. For more information, see the section "Set Up an E-Mail Account."

Import E-Mail from Other Applications

① Click File.

② Click Import Mailboxes.

The Import window appears.

③ Click the application from which you are importing e-mail (○ changes to ●).

④ Click Continue.

Note: *Different instructions appear, depending on the application that you choose.*

Mail imports your e-mail from the other application.

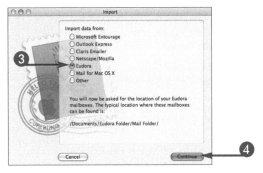

PART V

Create a Mailbox

Y ou can create new mailboxes in Mail. This feature allows you to organize your received and sent messages in different ways, for example, by project, sender, or month.

You can have as many mailboxes as you want. New mailboxes appear along in the left column of the Mail interface, under the Inbox, Outbox, and other default mailboxes. You can also create one mailbox for a specific account and another mailbox for another account, or a mailbox that receives e-mails from multiple accounts. You can even place a mailbox within another mailbox; these are

called subfolders. For example, you can have a 2005 mailbox, with 12 subfolders, one for each month, or you can have a Family mailbox with a subfolder for each family member.

In the Mail interface, some mailboxes are colored blue. These contain both e-mail messages and other mailboxes. This alerts you to messages, because mailboxes that only contain other mailboxes do not have a color.

Some IMAP e-mail servers may not allow you to create mailboxes with subfolders. Check with your ISP if you encounter problems.

Create a Mailbox

① Click Mailbox.

② Click New Mailbox.

A New Mailbox dialog appears.

③ Click ⊞ and select where you want to store your e-mail from the pull-down menu.

Note: *If you do not have an IMAP account, then your only option is On My Mac, which stores e-mail on your computer.*

④ Type a name for the mailbox.

⑤ Click OK.

A new mailbox appears.

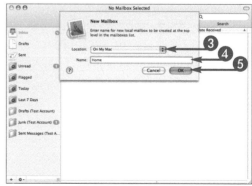

Rename a Mailbox

You can rename mailboxes in Mail. This is useful if you decide that you want to reorganize your mailboxes, or if you have made an error when you originally named a mailbox. Renaming a mailbox can also change the mailbox order, as mailboxes are arranged in alphabetical order within each account.

In an IMAP account, you cannot change the name of a mailbox unless you are online and connected to that mail server. You also cannot change a mailbox's name to the name of one that already exists on the server. Your ISP's

e-mail server may also forbid the use of certain characters, such as colons or slashes. If you cannot change the name of a mailbox, first make sure you are online; then try to rename it a different name. Check with your ISP's technical support to find out which characters are forbidden, and if you have further problems renaming mailboxes.

You also cannot rename the Inbox, Outbox, Drafts, Sent, or other special default mailboxes. You also cannot move these mailboxes.

Rename a Mailbox

① Click a mailbox.

② Click Mailbox.

③ Click Rename.

The mailbox name is highlighted.

④ Type a new name.

The mailbox is renamed.

Move a Mailbox

I n Mail, you can move a mailbox from within one account to within another in your mailbox list. This creates a copy of that mailbox. You can also move a mailbox into another mailbox within one user account, or move it outside another mailbox, changing a subfolder to a mailbox. This enables you to rearrange entire folders of e-mail, rather than having to drag many individual messages.

You cannot move mailboxes within a single account. By default, all mailboxes within an account are arranged

alphabetically. For example, if you have an e-mail account named "Joe" and have the folders A, B, and C in that account, the folders will always be in that order.

You can make a copy of a mailbox by holding down the Option key while dragging it. To back up all of your messages on an IMAP account, you can simply drag a mailbox from the IMAP account into your On My Mac folder. This ensures that you have a copy of all your e-mail messages on your own computer, not just on a remote server. This also enables you to access the e-mail messages even when you are offline.

① Click a mailbox.

② Drag the mailbox to a new location.

You can hold down the Option key while dragging to copy the mailbox to the new location.

The mailbox appears in a new location.

Delete a Mailbox

You can delete a mailbox from your mailbox list. This is useful if you have reorganized your e-mails, or if you have a folder full of old e-mails that you want to delete. You can also delete mailboxes that are local copies of mailboxes on an IMAP account, such as ones you have copied into the On My Mac account. For more information, see the section "Rename a Mailbox."

If you do not have proper permissions to delete local files, then when you try to delete a mailbox, a message appears, telling you that you cannot delete the mailbox.

You can select the mailbox and use the Get Info feature to see if this is the case. For more information on permissions, see Chapter 3. You may also not be able to delete a mailbox because of server-related issues; you can contact your ISP if this is the case.

You cannot delete the default mailboxes. These include the Inbox, Drafts, Sent, and others. You can delete Smart Mailboxes. For more information, see the section "Set Up a Smart Mailbox."

Delete a Mailbox

1 Click a mailbox.

2 Click Mailbox.

3 Click Delete.

The mailbox is deleted.

Compose and Send a Message

You can use Mail to send e-mail to any other e-mail user in the world. This allows you to share ideas, information, and messages with your family and friends, no matter where they are, as long as they have an e-mail account.

You can send a message to more than one person. If you enter multiple addresses in the To field, separated by commas, then Mail sends your message to all of the addresses.

You can send any message that you compose from any e-mail account that you have configured in Mail. If you

begin to type a new message without having selected an account from your In box, then Mail automatically assumes that you want to send it from the first account listed in your Accounts pane. You can change which account an e-mail is sent from at any time by entering one of your different e-mail account addresses in the From field. For more information, see the section, "Set Up an E-Mail Account."

You can select and drag e-mail addresses between fields. For example, you can drag an e-mail address from the To field to the Carbon copy (Cc) field.

Compose and Send a Message

① Click New.

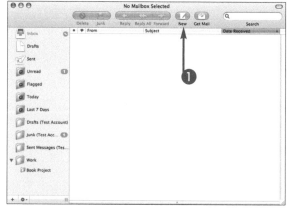

The New Message window appears.

② Type the e-mail address to which you want to send a message.

When you start to type the name of a contact that is in the Address Book, Mail automatically completes the address.

3 To send a carbon copy (Cc) of the message to another person, type that person's e-mail address in the Cc field.

4 Type the subject of your message.

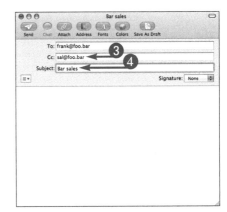

5 Type your message.

6 Click Send when you are finished typing your message.

Mail sends the message to the recipients in the To and Cc fields; it then stores a copy of the message in the Sent mailbox.

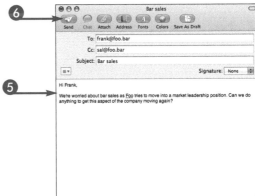

Can Mail check the spelling of a word in my messages?

▼ Yes. To have Mail check the spelling of any word in your message, press and hold down the Control key as you click to select the word in question. A pull-down menu appears, displaying suggestions for the proper spelling of the word. Click the suggestion that you want to use. Mail exchanges the correctly spelled word for the incorrectly spelled one.

Can I send myself a blind carbon copy (Bcc) or a carbon copy (cc) of a message?

▼ Yes. You can automatically include yourself in the Bcc or Cc field of all of the messages that you send by clicking Mail, then clicking Preferences, and then clicking Composing. In the Composing pane that appears, click the Always Cc or Always Bcc myself options. You can also click View and select Bcc Header.

Can I check the status of an e-mail that I am sending?

▼ Yes. Click Window; then select Activiy Viewer before you send your e-mail. A window appears that shows you the progress of the e-mail after you click Send.

Use a Contact
from Address Book

In Mail, you can access your personal contact information from the Address Book application. The information entered into Address Book is available to any other application programmed to access it. This enables you to address e-mails quickly if they are to people whose information you have stored in Address Book.

Address Book is Mac OS X's system-wide contact manager. You can find it in the Applications folder. Address Book stores and categorizes personal contact information, including name, phone number, address, e-mail address,

and company. You can organize the information fields within Address Book to match the way you work, and to only search for information within the Address Book data.

To send a message to someone from your Address Book, you must first have his or her e-mail address entered in his or her information card in your Address Book. If a person has sent you an e-mail, then you can easily add his or her e-mail information into your Address Book. For more information, see Chapter 7. You can also use a group in Address Book to send a message to a group of people at once.

Use a Contact from Address Book

① Click New.

The New Message window appears.

② Click Address to select a name from Address Book.

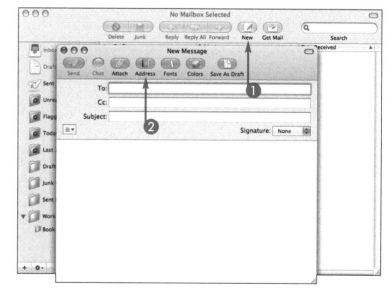

The Addresses window appears.

③ Click the group that contains your intended recipient.

④ Click the name in the list.

⑤ Click To.

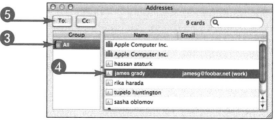

⑥ To carbon copy the message to someone, click the name of that person.

⑦ Click Cc.

You can repeat Steps *6* to *7* for each person that you want to receive a copy of the message.

⑧ Click to close the Addresses window.

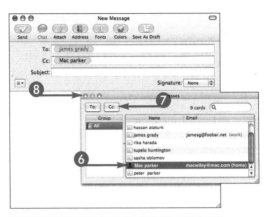

● This area shows the name of each person that you selected from Address Book. The name may appear in a blue highlighted area or it may include the person's e-mail address.

You can now finish composing the message.

PART V

MASTER IT

Can I add a person to Address Book without leaving Mail?

▼ Yes. If a person sends you an e-mail, then you can quickly add the sender's name and e-mail address to Address Book. Click a message that you received from this person and then press and hold ⌘-Y. The selected person's name and e-mail address appear in Address Book.

Can I delete a recipient from the e-mail message?

▼ Yes. If you have added a person's name to the To, Cc, or Bcc fields, and you want to remove it, then first select the name. If you see the person's name and e-mail address, then drag the cursor over the text and press Delete. If you see the person's name in a blue highlight, then click the highlight to select it, and then press Delete.

Can I send a message to every person in a group in Address Book?

▼ Yes. To send a message to every person in a group in Address Book, select the group in Step **3** and skip to Step **5**. To select more than one goup at a time, Shift-click to select adjacent addresses, or ⌘-click to select nonadjacent addresses.

Attach a File to an E-Mail

You can attach a file to any message that you send through Mail. This is useful if you need to share files such as text documents, photos, or PowerPoint presentations.

You can also attach multimedia items such as audio files and videos. Keep in mind that the larger the file is, the longer it takes to send. In addition, the larger the file is, the longer it takes the recipient to download. This is because the time that it takes for the file to transfer depends on the speed of both your and your recipient's Internet connections.

Although you can send any type of file as en e-mail attachment, this does not guarantee that the recipient can open the file. Before sending someone an attached file, you should ensure that the recipient has the necessary software to be able to read or play the file.

You can also compress files before attaching them. This not only makes the file smaller, and therefore quicker to transmit and download, but it can also protect against data corruption when the file is sent.

Attach a File to an E-Mail

① Create a new e-mail message.

Note: *For more information, see the section "Compose and Send a Message."*

② Click Attach.

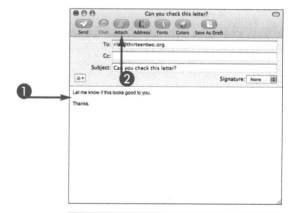

An Open dialog appears.

③ Click ![] to locate and select the file you want to attach to the e-mail message.

④ Click Choose File.

● An icon for the file appears in the message.

To attach additional files, repeat Steps **2** to **4** for each file.

5 Click Send.

Mail sends your message with the file or files attached.

PART V

Is there a maximum file size that I can attach to an e-mail?

▼ The size of the file that you can attach to an e-mail depends on the policies of your ISP. Most do not allow you to attach files that total more than 2MB for each message. However, you may be able to purchase a premium account that allows larger attachments. Check with your Internet Service Provider (ISP) for details.

Can I delete an attachment from an e-mail?

▼ Yes. If you select a file and attach it to an e-mail, and then decide that you do not want to include that file, then you can remove it from the e-mail. To remove the file, select the icon for that file, and then press Delete. The file's icon disappears.

Will deleting the attached file also delete the original file?

▼ No. Although you can delete the attachment from the e-mail before you send it, this does not delete the original file.

Manage E-Mail Threads

You can use Mail to view your e-mail message correspondence in threads. This is useful if you want to store and manage e-mails based on topics of discussion.

A thread is a series of e-mails that are linked as a conversation about a common topic. This means that you can sort and peruse all of your correspondence not just by who sent the e-mail, but also about a certain topic from all interested parties. For example, if you send an e-mail to Persons A, B, and C about the weather on Saturday, then you can group an e-mail thread entitled "Weather on

Saturday" that contains all messages to and from A, B, and C. Even if someone changes the subject line of his or her e-mail, Mail is still able to keep relevant e-mails in the proper thread.

You can collapse and expand threads in a view column, just as you can open and close folders in List view in the Finder. You can also collapse all threads at once.

Mail also features a Thread Summary pane, which presents information about the e-mails in a thread. This includes which e-mails you have read, who sent them, when they were sent, and whether the e-mails have attachments.

Manage E-Mail Threads

① Click View.

② Click Organize by Thread.

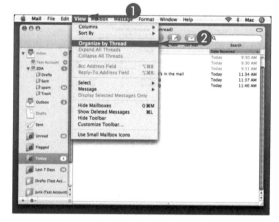

● Mail organizes your e-mails into threads.

③ To see all messages in a thread, click ▶ to the left of the thread (▶ changes to ▼).

④ To collapse all threads, click View.

⑤ Click Collapse All Threads.

All threads close.

Can I highlight all messages in a thread even when I am not viewing the messages as a thread?

▼ Yes. If you want to see which messages are in a thread, then click Mail, and then click Preferences. Then click Viewing to open the Viewing pane. Select the Highlight related messages using color check box (☐ changes to ☑).

Can I choose the highlight color?

▼ Yes. In the Viewing pane of the Mail Preferences window, click the color well next to the Highlight related messages using color option. In the Colors panel that appears, you can pick any color.

Can I switch back to normal organization after organizing my e-mails by thread?

▼ Yes. When your e-mail is organized by thread, this menu item is checkmarked. Click View, and then click Organize by Thread. The checkmark disappears.

Set Up a
Smart Mailbox

You can create Smart Mailboxes, which act like Smart Playlists in iTunes. This feature enables you to create rules that automatically redirect incoming messages to specific mailboxes.

For example, you can create a Smart Mailbox that automatically places any e-mails from an apple.com domain into a special Apple folder. You can also combine multiple rules, so that all e-mails from an apple.com domain go into the Apple folder unless they are from your friend Arisa, in which case they go into the Arisa folder.

By default, Mail has two Smart Mailboxes. The Unread mailbox contains all of your unread messages, and the

Viewed Today mailbox lists all messages that you have read today. After a day, e-mail messages move out of this mailbox.

These Smart Mailboxes can work with any of your e-mail accounts; as a result, incoming mail from any account is moved to a Smart Mailbox according to the rules that you have created. For more information about accounts, see the section "Set Up an E-Mail Account."

Unlike Mail's junk-mail filtering feature, the Smart Mailbox filtering feature is not adaptive. As a result, it does not create new rules as you move messages from one mailbox to another.

Set Up a Smart Mailbox

① Click Mailbox.

② Click New Smart Mailbox.

The Smart Mailbox window appears.

③ Type a name for your new Smart Mailbox.

④ Click 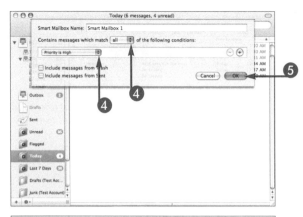 and select the rule criteria that you want to use from the pull-down menu.

⑤ Click OK.

● Your Smart Mailbox appears in Mail's mailbox list.

Can I change the criteria for a Smart Mailbox after I've clicked OK?

▼ Yes. If you have created a Smart Mailbox but later want to change its criteria, select the mailbox, and then click the Mailbox menu and select Edit Smart Mailbox. A sheet opens and you can change the conditions for including e-mail messages in the mailbox.

Can I delete a Smart Mailbox?

▼ Yes. If you no longer have use for a particular Smart Mailbox, you can delete it just as you would delete a regular mailbox. For more information, see the section "Delete a Mailbox."

If I create multiple Smart Mailboxes, does this mean that I will see one message in multiple mailboxes?

▼ No. Even if one e-mail fits the criteria for more than one Smart Mailbox, you will not see duplicate messages. Mail filters the incoming messages through a central content index. As a result, it does not create multiple copies of a single e-mail. Although you may see an e-mail listed in multiple mailboxes, each listing acts like an alias to the actual file, which saves disk space.

Turn HTML
E-Mail Off and On

You can disable or enable the display of HTML elements in e-mails that you have received in Mail. The HTML-disabling feature allows you to reduce the size of e-mails that you receive, which is useful if you have a slow Internet connection. If your connection speed is not an issue, then you can enable the HTML display to see graphics and type styles determined by HTML features.

When you receive a message that contains HTML graphics, Mail uses Safari's rendering engine to show you images, colors, and other items as they would appear on a Web page. However, many junk mails use graphic elements to embed hidden items that can send information. For

example, information about your computer address can be sent to remote servers when you open the message. As a result, viewing all the elements of an HTML mail can compromise the safety of your computer. Mail automatically prevents the display of such elements in messages that it has sent to the Junk folder.

Keep in mind that some e-mail client applications create e-mails that use HTML by default. If you receive an HTML e-mail from a friend, and you have disabled HTML viewing, then you may not be able to see all elements, such as styled text or text in a graphic, of the message that they have sent to you.

Turn HTML E-Mail Off

① Click Mail.

② Click Preferences.

The Mail Preferences window appears.

③ Click Viewing.

The Viewing pane appears.

④ Click the Display remote images in HTML messages option (☑ changes to ☐).

Mail will not display HTML elements of e-mail messages.

Turn HTML E-Mail On

① Click Mail.

② Click Preferences.

The Mail Preferences window appears.

③ Click Viewing.

The Viewing pane appears.

④ Click the Display remote images in HTML messages option (☐ changes to ☑).

HTML e-mail is enabled.

Can I change the size of the fonts in an HTML e-mail that I have received?

▼ Yes. If you have received a message in HTML format, and it uses fonts that are difficult to read, then you can change the size of the fonts. Click Format, and then click Style. In the submenu that appears, click Bigger. This does not affect the content of the message. However, it may affect how the message appears if you forward it or reply with quoted text.

Can I specify whether HTML formatting displays for a particular e-mail?

▼ Yes. You can specify whether formatting appears in individual e-mails. Click View, and then click Message. In the submenu that appears, click either the Plain Text Alternative option to disable HTML formatting, or the Show Best Alternative option. The options in this submenu depend on the fomat of the message that you are reading.

PART V

Search E-Mails Using Spotlight

You can search through all your e-mail messages using Spotlight, the search technology built into Mac OS X. You can look for specific items in an open message, all messages in a specific mailbox, or in all of your mailboxes, and you can search within the subject, addresses, or the body of the message. This is useful when you need to respond to an older e-mail, or look up the address of someone you have not added to the Address Book, or want to find when you discussed a topic with someone.

As with other Spotlight searches, as soon as you begin to enter a search term, Spotlight begins to return results. As you enter more text, Spotlight narrows down the results. To broaden the results, you can delete some of the text.

You can also save searches. After you enter the desired search text, you can click a Save button. This creates a Smart Mailbox that contains the result of the search. In addition, any future e-mail messages that meet the search criteria are placed in this Smart Mailbox.

Search E-Mails Using Spotlight

① Select the mailbox you want to search.

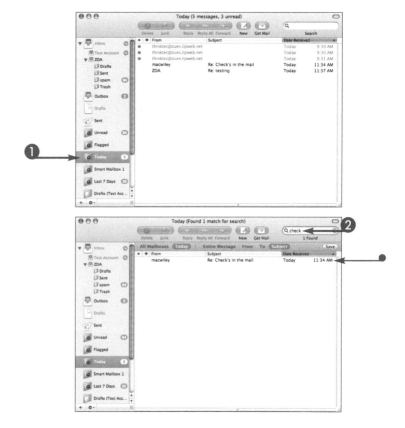

② Enter your search term.

- Results of your search appear.

③ To search all mailboxes, click All Mailboxes.

④ Click here to select what part of your e-mail message to search.

Specific results appear.

Can I search within attachments?

▼ No. You cannot use the search feature in Mail to search through documents, such as PDFs or text files, that you have sent as attachments. However, if you have downloaded and saved these documents to your computer, you can use Spotlight to search them.

Why do I not see the search field?

▼ If you have hidden the toolbar in the Mail window, you will not see the search field or any other of Mail's buttons. Click the oval button in the upper-right corner of the Mail window to show the Mail toolbar.

Can I refine my search by using the words "and" or "or"?

▼ Yes. You can use the words "and," "or," and "not" to add power to your search. For example, entering "red and blue" returns results where both "red" and "blue" appear. Entering "red or blue" shows results with either word, and "red not blue" shows messages that have the word "red" but not the word "blue."

Filter Junk E-Mails

You can teach Mail to recognize unwanted e-mails, such as commercial solicitations and other junk mail, also known as spam. This helps to keep your mailboxes uncluttered by spam, reduces the disk space required by your saved mail, and minimizes a major annoyance of electronic messaging.

When you first start using Mail, it is in training mode. This means that it flags questionable messages that it receives by highlighting them and placing them in the In mailbox. Mail flags certain e-mails, based on built-in rules that search for target words, domains of recognized spammers, and other criteria.

You can expand and fine-tune Mail's capabilities by turning on junk-mail filtering. Once you activate this feature, you can help Mail to identify which e-mails are spam. Initially, you can tell Mail to place all incoming e-mails into the In box, and to highlight the e-mails that it thinks are spam; this allows you to correct it if it marks a real message as junk. You can also tell Mail that a seemingly okay e-mail is, in fact, spam. Once you are confident that Mail has learned enough, you can set Mail to automatically redirect all spam to the Junk folder.

Filter Junk E-Mails

① Click Mail.

② Click Preferences.

The Mail Preferences window appears.

③ Click Junk Mail.

The Junk Mail pane appears.

④ Click Enable Junk Mail filtering (☐ changes to ☑).

⑤ Click the Leave it in my Inbox, but indicate it is junk mail (Training) option (◯ changes to ⦿).

Incoming junk mail appears highlighted in your Inbox.

6 Click an e-mail that you want to identify as junk mail.

7 Click Junk.

The Junk Mail dialog appears.

8 To automate the process, click the Move it to the Junk mailbox (Automatic) option (○ changes to ●).

Junk mail filtering is now automatic.

Can Mail work with my ISP's filtering services if my ISP uses them?

▼ Yes. In the Junk Mail pane of the Mail Preferences window, you can click the Trust Junk Mail headers set by your Internet Service Provider option. You can check your Junk Mail mailbox after activating this option to ensure that Mail does not identify any real e-mails as junk.

Can I tell Mail that an e-mail is not junk, even if it is identified as such?

▼ Yes. You can indicate that a message is not junk, even if it has been flagged as junk, either by you or by Mail. Simply click the message and then click the Not Junk icon in Mail's toolbar.

Can I specify my own rules for identifying junk mail?

▼ Yes. For example, you can tell Mail that all e-mails coming from a specific domain are junk. In the Junk Mail pane of the Mail Preferences window, click Advanced. A new window appears, in which you can set extensive personalized rules for identifying junk mail. You can edit these rules at any time.

Set Safe
E-Mail Addresses

You can specify certain safe Internet domains in Mail. This helps to ensure that you do not accidentally send messages to the wrong address. If you begin to compose a message to a recipient whose domain has not been entered as safe, then Mail displays the address in red.

An Internet domain is the part of an e-mail address after the @ sign. For example, in the e-mail address sjobs@apple.com, sjobs is the account name, while apple.com is the domain.

If you place the domain of your organization on the safe list, then this helps to ensure that you do not inadvertently

send e-mails to people outside your organization. If you regularly send e-mails to many people at many different domains, then you can add all of their information to the safe list.

You can also use the safe list to ensure that you only send e-mail from certain accounts, if you have multiple e-mail addresses. You can add the domain of the accounts from which you want to send e-mails; if you begin to compose a message from another account, then Mail displays the From address in red.

Set Safe E-Mail Addresses

① Click Mail.

② Click Preferences.

③ Click Composing.

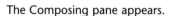

The Composing pane appears.

④ Click Mark addresses not in this domain
(☐ changes to ☑).

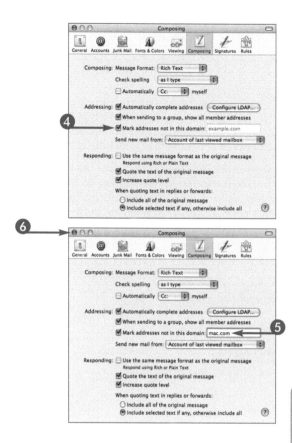

⑤ Type a safe domain name.

⑥ Click ⊙ to close the Mail Preferences window.

Mail adds the domain to the safe list.

Can I enter more than one safe domain?

▼ Yes. In Step **5**, type one safe domain, such as apple.com, and then type a comma, followed by the next domain name. You can add as many domains as you want.

Can I delete a domain from the safe list?

▼ Yes. Open the Mail Preferences window, and then click Composing. When the Composing pane appears, deselect the Mark addresses not in this domain option (☑ changes to ☐). Close the Mail Preferences window. Mail no longer marks e-mail addresses that are not on the safe list.

Does the safe list filter incoming messages?

▼ No. The safe list is only for outgoing messages that you compose. You can tell Mail to filter e-mails from specific domains either by using advanced rules in junk filtering, or by creating a Smart Mailbox. For more information, see the sections "Filter Junk E-Mails," and "Set Up a Smart Mailbox."

Show Header Information

You can reveal the header information of all messages that you have received in Mail. This enables you to examine technical details of the message such as the route that it took to get to you.

The header of an e-mail usually contains the names of all of the servers that transferred the message from the sender to you. It also contains data about any encoding of the message's content and information about the sender.

If there were problems in transmission, then you can use the header information to track them down. This can also give your ISP valuable information if you want to report other problems, such as junk mail.

If you are familiar with reading header information, you can create rules in Mail to filter incoming e-mail messages based on the contents of their headers. One example is that e-mail messages from online forums or mailing lists contain identifying data in their headers. If you have enabled header information, you can create rules to move these to mailboxes created for forum or mailing list notices.

Show Header Information

① With an e-mail open, click View.

② Select Message.

③ Click Long Headers.

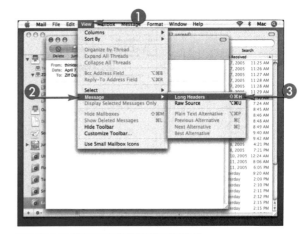

The header information appears for the e-mail.

Change Font and Color of Text

You can change how Mail displays the text in a message. Once you set new defaults, Mail displays all of your messages in the new font and color. This can be useful if you need Mail to use a larger font or higher contrast color for improved readability.

You can choose from any font available to you on the computer. For more information about fonts, see Chapter 10.

You can also set different colors for quoted text from other messages. This makes it easier to distinguish who has said

what in an e-mail conversation and track back the conversation.

When you change fonts or enable different colors or fonts for quotations, your correspondents will see the effect, if their e-mail clients support colors and fonts. If the recipients of your messages do not have the correct font on their computers, their e-mail clients will substitute another font in its place. As a result, you may see a change in font when they reply with the quoted text.

Change Font and Color of Text

① Click Mail.

② Click Preferences.

The Mail Preferences window appears.

③ Click Fonts & Colors.

The Fonts & Colors pane appears.

● You can select the font and size of text that you want from the pull-down menus.

● You can select the colors of quoted text that you want from the pull-down menu.

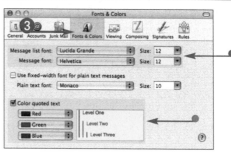

Add an Electronic Signature

You can add a signature to the end of the e-mails that you send. A signature is a line or two of text that recipients see at the bottom of all e-mails from you.

You can add your personal contact information such as your e-mail address or iChat name, your job title, or a quote. This can help to identify you to your recipients and can present a more professional image.

If you want more than one signature, instead of having one that appears on all of your e-mails, then you can create different signatures and select any of them from a list when you send a message. Either you can choose which signature you want to use each time you compose a message, or you can tell Mail to insert a signature in a random order.

You can also specify that your signature appear above quoted text when you reply to an e-mail. This ensures that the recipient can see your signature, which otherwise may be overlooked at the bottom of a long correspondence.

Add an Electronic Signature

① Click Mail.

② Click Preferences.

The Mail Preferences window appears.

③ Click Signatures.

The Signatures pane appears.

④ Click ⊞ to add the signature.

⑤ Type a description for the signature.

⑥ Type the text of the signature.

Note: You can repeat Steps **4** to **6** to create multiple
signatures.

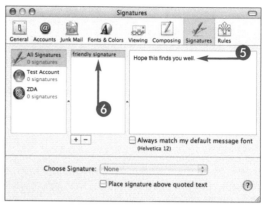

⑦ Select the signature that you want to use from
the pull-down menu.

⑧ Click ⬤ to close the Preferences window.

Your outgoing e-mails feature the signature
that you selected.

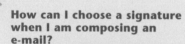

How can I choose a signature when I am composing an e-mail?

▼ To choose which signature
appears in your e-mail while you
are composing, select None in
Step **8**, and then select the
Show signature menu on
compose window option
(☐ changes to ☑). The next
time you compose an e-mail, a
pull-down menu appears in the
composition window that allows
you to select which signature
appears in your message.

Can I change the order of signatures?

▼ Yes. You can select and drag
signatures into any order within
the signature list in the
Signatures pane of the Mail
Preferences window.

Can I use styled text in a signature?

▼ Yes. You can use styled text,
such as bold, italic, or colored
text, in your signature. You can
use the Format menu to change
the font and other attributes of
your signature.

Set Up AIM and .Mac Accounts

Y ou can use iChat AV to access your AOL Instant Messenger (AIM) and .Mac accounts to chat with other members of these services. This allows you to use iChat AV to keep in touch with friends and family who use these services.

To access either the AIM or .Mac services, you need to have an account with them, which means that you must register a screen name and password. Both services offer free registration at their Web sites.

After you have configured iChat AV, you can chat with other users using your .Mac or AIM account. After you have added your friends to your Buddy List, you can chat with them as long as they are using either iChat AV or AIM. You can only see custom account icons for your friends who use iChat AV, while AIM users will appear first as AOL icons until they log in; then their icons will change to their customized ones.

If you want, you can start a group chat, so that all of your friends can talk to each other at once. When you use iChat AV to send instant messages to your friends, you can also send pictures and other files. You can also connect a Web cam, such as Apple's iSight, to your Mac and send live video and audio.

Set Up an AIM Account

① Click iChat.

② Click Preferences.

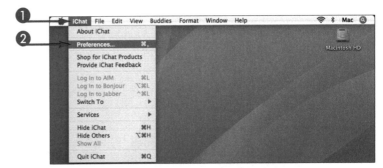

The iChat Preferences window appears.

③ Click the Add button (+).

④ Click Account Type ▣ and select AIM Account.

⑤ Type your AIM screen name and password.

⑥ Click Add.

iChat can access your AIM account.

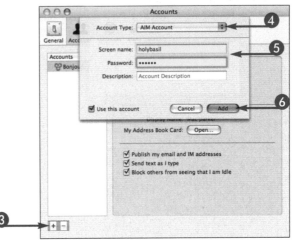

Set Up a .Mac Account

① Click iChat.

② Click Preferences.

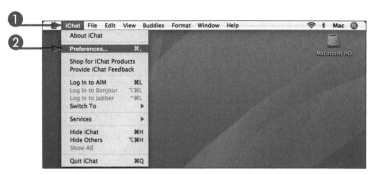

③ Click ⊞.

④ Click Account Type ⬍ and select .Mac Account.

⑤ Type your .Mac screen name and password.

● If this is a new account, click Create New .Mac Account.

⑥ Click Add.

You can chat using your .Mac account.

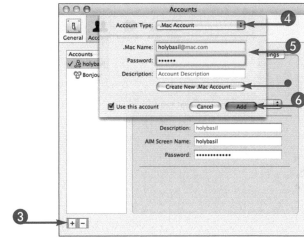

Can I use iChat AV to send messages to friends on other instant messenger (IM) clients, such as Yahoo Instant Messenger or MSN?

▼ No. You can chat with other iChat AV users, as well as AIM users, but not with friends who use Yahoo Instant Messenger or MSN. Other iChat users will be listed under their .Mac account names and AIM users will be listed under their AIM screen names.

Can I change my password and account information?

▼ Yes. For your .Mac account, go to the .Mac Web site at www.mac.com and log in to change your information. To change your AIM account information while using AIM, click the Edit menu, select Account Options, and then Change Password.

Can I use iChat AV to chat with all other AIM users?

▼ Yes. iChat AV is compatible with all current versions of AIM, so you are able to chat with all friends logged into the AIM network. However, only some versions of AIM are compatible with iChat AV's audio conference capabilities.

Change Your
iChat AV Icon

Y ou can customize the image that appears next to your screen name in chats and in the Buddy List. This is a useful way to help your friends find you more quickly than if you display a generic icon in your chats. You can use any picture, whether a photograph or illustration.

When you customize your user icon, you and other users can see this image whenever you are online in their Buddy Lists, or next to your instant messages when you chat. If

you do not want to see user's icons, you can click the View menu and deselect the Show Buddy Pictures option. If another user has deselected that option, he or she will not see your iChat AV icon.

If you choose an image that is much larger than 64 x 64 pixels, then a window appears, allowing you to resize and crop the image. If the image you choose is only a few pixels larger than 64 x 64 pixels, iChat automatically resizes the image.

Change Your iChat AV Icon

① Select the image file that you want to use as your icon.

② Drag the file to your name in the Buddy List.

iChat replaces the existing icon with the new icon that you have selected.

Change Your iChat AV Status

You can change your iChat AV status while you are online. For example, you can change it from Available, which means that you are ready and able to send and receive messages, to Away, which indicates that you are not at your computer; you can also change it to a custom message. This is useful if you want to let other users know that you will be back in a moment, or that you are only chatting with coworkers.

You can also create custom status messages, one for when you are available and one for when you are not. These do not replace the standard Available and Away messages, but you can use these instead of the standard messages. These will be visible only to other iChat AV users, not to AIM users.

If you have not touched the keyboard or mouse of your computer for a while, then iChat AV automatically changes your status to Idle. This indicates to other iChat AV users that, although you are logged in, you may not be at your desk.

Change Your iChat AV Status

① Click the status indicator.

A pull-down menu appears, displaying status message options.

② Click a new status message.

Note: *You can create a custom menu by clicking Custom and then typing your message in the text field that appears.*

PART V

Start a Video Chat

If you connect a Web cam or a Firewire-enabled camcorder to your Mac, then you can use iChat AV to conduct a video chat. This allows you to send real-time video while you are sending instant messages. If your friends who are using iChat AV also have similar cameras, then you can see their real-time video at the same time. If your camera has a microphone, or you have only a microphone connected to your computer, then you can have an audio chat over iChat AV.

The quality of the video and audio depends on the speed of your computers and of your Internet connections as well as the quality of your camera and microphone. The better your DSL or cable modem bandwidth, the better your audio and video connection will be. Video chat is not available to users with dial-up modem connections.

You can use Apple's iSight Web camera, which also features a built-in microphone, with iChat AV. Most digital camcorders with FireWire or iLink connectivity will also work.

Start a Video Chat

① Click the name of the buddy with whom you want to chat.

② Click the camera icon.

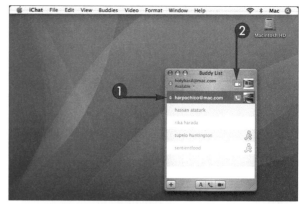

A preview window appears with your outgoing video.

● When your buddy accepts the invitation, your camera's image appears in the chat window.

Note: To send video to a buddy who does not have a camera, you can click the Buddies menu and then click Invite to One-Way Video Chat.

Change the Size of Your Video Chat Window

You can resize the video chat window in iChat AV. For example, you can fill the entire computer screen with the video image, as well as change the size of the preview image that appears before your buddies accept your invitations to chat. This allows you to view your buddy's video in a larger format, or move it out of the way so that you can access your Desktop.

The quality of the images depends on a few criteria. For example, the faster your computer is, the more easily it can process a large video image. In addition, the better the graphics card in your computer, the better the picture. The quality of the image also depends on you and your buddy's Internet connection speeds, as well as the quality of the Web cams that you use.

It is useful to decrease the size of the video chat window if you are conferencing for work. This way, you can more easily access the files and folders you need to work with. You can switch back and forth between window sizes at any time.

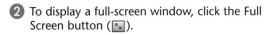
Change the Size of Your Video Chat Window

① Click the bottom-right corner of the chat window and drag it to resize the window.

② To display a full-screen window, click the Full Screen button (⬜).

The window fills the screen.

Note: *Not all computers and video cards can support full-screen video chat.*

To return to windowed video, click the Escape key on your keyboard.

Capture a Picture of Your Video Chat

Y ou can use iChat AV to take a picture of you and the buddy with whom you are chatting, provided you both have Web cameras and are using iChat AV to have a video chat. This allows you to take a snapshot of your conversation.

You can then use the image in a number of ways. For example, you can place it in a document, such as a Word file or a PDF. You can also send the image file to a friend on your Buddy List.

When you save a picture, it is in JPEG format. Although you can print out JPEG images, this format was not designed for high-resolution reproduction; therefore, it does not produce a high-quality printout. However, JPEGs are a preferred image format for Web pages, and so you can place pictures that you save from video chats on your personal Web site. You can use Preview or another image-editing application, such as Adobe Photoshop, to convert your picture to another format, depending on how you want to use the image.

Capture a Picture of Your Video Chat by Dragging

① ⌘-drag the image in the video chat window to your Desktop.

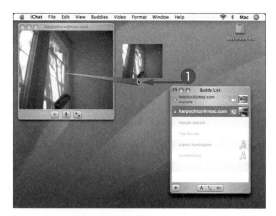

● An icon of the JPEG image of the video chat appears on your Desktop.

Capture a Picture of Your Video Chat by Copying

1 Click in the video chat window.

2 Press ⌘-C.

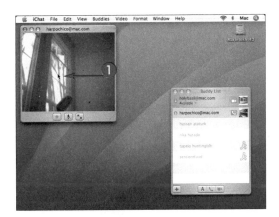

3 Open another application and press ⌘-V.

● The image is pasted to the new document.

How can I send the image to a buddy in iChat AV?

▼ After you ⌘-click the image in the video chat window, you can drag that file to the icon of a buddy in the iChat AV Buddy List. This sends the file to your buddy.

Can I place the copied image into Preview?

▼ Yes. You can place the image from your video chat into a Preview document. After you press ⌘-C to copy the image from iChat AV, you can switch to the Preview application, then click File, and then click New from Clipboard. This opens a new Preview window with your copied image.

Can I save the file in another file format other than JPEG?

▼ Yes. Although iChat initially saves the file in JPEG format, you can convert the file and save it in any other graphics format. You can paste or copy the file to any image-editing application, such as Preview, and use that application to convert the file.

PART V

Create a
Chat Room

Y ou can invite multiple people to have an instant
message chat at the same time. This enables you to
create a chat room in which all of your buddies can
interact with you and with each other. All messages appear
in a single chat window and are not threaded; therefore, a
response to your comment may be mixed in with other
people's comments.

After you create the chat room, you can invite any buddy,
or anyone whose AIM or .Mac username you know, to enter
the room. Other users are not able to enter the room until
you send them an invitation.

All chat in a chat room is public. Every message sent from
one user to another is visible to all users. You can leave a
room and have a private chat, whether text, audio, or
video, with another user if they also leave the chat room.

You can send files to other users and receive files from other
users when you are in a chat room. To send a file, you can
simply drag the file to that user's screen name in your
Buddy List.

Create a Chat Room

① Click File.

② Click New Chat.

A new Chat window appears.

③ Click ⊞ in the Participants pane of the Chat
window.

A list of online buddies appears.

④ Click each buddy that you want to include in the chat.

⑤ Type a message.

⑥ Press Return to send the invitation message to your buddies.

Your buddies can enter the chat room by responding.

Are there established AOL chat rooms that I and my buddies can join?

▼ Yes. You can find a list of established AOL chat rooms that iChat AV users can join at www.aim.com/chats.adp?aolp=. You can invite multiple buddies to join these rooms just as you would invite them to join a chat room that you create.

What can I do if I am in a chat room and I cannot tell who is chatting?

▼ If you are seeing chat messages and you do not see names and pictures of users next to these messages, then you can click iChat, then click View, and then click Show Names and Pictures. The names and pictures appear by the names of users as they send messages.

Can buddies turn down invitations to chat?

▼ Yes. If they are online with iChat AV when you send a message inviting them to chat but they do not want to chat at the moment, then they can simply not respond.

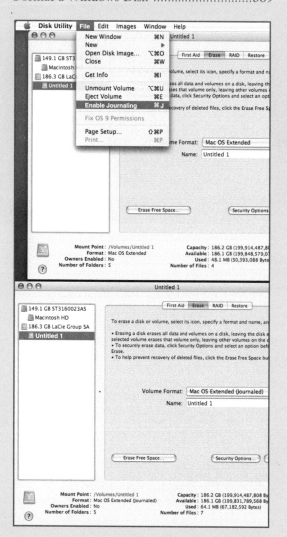

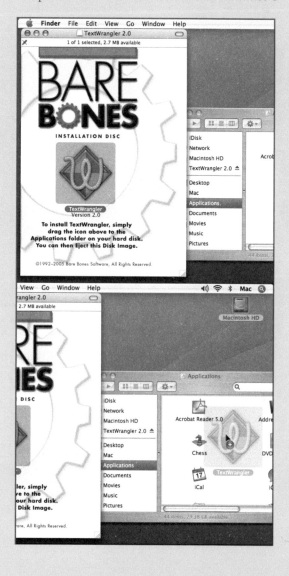

26 — Troubleshooting Problems on Your Mac

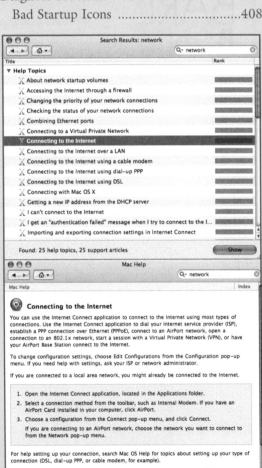

Repair Permissions

Y ou can use Disk Utility to examine and repair the permissions that you have set for all of the files and applications on your computer. This is a useful troubleshooting procedure as it can resolve small problems such as files that refuse to open, or when familiar program or file icons change their appearance on their own. Permissions tell the operating system which users can read, write, or run a file or application.

Permissions that are attached to files or applications can become damaged when you are installing new software, or if you have to force an application or the Finder to quit.

As a result, problems may arise when you try to use these files. For example, an application may not open when you attempt to launch it, or the entire computer may run more slowly.

Because Mac OS X is Unix-based, every item in the operating system is treated as a file. As a result, every item has permissions attached to it. The larger your hard drive and the greater the number of items that it contains, the longer it takes to verify and repair permissions. The processor and hard drive speed of your computer are also factors in the time that it takes Disk Utility to work.

Repair Permissions

Note: *Launch the Disk Utility that is located in the Utilities folder in the Applications folder.*

① In Disk Utility, click the hard drive or partition that you want to repair.

Disk Utility options appear in the right pane.

② Click First Aid.

The Permissions repair options appear.

③ Click Verify Disk Permissions.

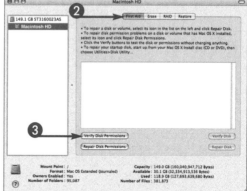

● Disk Utility shows whether permissions need to be repaired.

You can stop the verification process at any time by clicking Stop Permissions Verify.

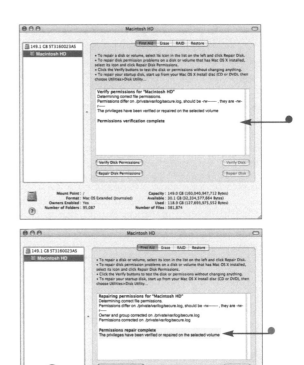

④ Click Repair Disk Permissions.

You can stop the repair process at any time by clicking Stop Permission Repair.

● Disk Utility repairs permissions on the drive partition that you selected.

Are there particular times that I should repair permissions?

▼ It is a good idea to repair permissions after updating your system software or installing new applications. These are most likely to cause minor permissions damage. You can also repair permissions if you see a slowdown in your computer's performance, or if custom file and folder icons are suddenly replaced by generic icons.

Can I repair any kind of disk with Disk Utility?

▼ No. You can verify and repair permissions on hard drives with any format that is supported by Mac OS X; this includes hard drives in HFS and HFS+ format. You cannot repair permissions on CD-ROMs, DVD-ROMs, or write-protected disks.

What should I do if Disk Utility cannot repair my disk?

▼ If you have serious problems with computer slowdowns or you are unable to launch programs even after running Disk Utility, then back up your data immediately and try another disk repair application.

Turn On Journaling

You can enable file system journaling for your computer's hard drive with Disk Utility. This provides an extra level of security for your data if you have to force restart your computer or if your computer restarts because of a power failure.

When you turn on journaling, the operating system makes a log of all changes that are made; this log is called the journal. When your computer shuts down improperly, the regular read-and-write process is interrupted, which can cause inconsistencies between the file system directory and the actual location and state of files.

In a file system without journaling activated, the operating system has to check the entire file system before it can restart services. This can take a long time on a large hard drive. When you have turned on journaling and the computer restarts after a shutdown, the operating system uses the journal to restore your computer to its prior state. This is not only a more secure way to restore your data, but it also takes less time. Keep in mind that journaling does not restore unsaved changes to documents and cannot be used to restore overwritten drafts of text files, for example.

1 Launch Disk Utility from the Utilities folder.

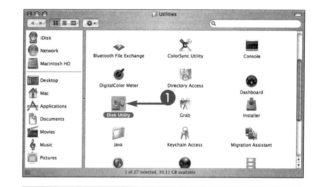

2 Click a disk.

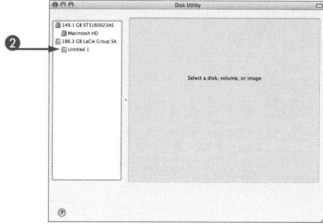

③ Click File.

④ Click Enable Journaling.

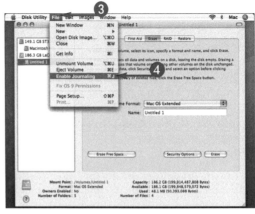

Disk Utility activates the Journaling feature.

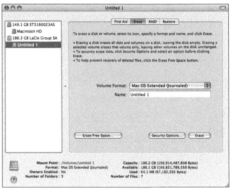

When I turn on journaling, does it cause my computer to run more slowly?

▼ Yes, but only slightly, and only in specific circumstances. Because journaling works by noting every change to the system, there is slightly more overhead for every task. However, any slowdown should be minimal. The exception is if you are working with large video, audio, or other high-bandwidth files that require constant and fast disk access.

Can I turn off journaling?

▼ Yes. If you decide that there is no benefit to journaling, then you can turn it off. In Disk Utility, select your hard drive, click File, and then click Disable Journaling.

Why can I not turn on journaling?

▼ If you install Mac OS X on a hard drive that has just been formatted in Mac OS X Extended format, then journaling is automatically enabled. You can still read, write, and access Mac OS Extended volumes that do not feature journaling.

Using
Disk Info

You can use Disk Utility to examine information about your hard drive or a partition on your hard drive. This helps you to compile data about your computer in case of problems. You can also use Disk Utility to determine how large your hard drive is, and how much disk space is available.

Disk Utility helps you to find the following information about your hard drive: format, capacity, amount of space available, whether permissions are enabled, how many folders and files reside on the volume, the disk's universal unique identifier number, and whether the disk can be verified or repaired. Some of this information, such as type

and format of the hard drive, is also available in the System Profiler. For more information on the System Profiler, see Chapter 26.

This information can be useful in troubleshooting. Experienced technicians can take some of this data and deduce if there are specific problems, such as bad sectors, on your drive.

You can also use the information feature of Disk Utility to examine external drives and even removable media, such as recordable CD-ROMs and DVDs. This can help you determine how much space is used and how much is still available on a multisession recordable disc.

Using Disk Info

① Click a disk.

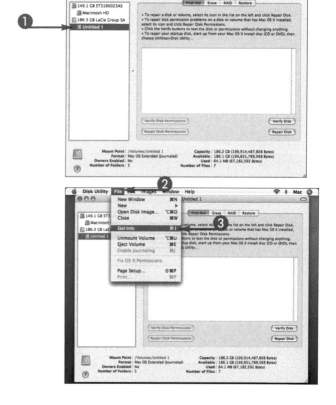

② Click File.

③ Click Get Info.

A window appears with the disk information.

Erase a Disk

Y ou can use Disk Utility to erase disks and partitions of disks. This is useful if you want to install a new operating system or a new version of an operating system, or if your operating system has become so corrupted that it has become unstable. However, erasing a disk will not solve a hardware-related problem, such as a corrupted drive with bad blocks.

Erasing a disk deletes all data on it. It is possible for an experienced technician to recover data from a simple

erase, but this data will be fragmentary and you will not be able to find complete files and applications. If you want to save any data on a disk that you plan to erase, then you must back it up to another hard drive, CD-R, CD-RW, recordable DVD, or other type of media.

You can erase a disk securely, so that no data will ever be recoverable. This is useful if you are selling a computer with personal or company data. To do this, click the Security Options and select the Zero Out, 7-Pass Erase, or 35-Pass erase options.

Erase a Disk

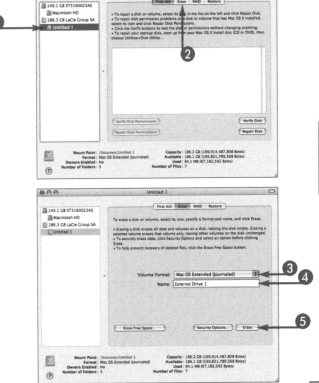

1 Click the disk that you want to erase.

2 Click Erase.

3 Click Volume Format and select a format from the pull-down menu.

4 Type a name for the disk.

5 Click Erase.

The data are permanently deleted from the disk.

Create a Disk Image

Y ou can use Disk Utility to create a *disk image*, a file that comprises the contents of a virtual disk. This method is a good way to back up hard drives or folders or to share data. Because disk images are stable, single files are easy to store and share. A disk image appears on your Desktop or in a Finder window as an icon with the name of the disk followed by the .dmg file extension.

You can open a disk image by double-clicking it. The Finder automatically expands the file. Depending on the nature

of the original item that was turned into a disk image, you may see either a new folder or a new hard drive icon on your Desktop. If the disk image was of a hard drive, then the operating system mounts the expanded image as if it were an actual hard drive connected to your computer. Once the image is expanded, you can drag files from the opened image to copy them to your own computer's hard drive.

Create a Disk Image

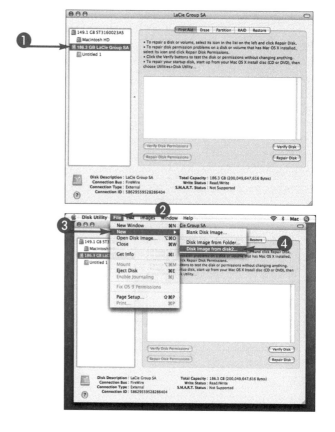

① Click a disk.

② Click File.

③ Select New.

④ Click Disk Image.

A dialog appears.

5 Type a name for the disk image.

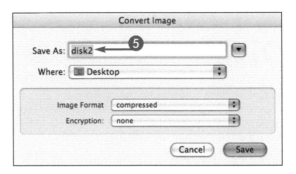

6 Click Image Format ⬍ and select a disk format from the pull-down menu.

7 Click Save.

Disk Utility creates a disk image.

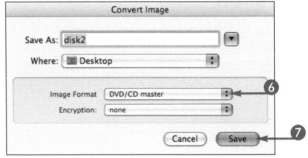

Can I use a disk image to back up data to a recordable CD-ROM or DVD?

▼ Yes. This is a good way to back up or copy data to a medium that you can easily share with others. Once you create a disk image, select it in the left column of the Disk Utility window. Then insert a blank recordable CD-ROM or DVD and click the Burn button at the top of the Disk Utility window. Disk Utility burns the disk image to the inserted disk, which you can then take anywhere.

Can I change the format and encryption of a disk image once I have created it?

▼ Yes. You can change both the image format and the level of encryption of a disk image after you have created it. In Disk Utility, select the disk image in the left column, then click Images, and then click Convert. Select a new image format and level of encryption and click Save. The new disk image has the same name as the old one but is now in the new format, or with the new level of encryption that you want.

Unmount a Disk

You can use Disk Utility to unmount a disk. Depending on the nature of the disk, this either ejects the disc, such as a CD-ROM, or enables you to disconnect the disk, such as an external hard drive.

In the case of a hard drive that has multiple partitions, you can use Disk Utility to unmount a single partition, rather than all partitions on the disk, which would happen if you disconnected the hard drive. This is useful if you want to run a disk repair program on that partition.

It is important to unmount disks before physically disconnecting them from your computer. Though most modern connectivity standards such as FireWire and USB are hot-pluggable, which means you can connect devices without turning them or your computer off, removing a hard drive without unmounting it runs the risk of disk corruption. If you have an iPod, the process is similar; you need to drag the iPod icon to the Trash or click the Eject button in the iTunes interface to unmount the iPod before disconnecting it physically.

Unmount a Disk

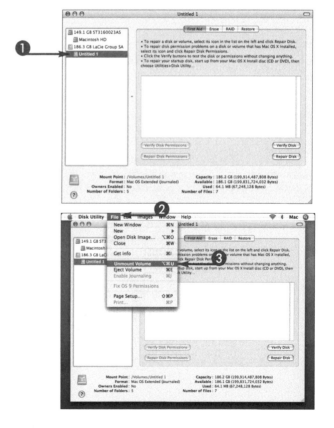

1 Click a disk or partition.

2 Click File.

3 Click Unmount.

The disk or partition is unmounted.

Format a Windows Disk

Y ou can use Disk Utility to format a hard drive in the native Windows MS-DOS disk format for use with a Windows-based computer. This is useful if you work in a multiplatform environment and want to repurpose an old hard drive.

Because you must first erase all data from the hard drive, you must remove and back up all valuable data before performing this task. Keep in mind that you cannot format part of a hard drive in the Windows format and another part of the hard drive in a Mac OS X format. This is

because the disk formats native to the two operating systems are different.

Depending with which version of Windows you plan to use the disk, you may be limited in what you name the hard drive. Some versions of Windows place a limit on the number of characters allowed in the name of a hard drive, or prohibit certain characters such as a colon. If this is a concern, check the Windows manual that came with the computer into which you want to place the formatted hard drive.

Format a Windows Disk

① Click the disk that you want to format.

② Click Erase.

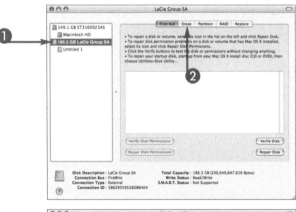

③ Click Volume Format ▣ and select MS-DOS File System from the pull-down menu.

④ Type a name for the disk.

⑤ Click Erase.

Note: You may need to click Erase again if a warning dialog appears.

The disk is erased and formatted for Windows.

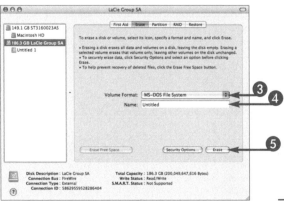

Install an Application

You can install a Max OS X-compatible application onto your computer at any time. This allows you to expand the capabilities of your computer indefinitely.

You can install Mac OS X applications in one of two ways. The first uses a small utility, called an installer, to place the application and support files into the relevant folders on your computer. Although the actual program may be installed in the Applications folder, some necessary files may need to be installed in the Library or Preferences folders.

The other type of installation does not use an installer. Instead, you simply drag a folder containing the program and support files and drop it into your Applications or other folder.

All applications specify which method you need to use. If it is not clear, you can open the Read Me file that comes with the application.

During the installation process, you may be asked for your username and password. You can type the username and password that you provided when you first configured Mac OS X, or any username and password for an account with Administrator privileges. This is to prevent malicious viruses or users from placing unwanted software on your computer.

Install an Application with an Installer

1 Double-click the application installer's icon.

The installer window appears.

2 Follow the on-screen instructions to install the software.

Install an Application by Drag and Drop

1 Select the application icon or folder.

Note: If you download an application, it may be distributed as a disk image, which Mac OS X will automatically expand.

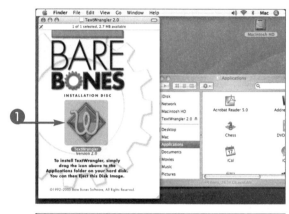

2 Drag the folder to your Applications folder.

The application is now installed.

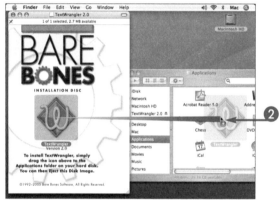

Can I easily tell which method I need to use to install an application?

▼ Yes. When you insert the CD-ROM or DVD-ROM containing the application or suite of applications that you want to install, a window appears in the Finder, showing the disc's contents. Usually, this window contains an icon with the label "Drag to install" or "Double-click to install." If you do not see clear instructions, then you can double-click the Read Me text file included on the disc and follow the instructions that it contains.

If there is a problem with applications that came bundled with Mac OS X, can I reinstall them?

▼ Yes. If you are having a problem with any of the applications that came with Mac OS X, then you can either reinstall Mac OS X or you can use the Restore feature that is available on the discs that were included with your computer. If you reinstall the operating system, then this deletes all information on your hard drive; as a result, you first need to back up all of your data to recordable media or an external hard drive.

Can I get more software for Mac OS X?

▼ Yes. To do this, you can click and then click Mac OS X Software. The Safari Web browser launches, and displays a Web page from which you can download free and commercial software and utilities for Mac OS X.

PART VI

391

Uninstall or Remove an Application

You can uninstall or remove any application from your Mac OS X computer at any time. This is useful if you have multiple copies of one application, an older version of an application that you have updated, or if you want to remove an application that you no longer use.

Unlike in other operating systems, you can use the drag-and-drop method of installing applications to keep multiple versions, such as older versions of Web browsers, on your computer. However, you may not want to keep some of the older versions, especially if you do not want to tax your system by running multiple versions at the same time.

Some applications keep their data files in the same folder as the application. As a result, removing an application can also remove all of the data and files that you have created with the application, unless you copy them to another location or back them up to recordable media or an external hard drive. However, some applications save files in other locations; for example, iTunes stores its music and other audio files in the Music folder in your User folder.

Uninstall or Remove an Application

① Locate the application that you want to uninstall.

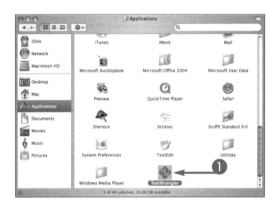

② Drag the application folder to the Trash.

③ Locate the folder with the application's name in the Preferences folder, as well as in the Library folder or in the Application Support folder in the Library folder.

Most, but not all, applications create a folder of support files in the Library or Preferences folders when they are installed.

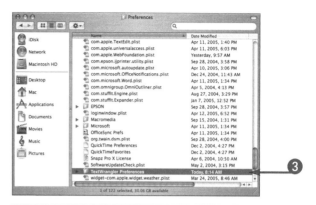

④ Drag the folder to the Trash.

⑤ Empty the Trash.

The application is uninstalled.

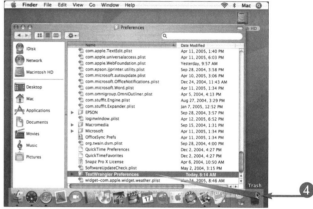

If I delete the alias to an application, am I also deleting the application?

▼ No. Aliases in Mac OS X are pointers to the actual item, whether the item is a file or an application. You can delete the alias without affecting the original item. As a result, you cannot delete the original file by deleting the alias.

Can I delete the application installer?

▼ Yes. You may have installed a program from an installer that you have downloaded from the Internet or copied from a CD-ROM. Once you have completed the process, you can delete the installer, unless you want to place copies of the application into other user directories.

Do all applications place support folders in the Library folder?

▼ No. Some applications are installed as packages. Packages appear as a single icon, but they contain the actual application as well as folders and support files. Such applications may not have related folders in the Library or other folders on your hard drive.

Install a Printer with Printer Setup Utility

You can add a USB, Firewire, or other type of printer to your Mac OS X system using Printer Setup Utility, which is located in your Utilities folder. This allows you to make physical copies of any type of file, including word-processing documents and digital images.

The Printer Setup Utility can also help you select which printer, if you have multiple printers available, will be your default printer. The default printer is the one that will output your document unless you specify otherwise in the Print dialog. For more information on the Print dialog,

see Chapter 4. The Show Info feature of the Printer Setup Utility can provide detailed information about your printer, including any features not automatically enabled.

You can connect inkjet, bubble-jet, or laser printers to your computer. Once you have installed a printer on your computer, you can enable other computers on your local network to print to it. For more information, see Chapter 18. You can also use a printer that is installed on another computer on your network, even if you are connected to that network wirelessly through AirPort.

see Chapter 4.

Install a Printer with Printer Setup Utility

1 Launch the Printer Setup Utility that is located in the Utilities folder inside the Applications folder.

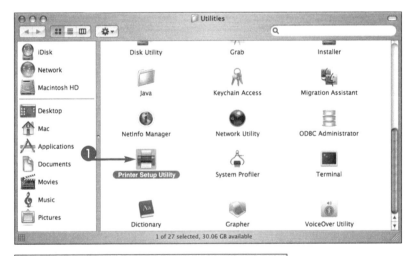

2 Click Add.

If the Printer List is not visible, click View and then click Show Printer List.

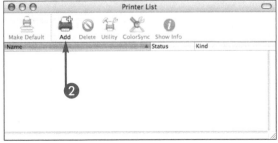

A Printer List window appears.

③ Click the printer you want.

④ Click Add.

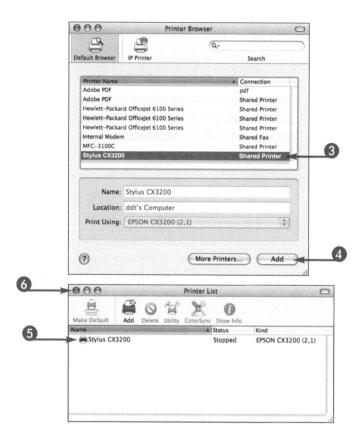

The printer now appears in the Printer List window.

⑤ Click Printer Setup Utility.

⑥ Click 🔘 to close the dialog.

You can now use the printer to print documents.

Can I change the default printer?

▼ Yes. To change the default printer, which is the printer selected by default when you choose to print a document, click View in the Printer Setup Utility toolbar, and then click Show Printer List. In the Printer List window that appears, click the name of the printer that you want to make the default printer, and then click the Make Default button. The name of the default printer appears in bold type.

What can I do if I am having trouble adding a printer to the list?

▼ If you are having trouble installing a printer, Mac OS X may not have the software drivers required to communicate with the printer. If your printer did not come with the required software — usually on a CD-ROM — then you may be able to download the correct software from the manufacturer's Web site. Once you have the software, you can perform Steps **1** to **5** to add the printer.

Check for Updates
with Software Update

You can use the Software Update feature of the System Preferences to check for and install updates to your operating system, as well as all of the applications from Apple that are included in Mac OS X. This provides you with a convenient way to keep your computer and applications up to date.

The Software Update feature contacts remote servers at Apple that host the most current versions of the relevant software. This includes security updates, which are vital to ensure that your computer has the latest changes that keep it safe from viruses and other security threats.

Software Update allows you to decide which of the updates you want to install. Some updates, such as for your operating system, require that you restart your computer, and so you may decide to install them later.

You can also schedule Software Update to look for new software versions on a regular basis. Following the schedule you have set, Software Update launches, connects to Apple, and then alerts you if it has found that your existing software needs updating.

Check for Updates with Software Update

① Click the Apple menu (⌘).

② Click System Preferences.

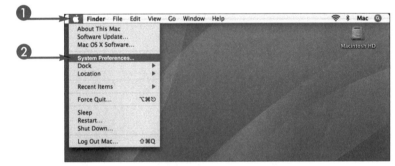

The System Preferences window appears.

③ Click Software Update.

The Software Update pane appears.

④ Click Check Now.

● You can set the Software Update preferences to check for updates on a daily, weekly, or monthly basis.

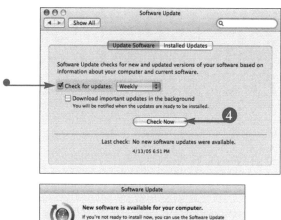

If new updates are available, then they appear in a new window.

⑤ Click to select the items that you want to update (☐ changes to ☑).

⑥ Click Install.

Your system installs the software updates.

Can I use Software Update if I am not connected to the Internet?

▼ No. Because Software Update needs to connect to remote servers, it does not work if you are not online.

How can I tell which updates require that I restart my computer?

▼ Software updates that require a computer restart for installation are indicated with an icon next to their names in the list that appears after Step **4**.

Why does Software Update check for updates again after I have installed new versions?

▼ After you have used Software Update to install updates of your operating system and applications, it checks for updates again. This is because if you have not checked often, you may need to install a series of updates to bring your software to the current version. For example, if you have Mac OS 10.4.0 on your computer and the current version is 10.4.5, you may need to download and install versions 10.4.1 and so on before you can install version 10.4.5.

PART VI

Get Help with the Help Viewer

Y ou can use the Help Viewer, Mac OS X's built-in help system, to look up information on how to use your computer. The Help Viewer can also show you how to identify and solve various problems.

When you open the Help Viewer in the Finder, a series of help topics appear, related to operating and troubleshooting the Finder. The Help Viewer also displays various topics, such as what features are new in this version of the software and top customer issues. You can also browse topics, as well as search for specific issues by entering key words or even entire questions into the search field at the top of the Help Viewer window.

In addition, you can use the Help Viewer to search for information about other applications. You can do this by activating the Help Viewer with the application you want to learn about in the foreground.

Although many of the files that the Help Viewer accesses are stored on your computer, the Help Viewer also updates its information by searching the Internet. Each time you open the Help Viewer, it checks its contents against what is hosted on remote servers at Apple. This ensures that your help system is up-to-date.

Get Help with the Help Viewer

① Click Help.

② Click the Help menu item.

The name of the Help menu item depends on the active application.

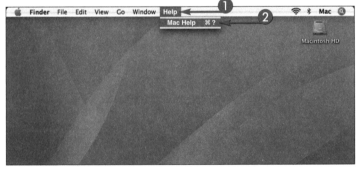

The Help window appears.

● This area may display links that you can click to find information about the active application.

③ Type a word or phrase that describes the topic of interest that you want the Help Viewer to search.

④ Press Return.

Help topics appear, based on the word or phrase that you typed.

⑤ Double-click a topic of interest.

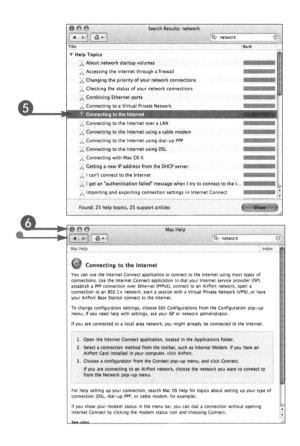

The information appears for the help topic that you selected.

● You can click the forward or backward buttons to move through the pages that you have viewed.

⑥ Click 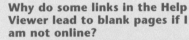 to close the Help Viewer when you are done.

Why do some links in the Help Viewer lead to blank pages if I am not online?

▼ The Help Viewer looks up some topics on remote servers to help keep the information current. As a result, some topics cannot be viewed unless you are connected to the Internet. Other topics may be visible, but not updated by remote information.

How can I decide what terms to use to search for in Help Viewer?

▼ You can access some topics by using different key words. For example, you can look up information about playing DVDs by typing the word "DVD" or the word "movie." If you are familiar with Windows, then you can search for "Windows to Mac Glossary," which is a help topic that guides Windows users on the terminology of the Mac OS.

What do some of the other links in the Help Viewer do?

▼ These links add other features that improve the usefullness of the Help Viewer. For example, you can click "Tell me more," if it appears in the Help Viewer window, to see a new list of related help topics. You can then double-click one of these topics to see a page with that information. You can have the Help Viewer launch the specific application or feature discussed in the help topic. You can also click the Go to the Web site link to open a Web site that contains the latest related information about the help topic.

Fix a Slow Help Viewer

If you notice that the performance of the Help Viewer degrades suddenly, then you can repair this problem. Slow performance can be due to the inability of the application to switch between Help libraries; this can slow down the Help Viewer when you switch between help topics.

You can delete the Help Viewer's cache, which is located in the Caches folder, in the Library folder within your user directory. Keep in mind that this is different from the Library folder in your computer's root folder. You must quit the Help Viewer before performing this operation.

This procedure is specific to the task of accelerating the Help Viewer. However, a similar fix can help restore the original speed of most Web browsers, including Safari. The cache for Web browsers contains previously viewed images, locations, and other information. Deleting a browser cache, though, can slow your overall browsing experience if you have a slow connection to the Internet, because your browser will have to reload the entire page rather than reloading from its cache.

Fix a Slow Help Viewer

① Click the com.apple.helpui folder.

This folder is in the Caches folder in the Library folder of your user directory.

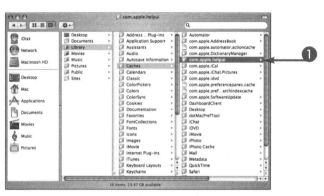

② Drag the folder to the Trash.

③ Empty the Trash.

The Help Viewer's performance should be restored.

Fix a Help Viewer That Crashes on Launch

You can repair the Help Viewer if it regularly crashes when you try to launch it. This is often caused by a corrupted Help Viewer Preferences file, which in turn can be caused by other applications crashing, the installation of new software, or the interruption of computer operations by a power failure. If this does not fix the problem, see Chapter 24 for information about Disk Utility.

The Help Viewer Preferences folder is located in the Library folder of your user directory. Keep in mind that this is different from the Library folder inside your computer's root directory, which is the top level of your computer's folder hierarchy.

You can also try to delete the Help Viewer cache folder. For more information, see the section "Fix a Slow Help Viewer."

Be careful when opening the Library and Preferences folder. Some applications place files in these folders that are necessary for these applications' operation. Consult the documentation for each application if you have questions. However, if you see a folder or file with the name of an application that you have uninstalled from your computer, it is safe to delete this folder or file.

Fix a Help Viewer That Crashes on Launch

① Open the Preferences folder in the Library folder of your user directory.

② Select the com.apple.help.plist and com.apple.helpviewer.plist files.

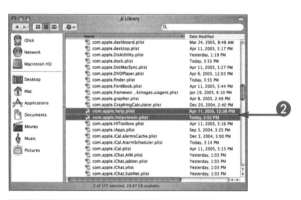

③ Drag these files to the Trash.

④ Empty the Trash.

You can now launch the Help Viewer.

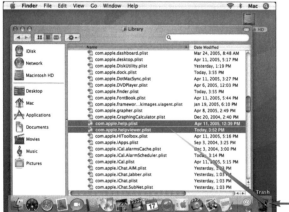

Boot in Safe Mode

You can start up your computer in Safe Mode, which is also called a Safe Boot. This enables you to restart a computer that is having serious problems, so that you can run repair software that you may not be able to run on the damaged computer in its normal boot mode.

Safe Mode performs an automatic disk check, which by itself may repair your computer's problems. After you restart your computer in Safe Mode, you can attempt to reboot the computer normally; if the computer does not exhibit any of the previously observed problems, then you may not need to perform any more repair work.

Booting in Safe Mode may take longer than a regular boot, due to the diagnostic procedures involved in a Safe Boot. Allow more time for this process.

Some applications or features you normally use may not work, or work properly, in Safe Mode. As a result, it is recommended not to run your computer regularly in Safe Mode, and to reboot into regular mode when you are done troubleshooting.

Boot in Safe Mode

① Click the Apple menu (🍎).

② Click Shut Down.

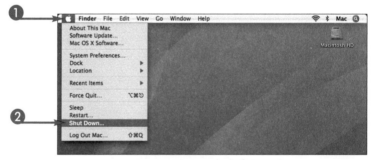

③ Press your computer's power button or key.

④ As soon as you hear the startup chime, press and hold the Shift key.

⑤ Release the Shift key when you see the gray Apple (🍎).

The computer boots into Safe Mode.

Zap PRAM

Y ou can reset, or zap, the parameter RAM (PRAM) of your computer. This often corrects common problems such as your computer displaying an incorrect time or date. Corrupted PRAM can also result in problems starting up your Mac, such as a blank screen.

PRAM is a type of memory that stores various software settings such as the current date, as well as information about the startup hard drive in your computer. After you zap the PRAM, you may need to reset your time zone, volume, and other settings in the System Preferences.

You may also need to reset some of these settings after regular firmware updates provided by Apple. Firmware updates may reset the PRAM without alerting you to this fact; you will notice that the clock on your computer is no longer correct.

Mac OS X does not store network settings in PRAM, so resetting the PRAM will not help with networking issues; it will not reset network settings, either. In addition, though Mac OS X also stores your DVD region choice in PRAM, resetting the PRAM does not allow you to change the DVD region settings.

Zap PRAM

① Click .

② Click Restart.

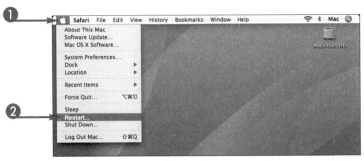

③ Press ⌘-Option-P-R until you hear the chime twice.

④ Release the keys.

The computer reboots with its PRAM reset.

PART VI

Look Up Problems in Apple's Online Tech Notes

You can use the technical support Web pages at Apple's Web site to research problems that you may be experiencing with your hardware and operating system software. This is useful if you do not have access to expert technical support or do not want to contact Apple directly.

In the support section of Apple's Web site (www.apple.com/support), you can select product support subsections for all hardware and software products developed by Apple, from iPods to Xserves. This includes services such as .Mac and consumer and professional applications such as iPhoto and Motion.

You can also check this Web site for recent software updates, if you do not want to use Mac OS X's Software Update feature. For more information, see Chapter 25. The Web page also includes a section showing less recent, but still popular, updates.

If you have a specific troubleshooting issue, you can use this Web page to search Apple's Knowledge Base, a collection of technical articles. These articles discuss not only current software and hardware, but also legacy products, so that you can search them for troubleshooting information for discontinued computers and operating systems.

Look Up Problems in Apple's Online Tech Notes

① Open www.apple.com/support in your Web browser.

② Select your computer model.

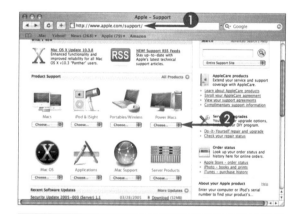

The product page appears.

③ Click a subject to read about common troubleshooting issues.

④ You can type key words and search for technical support articles.

⑤ Click the Search button.

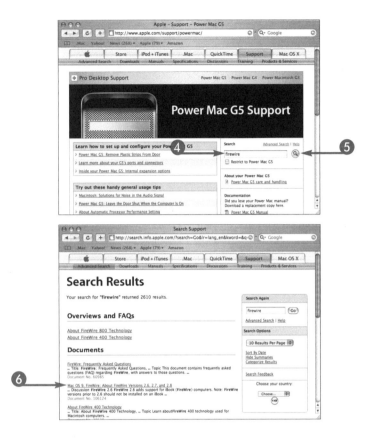

A page appears, showing the results of your search.

⑥ Click an article link to read it.

You can organize the results by date or categorize the results.

Do I need to have a current warranty with Apple to be able to access their support Web pages?

▼ No. Although there are sections of technical documents that are only available to software and hardware developers, and some sections with access restricted to dealers, you can browse Apple's library of support data without having to log in or have a warranty.

Can I tell whether I need to download and install any of the software updates listed on the support Web pages?

▼ You can check the version numbers of all of your software using the System Profiler utility located in the Utilities folder in your Applications folder. You can click Software in the left column of the System Profiler and then select Applications. This provides you with a comprehensive list of all applications installed on your computer as well as their version numbers.

Can I check anything else on the support Web pages?

▼ Yes. The Apple support Web site provides more than troubleshooting information. For example, you can register your new Apple product. You can check the status of any hardware that you have sent back for repair. You can also sign up for e-mail newsletters as well as extended service programs. You can even use this Web site to place orders at the Apple Store.

PART VI

Get System
Info

Y ou can gather information about your computer, both hardware- and software-related, so that you can learn exactly what version of the Mac OS X operating system you are using, as well as to find detailed data about the specifics of your computer hardware. This is useful to know, so that when you have a hardware or software problem, you can search more efficiently for possible solutions.

You can use a built-in feature of the Finder to view basic information about your computer. This tells you what

version of the Mac OS you are running, what speed and type of processor or processors are powering your computer, and how much memory you have installed. You can access this feature at any time, even when you are working in an application.

This feature also launches the System Profiler, which offers extensive data about your processor, your hard drive, your video card, other internal and external hardware, and even what software and extensions you have available on the computer's hard drive.

Get System Info

① Click .

② Click About This Mac.

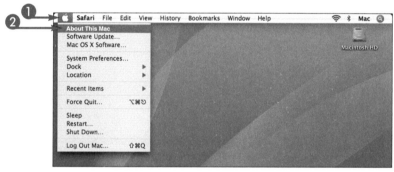

The About This Mac window appears.

● This window displays the Mac OS X version, processor type and speed, and installed memory.

③ Click More Info.

System Profiler launches.

④ Click the Hardware ▶ to view more information options about your system hardware (▶ changes to ▼).

⑤ Click an item in the left column to see detailed information about the item in the right pane.

⑥ Click the Software ▶ to see more information options about your system software (▶ changes to ▼).

⑦ Click an item in the left column to view detailed information about the item in the right pane.

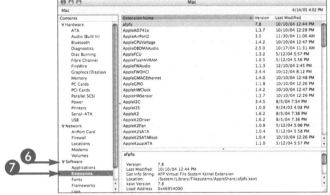

Can I use the About This Mac window to look for more current versions of Mac OS X?

▼ Yes. When the About This Mac window appears, click the Software Update button. This launches the Software Update feature of the System Preferences. For more information about using Software Update to search for new versions of applications and the operating system, see Chapter 25.

Can I use the System Profiler to get information about past problems with my computer?

▼ Yes. You can click Logs in the left column of the System Profiler. This presents you with the option of viewing the console log or the system log. These logs can provide you with detailed information about the state of your computer, as well as a record of what happened at a low level during application or system crashes.

How can I find out my computer's serial number?

▼ In the About This Mac window, double-click the version number below the words Mac OS X. This displays the serial number of your computer.

Diagnose Problems When You See Bad Startup Icons

You can diagnose some of the problems that your computer may be having if you understand the meaning of warning icons that appear on your computer screen at startup. These icons can help you to identify problems that are affecting your computer.

Normally, your Mac goes through a series of system checks and hardware initializations each time that you start it up. Much of this process happens in the hardware, before the operating system loads; the computer tests the RAM, the hard disk, and the communications systems such as Ethernet. If you have journaling turned on, then when the operating system loads, it checks the state of the computer's file system against the state of the file system when the computer was shut down.

The startup process can be a useful maintenance tool, purging caches, and checking the file system. In fact, rebooting your computer, which forces the computer to run these procedures, can sometimes alleviate system slowdowns that can occur after you have used your computer for days on end.

If serious problems are found that the computer cannot resolve during start up, then it may display a warning icon instead of the familiar startup screen. This section shows you what these icons tell you about your computer and how to fix the problems they signal.

Empty, Blue Screen

Your computer may go through most of the normal startup process, past the gray screen with the Apple logo, but then stall out, showing only a blue screen and possibly a spinning progress indicator, which looks like a colorful, spinning disk. The blue screen will be blank: no Dock and no menu bar. This means that the operating system has encountered a conflict in items that it is trying to load. This may be due to a bad font in the Mac OS 9 System Folder, in which case you can start up from the Mac OS 9 CD-ROM, which was included in your system software disks, by inserting the disc and restarting while holding down the C key. Drag the Fonts folder from the Mac OS 9 System Folder — not the Mac OS X System folder — to the Desktop, and restart in Mac OS X.

The blue screen may also be due to incompatible login items. Login items are files or applications that you have configured to launch when a user logs in to the computer. In this case, boot your computer in Safe Mode and open the Accounts pane of your System Preferences. Click the Startup Items tab, and then select all of the items that appear. Click the Remove (minus sign) button. After this, you can restart the computer. For more information on Safe Mode, see the section "Boot in Safe Mode."

In a normal startup process, you may see a blank, blue screen for a short time. This amount of time depends on your computer's processor speed and hard drive size, among other criteria. Do not take action unless this screen persists for an appreciable amount of time.

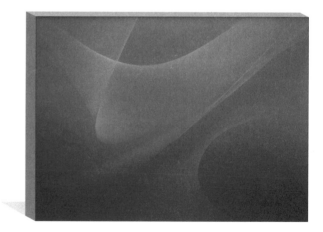

Black Screen or No Signal

You may see a dark screen, as though your computer were not even attached to the monitor. In fact, this may be the case. First, check to ensure that the connecting cable between your computer and monitor is seated properly. Some cables may appear connected but still need to be tightened down either by outboard screws or clamps. Apply a reasonable pressure but do not force the connection if it already feels snug.

If this is not the problem, then follow the instructions that came with your computer and check that your video card, if you have one, is seated properly inside the computer. Most desktop Macs are equipped with separate video cards that are connected on a PCI or PCI-X bus and that can therefore become unseated. With most Macintosh computers, you do not need to open the computer case to adjust the seating of the video card if it is loose.

There may also be a problem with your monitor. If it is an external monitor, disconnect it from your computer and try to use it with another one. Most monitors are both Mac- and PC-compatible, aside from those Apple-branded monitors using an Apple Display Connector (ADC), which can only connect to Macintosh computers with a compatible video card. This is a type of connector that combines the power, monitor, and USB cables into one port. Check the monitor's owner manual for details.

No Sign

After the startup process, you may see a circle with a diagonal bar drawn through it — the international "no" sign. This replaces the broken folder startup icon of earlier versions of Mac OS X. If you see this sign, this indicates that the operating system could not find certain files or folders that it needs to start up the computer. Some of these files are invisible when you are working in Mac OS X, but are visible if you have booted the computer into Mac OS 9. These include the files mach_kernel and automount. Applications, Library, System, and Users are required folders that are visible in both operating systems. If you have moved or deleted any of these files or folders, then you will see the No icon next time you start up your computer. However, this icon may appear even if the folders are in their proper places.

If this is the case, then you can reboot while resetting the PRAM. For more information, see the section Zap PRAM. You can also try holding the X key while restarting; this forces the computer to start up in Mac OS X. If you can boot into Mac OS X, then open the System Preferences, click Startup Disk, and ensure that your Mac OS X System folder is selected. If neither of these techniques works, then you may have to reinstall Mac OS X; you should contact your regular technical support before this, as reinstalling an operating system deletes all saved settings and documents.

continued

PART VI

Diagnose Problems When You
See Bad Startup Icons *(Continued)*

Blank, Gray Screen

If you see a blank, gray screen, aside from the initial gray screen that lasts a few seconds, this indicates that the computer has encountered a problem even before it has started to load the operating system. The normal gray screen leads to or features a darker gray Apple logo in its center.

First, disconnect all of your peripherals except for the keyboard and the mouse. This includes printers, external hard drives, scanners, speakers, and cameras. Then press and hold down the power key on your computer to attempt to reboot. If you still cannot boot past the gray screen, then turn off the computer and remove any third-party hardware upgrades such as PCI cards and extra RAM aside from the memory that came with your computer. Consult the computer's manual for specifics and make sure to ground yourself before touching the interior of the computer. After all items are removed, close and reboot the computer.

If the computer boots with no problem, then shut down the computer, reinstall one item, and try to restart. If the restart is successful, reinstall another item and repeat until you have isolated the problematic piece of hardware; it may be defective or incompatible with your computer.

If rebooting does not work, then boot the computer from your Mac OS X installation disk and run the copy of Disk Utility that is included on the CD-ROM.

Kernel Panic Screen

You may see a message telling you that you need to restart your computer. This message can appear during the startup process or during the course of otherwise normal operations. This indicates that what has happened is a kernel panic, which is a software error that occurs in Unix-based operating systems, including Mac OS X. In this type of error, the core, or kernel, of the operating system receives an instruction that does not come in a form that it expects, or it receives an instruction and does not execute it properly. This can happen after another type of error occurs from which the operating system is not able to recover. It is also more likely to happen after applications have crashed; these leave the equivalent of residue in the operating system's memory, and this can cause conflicts. Other causes of kernel panics include damaged software or damaged or incompatible hardware.

To escape from a kernel panic, you can press your computer's Power button for a few seconds or press the Restart button if your computer has one. Mac OS X versions 10.3 and later feature automatic kernel panic logging, which means that the computer records technical data as to why your computer failed. These data are stored in a file labeled panic.log, which is stored on your hard drive in the Logs folder, in the Library folder at the root level of your computer's hard drive.

The information in this file may not make much sense to the average user. However, it can be useful to expert users or when working with Apple technical support personnel.

You need to restart your computer. Hold down the Power button for several seconds or press the Restart button.

Veuillez redémarrer votre ordinateur. Maintenez la touche de démarrage enfoncée pendant plusieurs secondes ou bien appuyez sur le bouton de réinitialisation.

Sie müssen Ihren Computer neu starten. Halten Sie dazu die Einschalttaste einige Sekunden gedrückt oder drücken Sie die Neustart-Taste.

コンピュータを再起動する必要があります。パワーボタンを数秒間押し続けるか、リセットボタンを押してください。

A Flashing Question Mark

At times, you may see a flashing question mark appear on the screen when you attempt to start up your computer. This is often caused by the operating system not being able to find the system software that it needs to complete the startup process. This can occur when you have changed the settings of the Startup Disk System Preference, perhaps to an external drive that is no longer connected to the computer, or to a CD-ROM that you have ejected. The flashing question mark can appear and then disappear, leaving your computer to start up normally. In this case, you do not need to take any troubleshooting action other than checking to see which disk is selected in the Startup Disk System Preference.

If your computer displays a flashing question mark and then does not start up, then there are a variety of possible solutions for getting your computer to boot to Mac OS X. If one of these methods solves the problem, then you do not need to try any of the others.

First, place the system software CD-ROM or DVD that came with your computer into the disc drive and hold down the C key while rebooting. This forces the computer to boot from the disc. When you see the menu bar, click the Apple icon (■) and then click Disk Utility. Do not click Continue in the installer that also appears. When Disk Utility launches, click the First Aid tab, and then click Repair. After this process is complete, try to restart the computer.

If you still see the flashing question mark, try restarting the computer again while holding down the X key. This forces the computer to boot into Mac OS X. You may see the computer restart again during the boot process.

If this does not solve the problem, try to reset the computer's PRAM. You can do this by restarting the computer while holding down ⌘-Option-P-R. For more information, see the section "Zap PRAM."

If none of these procedures allows you to start the computer without stalling at the flashing question mark, then insert your Mac OS X Installation CD-ROM and reinstall Mac OS X. This overwrites and erases all of your stored documents and settings.

PART VI

A

C

continued

INDEX

continued

INDEX

continued

There's a Visual™ book for every learning level . . .

Simplified®
The place to start if you're new to computers. Full color.

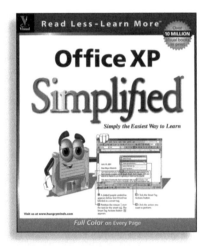

Also available:
- Windows XP Simplified, 2nd Edition
- Computers Simplified
- Microsoft Office 2000 Simplified
- Windows 98 Simplified
- Microsoft Word 2000 Simplified
- Excel 2002 Simplified
- Word 2002 Simplified
- PC Upgrade and Repair Simplified, 2nd Edition
- Creating Web Pages with HTML Simplified, 2nd Edition

Visual
An Imprint of ⊕WILEY
Now you know.

Teach Yourself VISUALLY™
Get beginning to intermediate level training in a variety of topics. Full color.

Also available:
- Teach Yourself VISUALLY Mac OS X Tiger
- Teach Yourself VISUALLY Digital Photography, 2nd Edition
- Teach Yourself VISUALLY Office 2003
- Teach Yourself VISUALLY Photoshop Elements 3
- Teach Yourself VISUALLY Photoshop CS
- Teach Yourself VISUALLY Windows XP Special Media Edition
- Teach Yourself VISUALLY Weight Training
- Teach Yourself VISUALLY Guitar

Master VISUALLY®
Step up to intermediate to advanced technical knowledge. Two-color.

Also available:
- Master VISUALLY Windows XP
- Master VISUALLY Office 2003
- Master VISUALLY Office XP
- Master VISUALLY eBay Business Kit
- Master VISUALLY iPod and iTunes
- Master VISUALLY Project 2003
- Master VISUALLY Windows Mobile 2003
- Master VISUALLY Dreamweaver MX and Flash MX
- Master VISUALLY Windows 2000 Server
- Master VISUALLY Web Design

...all designed for visual learners — just like you!

Top 100 Simplified® Tips & Tricks

Tips and techniques to take your skills beyond the basics. Full color.

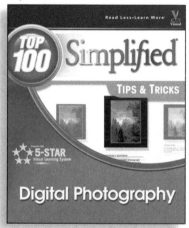

Visual Blueprint™

Where to go for professional level programming instruction. Two-color.

Read Less-Learn More®

For a complete listing of Visual books, go to wiley.com/go/visualtech

Also available:

- **Windows XP: Top 100 Simplified Tips & Tricks, 2nd Edition**
- **Photoshop Elements 3: Top 100 Simplified Tips & Tricks**
- **Mac OS X v.10.3 Panther: Top 100 Simplified Tips & Tricks**
- **eBay: Top 100 Simplified Tips & Tricks**
- **HTML: Top 100 Simplified Tips & Tricks**
- **Office 2003: Top 100 Simplified Tips & Tricks**
- **Excel 2003: Top 100 Simplified Tips & Tricks**
- **Photoshop CS: Top 100 Simplified Tips & Tricks**
- **Internet: Top 100 Simplified Tips & Tricks**

Also available:

- **HTML: Your visual blueprint for designing effective Web pages**
- **Excel Programming: Your visual blueprint for creating interactive spreadsheets**
- **Unix for Mac: Your visual blueprint to maximizing the foundation of Mac OS X**
- **MySQL: Your visual blueprint for creating open-source databases**
- **Active Server Pages 3.0: Your visual blueprint for developing interactive Web sites**

- **Visual Basic .NET: Your visual blueprint for building versatile programs on the .NET Framework**
- **Adobe Scripting: Your visual blueprint for scripting in Photoshop and Illustrator**
- **JavaServer Pages: Your visual blueprint for designing dynamic content with JSP**
- **Access 2003: Your visual blueprint for creating and maintaining real-world databases**

You can master all kinds of topics visually, including these

All designed for visual learners — just like you!

Visual Read Less-Learn More®

eBay Business Kit
0-7645-6816-7

MASTER VISUALLY
Step Up to Success — Visually
iPod and iTunes
0-7645-7702-6

Creating Web Pages
0-7645-7726-3

For a complete listing of *Master VISUALLY*® titles and other Visual books, go to wiley.com/go/visualtech

Visual
An Imprint of **WILEY**
Now you know.